PENGUIN BOOKS

THE FRANCHISE AFFAIR

The author of *The Franchise Affair*, whose death cut short a distinguished career as novelist and playwright, was born in the Highlands, her baptismal name being Elizabeth MacKintosh. Destined for art school, she preferred to devote three years to physical training, having no intention to make writing her profession. Her versatility, however, led to the creation of two remarkable literary personalities – Gordon Daviot, playwright, and Josephine Tey, detective novelist. As playwright she will be remembered by many as the author of *Richard of Bordeaux*, *Queen of Scots*, *The Laughing Woman*, and many other plays. Her first detective novel, *The Man in the Queue*, published under the name of Gordon Daviot, was written for a competition; for her second, *A Shilling for Candles*, she took the family name Josephine Tey. Then followed half a dozen crime stories in quick succession, beginning with *Miss Pym Disposes*, followed by *The Franchise Affair* (a success both as novel and film), *Brat Farrar*, *To Love and Be Wise*, and *The Singing Sands*. *The Daughter of Time*, because of its serious contribution to historical knowledge, was recognized as holding a unique place in detective fiction.

JOSEPHINE TEY

THE FRANCHISE
AFFAIR

PENGUIN BOOKS

PENGUIN BOOKS

Published by the Penguin Group
27 Wrights Lane, London w8 5tz, England
Viking Penguin Inc., 40 West 23rd Street, New York, New York 10010, USA
Penguin Books Australia Ltd, Ringwood, Victoria, Australia
Penguin Books Canada Ltd, 2801 John Street, Markham, Ontario, Canada l3r 1b4
Penguin Books (NZ) Ltd, 182–190 Wairau Road, Auckland 10, New Zealand

Penguin Books Ltd, Registered Offices: Harmondsworth, Middlesex, England

First published by Peter Davies 1948
Published in Penguin Books 1951
20

Made and printed in Great Britain by
Hazell Watson & Viney Limited
Member of BPCC plc
Aylesbury, Bucks, England
Set in Monotype Times

1

IT was four o'clock of a spring evening; and Robert Blair was thinking of going home.

The office would not shut until five, of course. But when you are the only Blair, of Blair, Hayward, and Bennet, you go home when you think you will. And when your business is mostly wills, conveyancing, and investments your services are in small demand in the late afternoon. And when you live in Milford, where the last post goes out at 3.45, the day loses whatever momentum it had long before four o'clock.

It was not even likely that his telephone would ring. His golfing cronies would by now be somewhere between the fourteenth and the sixteenth hole. No one would ask him to dinner, because in Milford invitations to dinner are still written by hand and sent through the post. And Aunt Lin would not ring up and ask him to call for the fish on his way home, because this was her bi-weekly afternoon at the cinema and she would at the moment be only twenty minutes gone with feature, so to speak.

So he sat there, in the lazy atmosphere of a spring evening in a little market town, staring at the last patch of sunlight on his desk (the mahogany desk with the brass inlay that his grandfather had scandalized the family by bringing home from Paris), and thought about going home. In the patch of sunlight was his tea-tray; and it was typical of Blair, Hayward, and Bennet that tea was no affair of a japanned tin tray and a kitchen cup. At 3.50 exactly on every working day Miss Tuff bore into his office a lacquer tray covered with a fair white cloth and bearing a cup of tea in blue-patterned china, and, on a plate to match, two biscuits: petit-beurre Mondays, Wednesdays, and Fridays, digestive Tuesdays and Thursdays.

Looking at it now, idly, he thought how much it represented the continuity of Blair, Hayward, and Bennet. The china he could remember as long as he could remember anything. The tray had been used when he was very small by the cook at home to take the bread in from the baker, and had been rescued by his young mother and brought to the office to bear the blue-patterned cups. The cloth had come years later with the advent of Miss Tuff. Miss Tuff was a war-time product: the first woman who had ever sat at a desk in a respectable solicitors' in Milford. A whole revolution Miss Tuff was in her single, gawky, thin, earnest person. But the firm had survived the revolution with hardly a jolt, and now, nearly a quarter of a century later, it was inconceivable that thin, grey, dignified Miss Tuff had ever been a sensation. Indeed her only disturbance of the immemorial routine was the introduction of the tray-cloth. In Miss Tuff's home no meal was ever put straight on to a tray; if it comes to that, no cakes were ever put straight on to a plate: a tray-cloth or a doyley must intervene. So Miss Tuff had looked askance at the bare tray. She had, moreover, considered the lacquered pattern distracting, unappetizing, and 'queer'. So one day she had brought a cloth from home; decent, plain, and white, as befitted something that was to be eaten off. And Robert's father, who had liked the lacquer tray, looked at the clean white cloth and was touched by young Miss Tuff's identification of herself with the firm's interests, and the cloth had stayed, and was now as much a part of the firm's life as the deed-boxes and the brass plate and Mr Heseltine's annual cold.

It was when his eyes rested on the blue plate where the biscuits had been that Robert experienced that odd sensation in his chest again. The sensation had nothing to do with the two digestive biscuits, at least not physically. It had to do with the inevitability of the biscuit routine: the placid certainty that it would be digestive on a Thursday and petit-beurre on a Monday. Until the last year or so he had found no fault with certainty or placidity. He had never wanted any other life but this: this quiet, friendly life in the place where he had grown up. He still did not want any other. But once or twice lately an odd, alien thought had crossed his mind, irrelevant and unbidden. As nearly as it could be put into words it was: 'This is all you are ever going to have.' And with the thought would come that moment's constriction in his chest. Almost a panic reaction, like the heart-squeezing that remembering a dentist appointment would cause in his ten-year-old breast.

This annoyed and puzzled Robert, who considered himself a happy and fortunate person, and adult at that. Why should this foreign thought thrust itself on him and cause that dismayed tightening under his ribs? What had his life lacked that a man might be supposed to miss?

A wife?

But he could have married if he had wanted to. At least he supposed he could; there were a great many unattached females in the district and they showed no sign of disliking him.

A devoted mother?

But what greater devotion could a mother have given him than Aunt Lin provided – dear, doting Aunt Lin?

Riches?

What had he ever wanted that he could not buy? And if that wasn't riches he didn't know what was.

An exciting life?

But he had never wanted excitement. No greater excitement, that is, than was provided by a day's hunting or being all-square at the sixteenth.

Then what?

Why the 'This is all you are ever going to have' thought?

Perhaps, he thought, sitting staring at the blue plate where the biscuits had been, it was just that childhood's attitude of something-wonderful-tomorrow persisted subconsciously in a man as long as it was capable of realization, and it was only after forty, when it became unlikely of fulfilment, that it obtruded itself into conscious thought, a lost piece of childhood crying for attention.

Certainly he, Robert Blair, hoped very heartily that his life would go on being what it was until he died. He had known since his schooldays that he would go into the firm and one day succeed his father; and he had looked with good-natured pity on boys who had no niche in life ready-made for them; who had no Milford, full of friends and memories, waiting for them; no part in English continuity as was provided by Blair, Hayward, and Bennet.

There was no Hayward in the firm nowadays: there had not been one since 1843; but a young sprig of the Bennets was occupying the back room at this moment. Occupying was the operative word, since it was very unlikely that he was doing any work, his chief interest in life being to write poems of an

7

originality so pristine that only Nevil himself could understand them. Robert deplored the poems but condoned the idleness, since he could not forget that when he had occupied that same back room he had spent his time practising mashie shots into the leather armchair.

The sunlight slipped off the edge of the tray and Robert decided it was time to go. If he went now he could walk home down the High Street before the sunlight was off the east-side pavement; and walking down Milford High Street was still one of the things that gave him conscious pleasure. Not that Milford was a show-place. It could be duplicated a hundred times anywhere south of Trent. But in its unselfconscious fashion it typified the goodness of life in England for the last three hundred years. From the old dwelling-house flush with the pavement that housed Blair, Hayward, and Bennet and had been built in the last years of Charles the Second's reign, the High Street flowed south in a gentle slope – Georgian brick, Elizabethan timber-and-plaster, Victorian stone, Regency stucco – to the Edwardian villas behind their elm trees at the other end. Here and there, among the rose and white and brown, appeared a front of black glass, brazening it out like an overdressed parvenu at a party; but the good manners of the other buildings discounted them. Even the multiple businesses had dealt leniently with Milford. True, the scarlet and gold of an American bazaar flaunted its bright promise down at the south end and daily offended Miss Truelove, who ran the Elizabethan relic opposite as a tea-shop with the aid of her sister's baking and Anne Boleyn's reputation. But the Westminster Bank, with a humility rare since the days of usury, had adapted the Weavers' Hall to their needs without so much as a hint of marble; and Soles, the wholesale chemists, had taken the old Wisdom residence and kept its tall, surprised-looking front intact.

It was a fine, gay, busy little street, punctuated with pollarded lime trees growing out of the pavement; and Robert Blair loved it.

He had gathered his feet under him preparatory to getting up when his telephone rang. In other places in the world, one understands, telephones are made to ring in outer offices, where a minion answers the thing and asks your business and says that

8

if you will be good enough to wait just a moment she will 'put you through', and you are then connected with the person you want to speak to. But not in Milford. Nothing like that would be tolerated in Milford. In Milford if you call John Smith on the telephone you expect John Smith to answer in person. So when the telephone rang on that spring evening in Blair, Hayward, and Bennet's it rang on Robert's brass-and-mahogany desk.

Always, afterwards, Robert was to wonder what would have happened if that telephone call had been one minute later. In one minute, sixty worthless seconds, he would have taken his coat from the peg in the hall, popped his head into the opposite room to tell Mr Heseltine that he was departing for the day, stepped out into the pale sunlight, and been away down the street. Mr Heseltine would have answered his telephone when it rang and told the woman that he had gone. And she would have hung up and tried someone else. And all that followed would have had only academic interest for him.

But the telephone rang in time; and Robert put out his hand and picked up the receiver.

'Is that Mr Blair?' a woman's voice asked – a contralto voice that would normally be a confident one, he felt, but now sounded breathless or hurried. 'Oh, I am so glad to have caught you. I was afraid you would have gone for the day. Mr Blair, you don't know me. My name is Sharpe, Marion Sharpe. I live with my mother at The Franchise – the house out on the Larborough road, you know.'

'Yes, I know it,' Blair said. He knew Marion Sharpe by sight, as he knew everyone in Milford and the district: a tall, lean, dark woman of forty or so; much given to bright silk kerchiefs which accentuated her gipsy swarthiness. She drove a battered old car, from which she shopped in the mornings while her white-haired old mother sat in the back, upright and delicate and incongruous and somehow silently protesting. In profile old Mrs Sharpe looked like Whistler's mother; when she turned full-face and you got the impact of her bright, pale, cold, seagull's eye, she looked like a sibyl. An uncomfortable old person.

'You don't know me,' the voice went on, 'but I have seen you in Milford and you look a kind person, and I need a lawyer. I

9

mean, I need one now, this minute. The only lawyer we ever have business with is in London – a London firm, I mean – and they are not actually ours. We just inherited them with a legacy. But now I am in trouble and I need legal backing, and I remembered you and thought that you would – '

'If it is your car –' Robert began. 'In trouble' in Milford meant one of two things: an affiliation order or an offence against the traffic laws. Since the case involved Marion Sharpe, it would be the latter; but it made no difference, because in neither case was Blair, Hayward, and Bennet likely to be interested. He would pass her on to Carley, the bright lad at the other end of the street, who revelled in court cases and was popularly credited with the capacity to bail the Devil out of hell. ('Bail him out!' someone said one night at the Rose and Crown. 'He'd do more than that. He'd get all our signatures to a guinea testimonial to the Old Sinner.')

'If it is your car –'

'Car?' she said vaguely; as if in her present world it was difficult to remember what a car was. 'Oh, I see. No. Oh no, it isn't anything like that. It is something more serious. It's Scotland Yard.'

'Scotland Yard!'

To that *douce* country lawyer and gentleman Robert Blair Scotland Yard was as exotic as Xanadu, Hollywood, or parachuting. As a good citizen he was on comfortable terms with the local police, and there his connexion with crime ended. The nearest he had ever come to Scotland Yard was to play golf with the local Inspector: a good chap who played a very steady game and occasionally, when it came to the nineteenth, expanded into mild indiscretions about his job.

'I haven't *murdered* anyone, if that is what you are thinking,' the voice said hastily.

'The point is: are you *supposed* to have murdered anyone?' Whatever she was supposed to have done, this was clearly a case for Carley. He must edge her off on to Carley.

'No; it isn't murder at all. I'm supposed to have kidnapped someone. Or abducted them, or something. I can't explain over the telephone. And, anyhow, I need someone now, at once, and – '

10

'But, you know, I don't think it is me you need at all,' Robert said. 'I know practically nothing about criminal law. My firm is not equipped to deal with a case of that sort. The man you need –'

'I don't want a criminal lawyer; I want a friend. Someone who will stand by me and see that I am not put-on. I mean, tell me what I need not answer if I don't want to, and that sort of thing. You don't need a training in crime for that, do you?'

'No; but you would be much better served by a firm who were used to police cases. A firm that –'

'What you are trying to tell me is that this is not "your cup of tea". That's it, isn't it?'

'No, of course not,' Robert said hastily. 'I quite honestly feel that you would be wiser –'

'You know what I feel like?' she broke in. 'I feel like someone drowning in a river because she can't drag herself up the bank, and instead of giving me a hand out you point out that the other bank is much better to crawl out on.'

There was a moment's silence.

'But on the contrary,' Robert said, 'I can provide you with an expert puller-out-of-rivers; a great improvement on my amateur self, I assure you. Benjamin Carley knows more about defending accused persons than anyone between here and –'

'What! That awful little man with the striped suits?' Her deep voice ran up and cracked, and there was another momentary silence. 'I am sorry,' she said presently in her normal voice. 'That was silly. But you see, when I rang you up just now it wasn't because I thought you would be clever about things' ('*Wasn't* it, indeed,' thought Robert) 'but because I was in trouble and wanted the advice of someone of my own sort. And you looked my sort. Mr Blair, do please come. I need you *now*. There are people from Scotland Yard here in the house. And if you feel that it isn't something you want to be mixed up in, you could always pass it on to someone else afterwards, couldn't you? But there may be nothing after all, to be mixed up in. If you would just come out here and "watch my interests", or whatever you call it, for an hour, it may all pass over. I'm sure there is a mistake somewhere. Couldn't you please do that for me?'

On the whole Robert Blair thought that he could. He was too good-natured to refuse any reasonable appeal – and she had given him a loophole if things grew difficult. And he did not, after all, now he came to think of it, want to throw her to Ben Carley. In spite of her *bêtise* about striped suits he saw her point of view. If you had done something you wanted to get away with, Carley was no doubt God's gift to you; but if you were bewildered and in trouble and innocent, perhaps Carley's brash personality was not likely to be a very present help.

All the same, he wished as he laid down the receiver that the front he presented to the world were a more forbidding one – Calvin or Caliban, he did not care, so long as strange females were discouraged from flinging themselves on his protection when they were in trouble.

What possible kind of trouble could 'kidnapping' be, he wondered as he walked round to the garage in Sin Lane for his car? *Was* there such an offence in English law? And whom could she possibly be interested in kidnapping? A child? Some child with 'expectations'? In spite of the large house out on the Larborough road they gave the impression of having very little money. Or some child that they considered 'ill-used' by its natural guardians? That was possible. The old woman had a fanatic's face if ever he saw one; and Marion Sharpe herself looked as if the stake would be her natural prop if stakes were not out of fashion. Yes, it was probably some ill-judged piece of philanthropy. Detention 'with intent to deprive parent, guardian, etc., of its possession.' He wished he could remember more of his *Harris and Wilshere*. He could not remember offhand whether that was a felony, with penal servitude in the offing, or a mere misdemeanour. 'Abduction and Detention' had not sullied the Blair, Hayward, and Bennet files since December 1798, when the squire of Lessows, much flown with seasonable claret, had taken across his saddle-bow the young Miss Gretton from a ball at the Gretton home and ridden away with her through the floods; and there was no doubt at all, of course, as to the squire's motive on that occasion.

Ah, well; they would no doubt be open to reason now that they had been startled by the irruption of Scotland Yard into their plans. He was a little startled by Scotland Yard himself.

Was the child so important that it was a matter for Head-quarters?

Round in Sin Lane he ran into the usual war, but extricated himself. (Etymologists, in case you are interested, say that the 'Sin' is merely a corruption of 'sand', but the inhabitants of Milford of course know better: before those council houses were built on the low meadows behind the town the lane led direct to the lovers' walk in High Wood.) Across the narrow lane, face to face in perpetual enmity, stood the local livery stable and the town's newest garage. The garage frightened the horses (so said the livery stable) and the livery stable blocked up the lane continually with delivery loads of straw and fodder and what not (so the garage said). Moreover the garage was run by Bill Brough, ex-R.E.M.E., and Stanley Peters, ex-Royal Corps of Signals; and old Matt Ellis, ex-King's Dragoon Guards, looked on them as representatives of a generation that had destroyed the cavalry and an offence to civilization.

In winter, when he hunted, Robert heard the cavalry side of the story; for the rest of the year he listened to the Royal Corps of Signals while his car was being wiped, oiled, filled, or fetched. Today the Signals wanted to know the difference between libel and slander and what exactly constituted defamation of charac-ter. Was it defamation of character to say that a man was 'a tinkerer with tin cans who wouldn't know a nut from an acorn'?

'Don't know, Stan. Have to think it over,' Robert said hastily, pressing the starter. He waited while three tired hacks brought back two fat children and a groom from their after-noon ride ('See what I mean?' said Stanley in the background) and then swung the car into the High Street.

Down at the south end of the High Street the shops faded gradually into dwelling-houses with doorsteps on the pavement, then to houses set back a pace and with porticos to their doors, and then to villas with trees in their gardens, and then, quite suddenly, to fields and open country.

It was farming country: a land of endless hedged fields and few houses; a rich country but lonely – one could travel mile after mile without meeting another human being. Quiet and confident and unchanged since the Wars of the Roses, hedged field succeeded hedged field and skyline faded into skyline, without any break in pattern. Only the telegraph posts betrayed the century.

Away beyond the horizon was Larborough. Larborough was bicycles, small arms, tin-tacks, Cowan's Cranberry Sauce, and a million human souls living cheek by jowl in dirty red brick; and periodically it broke bounds in an atavistic longing for grass and earth. But there was nothing in the Milford country to attract a race who demanded with their grass and earth both views and tea-houses; when Larborough went on holiday it went as one man west to the hills and the sea, and the great stretch of country north and east of it stayed lonely and quiet and unlittered, as it had been in the days of the Sun in Splendour. It was 'dull' and by that damnation was saved.

Two miles out on the Larborough road stood the house known as The Franchise, set down by the roadside with the inconsequence of a telephone kiosk. In the last days of the Regency someone had bought the field known as The Franchise, built in the middle of it a flat white house, and then surrounded the whole with a high, solid wall of brick with a large double gate, of wall height, in the middle of the road frontage. It had no relation with anything in the countryside: no farm buldings in the background; no side-gates, even, into the surrounding fields. Stables were built, in accordance with the period, at the back of the house, but they were inside the wall. The place was as irrelevant, as isolated as a child's toy dropped by the wayside. It had been occupied as long as Robert could remember by an old man, presumably the same old man; but since The Franchise people had always shopped at Ham Green, the village on the Larborough side of them, they had never been seen in Milford. And then Marion Sharpe and her mother had begun to be part of the morning shopping scene in Milford, and it was understood that they had inherited The Franchise when the old man died.

How long had they been there, Robert wondered. Three years? Four years?

That they had not entered Milford socially was nothing to reckon by. Old Mrs Warren, who had bought the first of the elm-shaded villas at the end of the High Street a small matter of twenty-five years ago in the hope that Milford air would be better for her rheumatism than the sea, was still referred to as 'that lady from Weymouth'. (It was Swanage, incidentally.)

The Sharpes, moreover, might not have sought social contacts. They had an odd air of being self-sufficient. He had seen the daughter once or twice on the golf course, playing (presumably as a guest) with Dr Borthwick. She drove a long ball like a man and used her thin brown wrists like a professional. And that was all Robert knew about her.

As he brought the car to a stop in front of the tall iron gates, he found that two other cars were already there. It needed only one glance at the nearer – so inconspicuous, so well groomed, so discreet – to identify it. In what other country in this world, he wondered as he got out of his own car, does the police force take pains to be well-mannered and quiet?

His eye lighted on the farther car and he saw that it was Hallam's, the local Inspector, who played such a steady game on the golf-course.

There were three people in the police car: the driver and, in the back, a middle-aged woman and what seemed to be either a child or a young girl. The driver regarded him with that mild, absent-minded, all-observing police eye, and then withdrew his gaze; but the faces in the back he could not see.

The tall iron gates were shut – Robert could not remember ever seeing them open – and Robert pushed open one heavy half with frank curiosity. The iron lace of the original gates had been lined, in some Victorian desire for privacy, by flat sheets of iron, and the wall was too high for anything inside to be visible, so that, except for a distant view of its roof and chimneys, he had never seen The Franchise.

His first feeling was disappointment. It was not the fallen-on-evil-times look of the house – although that was evident; it was the sheer ugliness of it. Either it had been built too late to share in the grace of a graceful period or the builder had lacked an architect's eye. He had used the idiom of the time, but it had apparently not been native to him. Everything was just a little wrong: the windows the wrong size by half a foot, wrongly placed by not much more; the doorway the wrong width and the flight of steps the wrong height. The total result was that

15

instead of the bland contentment of its period the house had a hard stare. An antagonistic, questioning stare. As he walked across the courtyard to the unwelcoming door Robert knew what it reminded him of: a dog that has been suddenly wakened from sleep by the advent of a stranger, propped on his forelegs, uncertain for a moment whether to attack or merely bark. It had the same what-are-you-doing-here? expression.

Before he could ring the bell the door was opened – not by a maid but by Marion Sharpe.

'I saw you coming,' she said, putting out her hand. 'I didn't want you to ring, because my mother lies down in the afternoons and I am hoping that we can get this business over before she wakes up. Then she need never know anything about it. I am more grateful than I can say to you for coming.'

Robert murmured something and noticed that her eyes, which he had expected to be a bright gipsy brown, were actually a grey hazel. She drew him into the hall, and he noticed as he put his hat down on a chest that the rug on the floor was threadbare.

'The Law is in here,' she said, pushing open a door and ushering him into a drawing-room. Robert would have liked to talk to her alone for a moment, to orientate himself ; but it was too late now to suggest that. This was evidently the way she wanted it.

Sitting on the edge of a bead-work chair was Hallam, looking sheepish. And by the window, entirely at his ease in a very nice piece of Hepplewhite, was Scotland Yard in the person of a youngish spare man in a well-tailored suit.

As they got up, Hallam and Robert nodded to each other.

'You know Inspector Hallam, then?' Marion Sharpe said. 'And this is Detective-Inspector Grant from Headquarters.'

Robert noticed the 'Headquarters', and wondered. Had she already at some time had dealings with the police or was it that she just didn't like the slightly sensational sound of 'the Yard'?

Grant shook hands, and said: 'I'm glad you've come, Mr Blair. Not only for Miss Sharpe's sake but for my own.'

'Yours?'

'I couldn't very well proceed until Miss Sharpe had some

kind of support; friendly support if not legal, but if legal so much the better.'

'I see. And what are you charging her with?'

'We are not charging her with anything – ' Grant began, but Marion interrupted him.

'I am supposed to have kidnapped and beaten up someone.'

'*Beaten up?*' Robert said, staggered.

'Yes,' she said, with a kind of relish in enormity. 'Beaten her black and blue.'

'Her?'

'A girl. She is outside the gate in a car now.'

'I think we had better begin at the beginning,' Robert said, clutching after the normal.

'Perhaps I had better do the explaining,' Grant said mildly.

'Yes,' said Miss Sharpe, 'do. After all, it is your story.'

Robert wondered if Grant were aware of the mockery. He wondered a little, too, at the coolness that could afford mockery with Scotland Yard sitting in one of her best chairs. She had not sounded cool over the telephone; she had sounded driven, half-desperate. Perhaps it was the presence of an ally that had heartened her, or perhaps she had just got her second wind.

'Just before Easter,' Grant began, in succinct police-fashion, 'a girl called Elisabeth Kane, who lived with her guardians near Aylesbury, went to spend a short holiday with a married aunt in Mainshill, the suburb of Larborough. She went by coach, because the London-Larborough coaches pass through Aylesbury and also pass through Mainshill before reaching Larborough; so that she could get off the coach in Mainshill and be within a three-minute walk of her aunt's house, instead of having to go into Larborough and come all the way out again, as she would have to if she travelled by train. At the end of a week her guardians – a Mr and Mrs Wynn – had a postcard from her saying that she was enjoying herself very much and was staying on. They took this to mean staying on for the duration of her school holiday, which would mean another three weeks. When she didn't turn up on the day before she was supposed to go back to school, they took it for granted that she was merely playing truant and wrote to her aunt to send her back. The aunt, instead of going to the nearest call-box or telegraph office, broke it to the Wynns in a letter that her niece had left on her way back to Aylesbury a fortnight previously. The exchange of letters had taken the best part of another week, so that by the time the guardians went to the police about it the girl had been missing for three weeks. The police took all the usual measures, but before they could really get going the girl turned up. She walked into her home near Aylesbury late one night, wearing only a dress and shoes and in a state of complete exhaustion.'

'How old is the girl?'

'Fifteen – nearly sixteen.' He waited a moment to see if Robert had further questions, and then went on. (As one counsel to another, thought Robert appreciatively, a manner to match the car that stood so unobtrusively at the gate.) 'She said she had been "kidnapped" in a car, but that was all the information anyone got from her for two days. She lapsed into a semi-conscious condition. When she recovered, about forty-eight hours later, they began to get her story from her.'

'They?'

'The Wynns. The police wanted it, of course, but she grew hysterical at any mention of police, so they had to acquire it second-hand. She said that while she was waiting for her return coach at the cross-roads in Mainshill a car pulled up at the kerb with two women in it. The younger woman, who was driving, asked her if she was waiting for a bus and if they could give her a lift.'

'Was the girl alone?'

'Yes.'

'Why? Didn't anyone go to see her off?'

'Her uncle was working and her aunt had gone to be god-mother at a christening.' Again he paused to let Robert put further questions if he was so minded. 'The girl said that she was waiting for the London coach, and they told her that it had already gone by. Since she had arrived at the cross-roads with very little time to spare and her watch was not a particularly accurate one, she believed this. Indeed, she had begun to be afraid, even before the car stopped, that she had missed the coach. She was distressed about it because it was then four o'clock, beginning to rain, and growing dark. They were very sympathetic and suggested that they should give her a lift to a place whose name she did not catch, where she could get a different coach to London in half an hour's time. She accepted this gratefully and got in beside the elder woman in the back of the car.'

A picture swam into Robert's mind of old Mrs Sharpe, upright and intimidating, in her usual place in the back of the car. He glanced at Marion Sharpe, but her face was calm. This was a story she had heard already.

'The rain blurred the windows and she talked to the older woman about herself as they went along, so that she paid little attention to where they were going. When she at last took notice of her surroundings the evening outside the windows had become quite dark and it seemed to her that they had been travelling for a long time. She said something about its being extraordinarily kind of them to take her so far out of their way, and the younger woman, speaking for the first time, said that as it happened it was not out of their way; and that, on the contrary, she would have time to come in and have a cup of something hot with them before they took her on to her new crossroads. She was doubtful about this, but the younger woman said it would be of no advantage to wait for twenty minutes in the rain when she could be warm and dry and fed in those same twenty minutes; and she agreed that this seemed sensible. Eventually the younger woman got out, opened what appeared to the girl to be drive gates, and the car was driven up to a house which it was too dark to see. She was taken into a large kitchen —'

'A kitchen?' Robert repeated.

'Yes, a kitchen. The older woman put some cold coffee on the stove to heat while the younger one cut sandwiches. "Sandwiches without tops" the girl called them.'

'Smorgasbrod.'

'Yes. While they ate and drank, the younger woman told her that they had no maid at the moment and asked her if she would like to be a maid for them for a little. She said that she wouldn't. They tried persuasion, but she stuck to it that that was not at all the kind of job she would take. Their faces began to grow blurred as she talked, and when they suggested that she might at least come upstairs and see what a nice bedroom she would have if she stayed, she was too fuddled in her mind to do anything but follow their suggestion. She remembers going up a first flight with a carpet and a second flight with what she calls "something hard" underfoot, and that was all she remembered until she woke in the daylight on a truckle bed in a bare little attic. She was wearing only her slip and there was no sign of the rest of her clothes. The door was locked and the small round window would not open. In any case – '

'*Round* window!' said Robert uncomfortably.

But it was Marion who answered him. 'Yes,' she said, meaningly, 'a round window up in the roof.'

Since his last thought as he came to her front door a few minutes ago had been how badly placed was the little round window in the roof, there seemed to Robert to be no adequate comment. Grant made his usual pause for courtesy's sake and went on.

'Presently the younger woman arrived with a bowl of porridge. The girl refused it and demanded her clothes and her release. The woman said that she would eat it when she was hungry enough, and went away, leaving the porridge behind. She was alone till evening, when the same woman brought her tea on a tray with fresh cakes and tried to talk her into giving the maid's job a trial. The girl again refused; and for days, according to her story, this alternate coaxing and bullying went on, sometimes by one of the women and sometimes by the other. Then she decided that if she could break the small round window she might be able to crawl out of it on to the roof which was protected by a parapet, and call the attention of some passer-by or some visiting tradesmen to her plight. Unfortunately her only implement was a chair, and she had managed only to crack the glass before the younger woman interrupted her in a great passion. She snatched the chair from the girl and belaboured her with it until she was breathless. She went away, taking the chair with her, and the girl thought that was the end of it. But in a few moments the woman came back with what the girl thinks was a dog whip and beat her until she fainted. Next day the older woman appeared with an armful of bed-linen and said that if she would not work she would at least sew. No sewing, no food. She was too stiff to sew and so had no food. The following day she was threatened with another beating if she did not sew. So she mended some of the linen and was given stew for supper. This arrangement lasted for some time, but if her sewing was bad or insufficient she was either beaten or deprived of food. Then one evening the older woman brought the usual bowl of stew and went away leaving the door unlocked. The girl waited, thinking it was a trap that would end in another beating; but in the end she ventured on to the landing. There was no sound, and she ran down a flight of uncarpeted stairs. Then down a second flight to the first landing. Now she could hear the two women talking in the kitchen. She crept down the last flight and dashed for the door. It was unlocked and she ran out just as she was into the night.'

'In her slip?' Robert asked.

'I forgot to say that the slip had been exchanged for her dress. There was no heating in the attic, and in nothing but a slip she would probably have died.'

'If she ever was in an attic,' Robert said.

'If, as you say, she was ever in an attic,' the Inspector agreed smoothly. And without his customary pause of courtesy went on: 'She does not remember much after that. She walked a great distance in the dark, she says. It seemed a highroad, but there was no traffic and she met no one. Then, on a main road some time later, a lorry driver saw her in his headlight and stopped to give her a lift. She was so tired that she fell straight asleep. She woke as she was being set on her feet at the roadside. The lorry driver was laughing at her and saying that she was like a sawdust doll that had lost its stuffing. It seemed to be still night-time. The lorry driver said this was where she said she wanted to be put off, and drove away. After a little she recognized the corner. It was less than two miles from her home. She heard a clock strike eleven. And shortly before midnight she arrived home.'

2

THERE was a short silence.

'And this is the girl who is sitting in a car outside the gates of The Franchise at this moment?' said Robert.

'Yes.'

'I take it you have reasons for bringing her here.'

'Yes. When the girl had recovered sufficiently she was induced to tell her story to the police. It was taken down in shorthand as she told it, and she read the typed version and signed it. In that statement there were two things that helped the police a lot. These are the relevant extracts:

"When we had been going for some time we passed a bus that had MILFORD in a lighted sign on it. No, I don't know where Milford is. No, I have never been there."

'That is one. The other is:

"From the window of the attic I could see a high brick wall with a big iron gate in the middle of it. There was a road on the farther side of the wall, because I could see the telegraph posts. No, I couldn't see the traffic on it, because the wall was too high. Just the tops of lorry-loads sometimes. You couldn't see through the gate because it had sheets of iron on the inside. Inside the gate the carriageway went straight for a little and then divided in two into a circle up to the door. No, it wasn't a garden, just grass. Yes, lawn, I suppose. No, I don't remember any shrubs; just the grass and the paths." '

Grant shut the little notebook he had been quoting from.

'As far as we know – and the search has been thorough – there is no other house between Larborough and Milford which fulfils the girl's description except The Franchise. The Franchise, moreover, fulfils it in every particular. When the girl saw the wall and the gate today she was sure that this was the place; but she has not so far seen inside the gate, of course. I had first to explain matters to Miss Sharpe and find out if she was willing to be confronted with the girl. She very rightly suggested that some legal witness should be present.'

'Do you wonder that I wanted help in a hurry?' Marion

Sharpe said, turning to Robert. 'Can you imagine a more nightmare piece of nonsense?'

'The girl's story is certainly the oddest mixture of the factual and the absurd. I know that domestic help is scarce,' Robert said; 'but would anyone hope to enlist a servant by forcibly detaining her, to say nothing of beating and starving her?'

'No normal person, of course,' Grant agreed, keeping his eye steadily fixed on Robert's so that it had no tendency to slide over to Marion Sharpe. 'But believe me, in my first twelve months in the force I had come across a dozen things much more incredible. There is no end to the extravagances of human conduct.'

'I agree; but the extravagance is just as likely to be in the girl's conduct. After all, the extravagance begins with her. She is the one who has been missing for – ' He paused in question.

'A month,' Grant supplied.

'For a month; while there is no suggestion that the household at The Franchise has varied at all from its routine. Would it not be possible for Miss Sharpe to provide an alibi for the day in question?'

'No,' Marion Sharpe said. 'The day, according to the Inspector, is the 28th of March. That is a long time ago, and our days here vary very little, if at all. It would be quite impossible for us to remember what we were doing on March the 28th – and most unlikely that anyone would remember for us.'

'Your maid?' Robert suggested. 'Servants have ways of marking their domestic life that are often surprising.'

'We have no maid,' she said. 'We find it difficult to keep one: The Franchise is so isolated.'

The moment threatened to become awkward and Robert hastened to break it.

'This girl – I don't know her name, by the way.'

'Elisabeth Kane; known as Betty Kane.'

'Oh yes; you did tell me. I'm sorry. This girl – may we know something about her? I take it that the police have investigated her before accepting so much of her story. Why guardians and not parents, for instance?'

'She is a war orphan. She was evacuated to the Aylesbury district as a small child. She was an only child, and was billeted

23

with the Wynns, who had a boy four years older. About twelve months later both parents were killed in the same "incident", and the Wynns, who had always wanted a daughter and were very fond of the child, were glad to keep her. She looks on them as her parents, since she can hardly remember the real ones.'

'I see. And her record?'

'Excellent. A very quiet girl, by every account. Good at her school work, but not brilliant. Has never been in any kind of trouble, in school or out of it. "Transparently truthful" was the phrase her form mistress used about her.'

'When she eventually turned up at her home, after her absence, was there any evidence of the beatings she said she had been given?'

'Oh yes ; very definitely. The Wynns' own doctor saw her early next morning, and his statement is that she had been very extensively knocked about. Indeed, some of the bruises were still visible much later when she made her statement to us.'

'No history of epilepsy?'

'No ; we considered that very early in the inquiry. I should like to say that the Wynns are very sensible people. They have been greatly distressed, but they have not tried to dramatize the affair or allowed the girl to be an object of interest or pity. They have taken the affair admirably.'

'And all that remains is for me to take my end of it with the same admirable detachment,' Marion Sharpe said.

'You see my position, Miss Sharpe. The girl not only describes the house in which she says she was detained, she describes the two inhabitants – and describes them very accurately. "A thin, elderly woman with soft white hair and no hat, dressed in black ; and a much younger woman, thin and tall and dark like a gipsy, with no hat and a bright silk scarf round her neck."'

'Oh yes. I can think of no explanation, but I understand your position. And now I think we had better have the girl in, but before we do I should like to say – '

The door opened noiselessly and old Mrs Sharpe appeared on the threshold. The short pieces of white hair round her face stood up on end, as her pillow had left them, and she looked more than ever like a sibyl.

She pushed the door to behind her and surveyed the gathering with a malicious interest.

'Hah!' she said, making a sound like the throaty squawk of a hen. '*Three* strange men!'

'Let me present them, mother,' Marion said, as the three got to their feet.

'This is Mr Blair, of Blair, Hayward, and Bennet – the firm who have that lovely house at the top of the High Street.'

As Robert bowed the old woman fixed him with her seagull's eye.

'Needs re-tiling,' she said.

It did, but it was not the greeting he had expected.

It comforted him a little that her greeting to Grant was even more unorthodox. Far from being impressed or agitated by the presence of Scotland Yard in her drawing-room of a spring afternoon, she merely said in her dry voice: 'You should not be sitting in that chair; you are much too heavy for it.'

When her daughter introduced the local Inspector she cast one glance at him, moved her head an inch, and quite obviously dismissed him from further consideration. This Hallam, to judge by his expression, found peculiarly shattering.

Grant looked inquiringly at Miss Sharpe.

'I'll tell her,' she said. 'Mother, the Inspector wants us to see a young girl who is waiting in a car outside the gate. She was missing from her home near Aylesbury for a month, and when she turned up again – in a distressed condition – she said that she had been detained by people who wanted to make a servant of her. They kept her locked up when she refused, and beat and starved her. She described the place and the people minutely, and it so happens that you and I fit the description admirably. So does our house. The suggestion is that she was detained up in our attic with the round window.'

'Remarkably interesting,' said the old lady, seating herself with deliberation on an Empire sofa. 'What did we beat her with?'

'A dog whip, I understand.'

'Have we got a dog whip?'

'We have one of those "lead" things, I think. They make a whip if necessary. But the point is, the Inspector would like us to meet this girl, so that she can say if we are the people who detained her or not.'

'Have you any objections, Mrs Sharpe?' Grant asked.

'On the contrary, Inspector. I look forward to the meeting with impatience. It is not every afternoon, I assure you, that I go to my rest a dull old woman and rise a potential monster.'

'Then if you will excuse me, I shall bring – '

Hallam made a motion, offering himself as messenger, but Grant shook his head. It was obvious that he wanted to be present when the girl first saw what was beyond the gate.

As the Inspector went out Marion Sharpe explained Blair's presence to her mother. 'It was extraordinarily kind of him to come at such short notice and so quickly,' she added, and Robert felt again the impact of that bright, pale old eye. For his money, old Mrs Sharpe was quite capable of beating seven different people between breakfast and lunch any day of the week.

'You have my sympathy, Mr Blair,' she said unsympathetically.

'Why, Mrs Sharpe?'

'I take it that Broadmoor is a little out of your line.'

'Broadmoor!'

'Criminal lunacy.'

'I find it extraordinarily stimulating,' Robert said, refusing to be bullied by her.

This drew a flash of appreciation from her, something that was like the shadow of a smile. Robert had the odd feeling that she suddenly liked him; but if so she was making no verbal confession of it. Her dry voice said tartly: 'Yes, I expect the distractions of Milford are scarce and mild. My daughter pursues a piece of gutta-percha round the golf-course – '

'It is not gutta-percha any more, mother,' her daughter put in.

'But at my age Milford does not provide even that distracttion. I am reduced to pouring weedkiller on weeds – a legitimate form of sadism, on a par with drowning fleas. Do you drown your fleas, Mr Blair?'

'No, I squash them. But I have a sister who used to pursue them with a cake of soap.'

'Soap?' said Mrs Sharpe, with genuine interest.

'I understand that she hit them with the soft side and they stuck to it.'

'How *very* interesting. A technique I have not met before. I must try that next time.'

With his other ear he heard that Marion was being nice to the snubbed Inspector. 'You play a very good game, Inspector,' she was saying.

He was conscious of the feeling you get near the end of a dream, when waking is just round the corner, that none of the inconsequence really matters because presently you'll be back in the real world.

This was misleading because the real world came through the door with the return of Inspector Grant. Grant came in first, so that he was in a position to see the expressions on all the faces concerned, and held the door open for a police matron and a girl.

Marion Sharp stood up slowly, as if better to face anything that might be coming to her, but her mother remained seated on the sofa as one giving an audience, her Victorian back as flat as it had been when she was a young girl, her hands lying composedly in her lap. Even her wild hair could not detract from the impression that she was mistress of the situation.

The girl was wearing her school coat and childish, low-heeled clumpish black school shoes; and consequently looked younger than Blair had anticipated. She was not very tall and certainly not pretty. But she had – what was the word? – appeal. Her eyes, a darkish blue, were set wide apart in a face of the type popularly referred to as heart-shaped. Her hair was mouse-coloured, but grew off her forehead in a good line. Below each cheek-bone a slight hollow, a miracle of delicate modelling, gave the face charm and pathos. Her lower lip was full, but the mouth was too small. So were her ears. Too small and too close to her head.

An ordinary sort of girl, after all – not the sort you would notice in a croc.; not at all the type to be the heroine of a sensation. Robert wondered what she would look like in other clothes.

27

The girl's glance rested first on the old woman and then went on to Marion. The glance held neither surprise nor triumph, and not much interest.

'Yes, these are the women,' she said.

'You have no doubt about it?' Grant asked her; and added: 'It is a very grave accusation, you know.'

'No, I have no doubt. How could I?'

'These two ladies are the women who detained you, took your clothes from you, forced you to mend linen, and whipped you?'

'Yes, these are the women.'

'A remarkable liar,' said old Mrs Sharpe, in the tone in which one says: A remarkable likeness.

'You say that we took you into the kitchen for coffee,' Marion said.

'Yes, you did.'

'Can you describe the kitchen?'

'I didn't pay much attention. It was a big one – with a stone floor, I think – and a row of bells.'

'What kind of stove?'

'I didn't notice the stove, but the pan the old woman heated the coffee in was a pale blue enamel one with a dark blue edge and a lot of chips off round the bottom edge.'

'I doubt if there is any kitchen in England that hasn't a pan exactly like that,' Marion said. 'We have three of them.'

'Is the girl a virgin?' asked Mrs Sharpe, in the mildly interested tone of a person inquiring: Is it a Chanel?

In the startled pause that this produced Robert was aware of Hallam's scandalized face, the hot blood running up into the girl's, and the fact that there was no protesting 'Mother!' from the daughter, as he unconsciously but confidently expected. He wondered whether her silence was tacit approval or whether after a lifetime with Mrs Sharpe she was shock-proof.

Grant said in cold reproof that the matter was irrelevant.

'You think so?' said the old lady. 'If I had been missing for a month from my house it is the first thing that my mother would have wanted to know about me. However. Now that the girl has identified us, what do you propose to do? Arrest us?'

'Oh no. Things are a long way from that at the moment. I

want to take Miss Kane to the kitchen and the attic, so that her descriptions of them can be verified. If they are, I report on the case to my superior and he decides in conference what further steps to take.'

'I see. A most admirable caution, Inspector.' She rose slowly to her feet. 'Ah well, if you will excuse me I shall go back to my interrupted rest.'

'But don't you want to be present when Miss Kane inspects – to hear the –' blurted Grant, surprised for once out of his composure.

'Oh dear, no.' She smoothed down her black gown with a slight frown. 'They split invisible atoms,' she remarked testily, 'but no one so far has invented a material that does not crease. I have not the faintest doubt,' she went on, 'that Miss Kane will identify the attic. Indeed, I should be surprised beyond belief if she failed to.'

She began to move towards the door, and consequently towards the girl; and for the first time the girl's eyes lit with expression. A spasm of alarm crossed her face. The police matron came forward a step protectively. Mrs Sharpe continued her unhurried progress and came to rest a yard or so from the girl, so that they were face to face. For a full five seconds there was silence while she examined the girl's face with interest.

'For two people who are on beating terms we are distressingly ill acquainted,' she said at last. 'I hope to know you much better before this affair is finished, Miss Kane.' She turned to Robert and bowed. 'Good-bye, Mr Blair. I hope you will continue to find us stimulating.' And, ignoring the rest of the gathering, she walked out of the door that Hallam held open for her.

There was a distinct feeling of anticlimax now that she was no longer there, and Robert paid her the tribute of a reluctant admiration. It was no small achievement to steal the interest from an outraged heroine.

'You have no objections to letting Miss Kane see the relevant parts of the house, Miss Sharpe?' Grant asked.

'Of course not. But before we go farther I should like to say what I was going to say before you brought Miss Kane in. I am glad that Miss Kane is present to hear it now. It is this. I have never to my knowledge seen this girl before, I did not give her a lift anywhere, on any occasion. She was not brought into this house either by me or by my mother, nor was she kept here. I should like that to be clearly understood.'

'Very well, Miss Sharpe. It is understood that your attitude is a complete denial of the girl's story.'

'A complete denial from beginning to end. And now, will you come and see the kitchen?'

3

GRANT and the girl accompanied Robert and Marion Sharpe on the inspection of the house, while Hallam and the police matron waited in the drawing-room.

As they reached the first-floor landing, after the girl had identified the kitchen, Robert said: 'Miss Kane said that the second flight of stairs was covered in "something hard", but the same carpet continues up from the first flight.'

'Only to the curve,' Marion said. 'The bit that shows. Round the corner it is drugget. A Victorian way of economizing. Nowadays if you are poor you buy less expensive carpet and use it all the way up. But those were still the days when what the neighbours thought mattered. So the lush stuff went as far as the eye could see and no farther.'

The girl had been right about the third flight, too. The treads of the short flight to the attic were bare.

The all-important attic was a low, square little box of a room, with the ceiling slanting abruptly down on three sides in conformity with the slate roof outside. It was lit only by the round window looking out to the front. A short stretch of slates sloped from below the window to the low white parapet. The window was divided into four panes, one of which showed a badly starred crack. It had never been made to open.

The attic was completely bare of furnishing. Unnaturally bare, Robert thought, for so convenient and accessible a store-room.

'There used to be stuff here when we first came,' Marion said, as if answering him. 'But when we found that we should be without help half the time, we got rid of it.'

Grant turned to the girl with a questioning air.

'The bed was in that corner,' she said, pointing to the corner away from the window. 'And next to it was the wooden commode. And in this corner behind the door there were three empty travelling-cases – two suitcases and a trunk with a flat top. There was a chair, but she took it away after I tried to break the window.' She referred to Marion without emotion, as if she were not present. 'There is where I tried to break the window.'

It seemed to Robert that the crack looked much more than a few weeks old; but there was no denying that the crack was there.

Grant crossed to the far corner and bent to examine the bare floor, but it did not need close examination. Even from where he was standing by the door Robert could see the marks of castors on the floor where the bed had stood.

'There was a bed there,' Marion said. 'It was one of the things we got rid of.'

'What did you do with it?'

'Let me think. Oh, we gave it to the cowman's wife over at Staples Farm. Her eldest boy got too big to share a room with the others any more and she put him up in their loft. We get our dairy stuff from Staples. You can't see it from here, but it is only four fields away over the rise.'

'Where do you keep your spare trunks, Miss Sharpe? Have you another box-room?'

For the first time Marion hesitated. 'We do have a large square trunk with a flat top, but my mother uses it to store things in. When we inherited The Franchise there was a very valuable tall-boy in the bedroom my mother has, and we sold it, and used the big trunk instead – with a chintz cover on it. My suitcases I keep in the cupboard on the first-floor landing.'

'Miss Kane, do you remember what the cases looked like?'

'Oh yes. One was a brown leather with those sort of caps at the corners and the other was one of those American-looking canvas-covered ones with stripes.'

Well, that was definite enough.

Grant examined the room a little longer, studied the view from the window, and then turned to go.

'May we see the suitcases in the cupboard?' he asked Marion.

'Certainly,' Marion said, but she seemed unhappy.

On the lower landing she opened the cupboard door and stood back to let the Inspector look. As Robert moved out of their way he caught the unguarded flash of triumph on the girl's face. It so altered her calm, rather childish face that it shocked him. It was a savage emotion, primitive and cruel; and very startling on the face of a demure schoolgirl who was the pride of her guardians and preceptors.

The cupboard contained shelves bearing household linen and on the floor four suitcases. Two were expanding ones, one of pressed fibre and one of rawhide; the other two were: a brown cowhide with protected corners and a square, canvas-covered hat-box with a broad band of multi-coloured stripes down the middle.

'Are these the cases?' Grant asked.

'Yes,' the girl said. 'Those two.'

'I am not going to disturb my mother again this afternoon,' Marion said, with sudden anger. 'I acknowledge that the trunk in her room is large and flat-topped. It has been there without interruption for the last three years.'

'Very good, Miss Sharpe. And now the garage, if you please.'

Down at the back of the house, where the stables had been converted long ago into a garage, the little group stood and surveyed the battered old grey car. Grant read out the girl's un-technical description of it as recorded in her statement. It fitted, but it would fit equally well at least a thousand cars on the roads of Britain today, Blair thought. It was hardly evidence at all. ' "One of the wheels was painted a different shade from the others and didn't look as if it belonged. The different wheel was the one in front on my side as it was standing at the pavement," ' Grant finished.

In the silence the four people looked at the darker grey of the near front wheel. There seemed nothing to say.

'Thank you very much, Miss Sharpe,' Grant said at length, shutting his notebook and putting it away. 'You have been very courteous and helpful, and I am grateful to you. I shall be able to get you on the telephone any time in the next few days, I suppose, if I want to talk to you further?'

'Oh yes, Inspector. We have no intention of going any-where.'

If Grant was aware of her too-ready comprehension he did not show it.

He handed over the girl to the matron and they left without

a backward glance. Then he and Hallam took their leave, Hallam still with an air of apologizing for trespass.

Marion had gone out into the hall with them, leaving Blair in the drawing-room, and when she came back she was carrying a tray with sherry and glasses.

'I don't ask you to stay for dinner,' she said, putting down the tray and beginning to pour the wine, 'partly because our "dinner" is usually a very scratch supper and not at all what you are used to. (Did you know that your aunt's meals are famous in Milford? Even I have heard about them.) And partly because – well, because, as my mother said, Broadmoor is a little out of your line, I expect.'

'About that,' Robert said, 'you do realize, don't you, that the girl has an enormous advantage over you – in the matter of evidence, I mean. She is free to describe almost any object she likes as being part of your household. If it happens to be there, that is strong evidence for her. If it happens not to be there, that is not evidence for you: the inference is merely that you have got rid of it. If the suitcases, for instance, had not been there, she could say that you had got rid of them because they had been in the attic and could be described.'

'But she did describe them, without ever having seen them.'

'She described two suitcases, you mean. If your four suitcases had been a matching set she would have only one chance in perhaps five of being right. But because you happened to have one of each of the common kinds her chances worked out at about even.'

He picked up the glass of sherry that she had set down beside him, took a mouthful, and was astonished to find it admirable.

She smiled a little at him and said, 'We economize, but not on wine,' and he flushed slightly, wondering if his surprise had been as obvious at that.

'But there was the odd wheel of the car. How did she know about that? The whole set-up is extraordinary. How did she know about my mother and me, and what the house looked like? Our gates are never open. Even if she opened them – though what she could be doing on that lonely road I can't imagine – even if she opened them and looked inside she would not know about my mother and me.'

'No chance of her having made friends with a maid? Or a gardener?'

'We have never had a gardener, because there is nothing but grass. And we have not had a maid for a year. Just a girl from the farm who comes in once a week and does the rough cleaning.'

Robert said sympathetically that it was a big house to have on her hands unaided.

'Yes; but two things help. I am not a house-proud woman. And it is still so wonderful to have a home of our own that I am willing to put up with the disadvantages. Old Mr Crowle was my father's cousin, but we didn't know him at all. My mother and I had always lived in a Kensington boarding-house.' One corner of her mouth moved up in a wry smile. 'You can't imagine how popular mother was with the residents.' The smile faded. 'My father died when I was very little. He was one of those optimists who are always going to be rich tomorrow. When he found one day that his speculations had not left even enough for a loaf of bread on the morrow, he committed suicide and left my mother to face things.'

Robert felt that this to some extent explained Mrs Sharpe.

'I was not trained for a profession, so my life has been spent in odd jobs. Not domestic ones – I loathe domesticity – but helping in those lady-like businesses that abound in Kensington. Lampshades, or advising on holidays, or flowers, or bric-à-brac. When old Mr Crowle died I was working in a tea-shop – one of those morning-coffee gossip shops. Yes, it is a little difficult.'

'What is?'

'To imagine me among the tea-cups.'

Robert, unused to having his mind read – Aunt Lin was incapable of following anyone's mental processes even when they were explained to her – was disconcerted. But she was not thinking of him.

'We had just begun to feel settled down and at home and safe when this happened.'

For the first time since she had asked his help Robert felt the stirring of partisanship. 'And all because a slip of a girl needs an alibi,' he said. 'We must find out more about Betty Kane.'

'I can tell you one thing about her. She is over-sexed.'

'Is that feminine intuition?'

'No. I am not very feminine and I have no intuition. But I have never known anyone – man or woman – with that colour of eye who wasn't. That opaque dark blue, like a very faded navy – it's infallible.'

Robert smiled at her indulgently. She was very feminine after all.

'And don't feel superior because it happens not to be law-yers' logic,' she added. 'Have a look round at your own friends and see.'

Before he could stop himself he thought of Gerald Blunt, the Milford scandal. Assuredly Gerald had slate-blue eyes. So had Arthur Wallis, the potman at the White Hart, who was paying three different monetary levies weekly. So had – Damn the wo-man, she had no right to make a silly generalization like that and be right about it.

'It is fascinating to speculate on what she really did during that month,' Marion said. 'It affords me intense satisfaction that someone beat her black and blue. At least there is one per-son in this world who has arrived at a correct estimate of her. I hope I meet him some day, so that I may shake his hand.'

'Him?'

'With those eyes it is bound to be a "him".'

'Well,' Robert said, preparing to go, 'I doubt very much whether Grant has a case that he will want to present in court. It would be the girl's word against yours, with no other back-ing on either side. Against *you* would be her statement – so de-tailed, so circumstantial. Against *her* would be the inherent unlikeliness of the story. I don't think he could hope to get a verdict.'

'But the thing is there, whether he brings it into court or not ; and not only in the files of Scotland Yard. Sooner or later a thing like that begins to be whispered about. It would be no comfort to us not to have the thing cleared up.'

'Oh, it will be cleared up, if I have anything to do with it. But I think we must wait for a day or two to see what the Yard mean to do about it. They have far better facilities for arriving at the truth than we are ever likely to have.'

'Coming from a lawyer, that is a touching tribute to the honesty of the police.'

'Believe me, truth may be a virtue, but Scotland Yard discovered long ago that it is a business asset. It doesn't pay them to be satisfied with anything less.'

'If he *did* bring it to court,' she said, coming to the door with him, 'and *did* get a verdict, what would that mean for us?'

'I'm not sure whether it would be two years' imprisonment or seven years' penal servitude. I told you I was a broken reed where criminal procedure is concerned. But I shall look it up.'

'Yes, do,' she said. 'There's quite a difference.'

He decided that he liked her habit of mockery. Especially in the face of a criminal charge.

'Good-bye,' she said. 'It was kind of you to come. You have been a great comfort to me.'

And Robert, remembering how nearly he had thrown her to Ben Carley, blushed to himself as he walked to the gate.

4

'HAVE you had a busy day, dear?' Aunt Lin asked, opening her table napkin and arranging it across her plump lap.

This was a sentence that made sense but had no meaning. It was as much an overture to dinner as the spreading of her napkin and the exploratory movement of her right foot as she located the footstool which compensated for her short legs. She expected no answer; or rather, being unaware that she had asked the question, she did not listen to his answer.

Robert looked up the table at her with a more conscious benevolence than usual. After his uncharted step-picking at The Franchise, the serenity of Aunt Lin's presence was very comforting, and he looked with a new awareness at the solid little figure with the short neck and the round pink face and the iron-grey hair that frizzed out from its large hairpins. Linda Bennet led a life of recipes, film stars, godchildren, and church bazaars, and found it perfect. Well-being and contentment enveloped her like a cloak. She read the Women's Page of the daily paper (How to Make a Boutonnière from Old Kid Gloves) and nothing else as far as Robert was aware. Occasionally when she tidied away the paper that Robert had left lying about she would pause to read the headlines and comment on them. ('MAN ENDS EIGHTY-TWO DAY FAST' – silly creature! 'OIL DISCOVERY IN BAHAMAS' – did I tell you that paraffin is up a penny, dear?) But she gave the impression of never really believing that the world the papers reported did in fact exist. The world for Aunt Lin began with Robert Blair and ended within a ten-mile radius of him.

'What kept you so late tonight, dear?' she asked, having finished her soup.

From long experience Robert recognized this as being in a different category from: 'Have you had a busy day, dear?'

'I had to go out to The Franchise – that house on the Larborough road. They wanted some legal advice.'

'Those odd people? I didn't know you knew them.'

'I didn't. They just wanted my advice.'

'I hope they pay you for it, dear. They have no money at all, you know. The father was in some kind of importing business – monkey-nuts or something – and drank himself to death. Left them without a penny, poor things. Old Mrs Sharpe ran a boarding-house in London to make ends meet, and the daughter was maid-of-all-work. They were just going to be turned into the street with their furniture when the old man at The Franchise died. So providential!'

'Aunt Lin! Where do you get those stories?'

'But it's true, dear. Perfectly true. I forgot who told me – someone who had stayed in the same street in London – but it was first-hand, anyhow. I am not one to pass on idle gossip, as you know. Is it a nice house? I always wondered what was inside that iron gate.'

'No, rather ugly. But they have some nice pieces of furniture.'

'Not as well kept as ours, I'll be bound,' she said, looking complacently at the perfect sideboard and the beautiful chairs ranged against the wall. 'The Vicar said yesterday that if this house were not so obviously a home it would be a show-place.' Mention of the clergy seemed to remind her of something. 'By the way, will you be extra patient with Christina for the next few days? I think she is going to be "saved" again.'

'Oh, poor Aunt Lin, what a bore for you! But I was afraid of it. There was a text in the saucer of my early-morning tea today: "Thou God seest me" on a scroll, with a tasteful design of Easter lilies in the background. Is she changing her church again, then?'

'Yes. She has discovered that the Methodists are "whited sepulchres", it seems, so she is going to those "Bethel" people above Benson's bakery, and is due to be "saved" any day now. She has been shouting hymns all the morning.'

'But she always does.'

'Not "sword of the Lord" ones. As long as she sticks to "pearly crowns" or "streets of gold" I know it is all right. But once she begins on the "sword of the Lord" I know that it will be my turn to do the baking presently.'

'Well, darling, you bake just as well as Christina.'

'Oh no, she doesn't,' said Christina, coming in with the meat course. A big soft creature with untidy, straight hair and a vague eye. 'Only one thing your Aunt Lin makes better than me, Mr Robert, and that's hot cross buns, and that's only once a year. So there! And if I'm not appreciated in this house, I'll go where I will be.'

'Christina, my love,' Robert said, 'you know very well that no one could imagine this house without you, and if you left I should follow you to the world's end. For your butter tarts, if for nothing else. Can we have butter tarts tomorrow, by the way?'

'Butter tarts are no food for unrepentant sinners. Besides, I don't think I have the butter. But we'll see. Meanwhile, Mr Robert, you examine your soul and stop casting stones.'

Aunt Lin sighed gently as the door closed behind her. 'Twenty years,' she said meditatively. 'You won't remember her when she first came from the orphanage. Fifteen, and so skinny, poor little brat. She ate a whole loaf for her tea, and said she would pray for me all her life. I think she has, you know.'

Something like a tear glistened in Miss Bennet's blue eye.

'I hope she postpones the salvation until she has made those butter tarts,' said Robert, brutally materialistic. 'Did you enjoy your picture?'

'Well, dear, I couldn't forget that he had five wives.'

'Who has?'

'*Had* dear – one at a time. Gene Darrow. I must say, those little programmes they give away are very informative, but a little disillusioning. He was a student, you see. In the picture, I mean. Very young and romantic. But I kept remembering those five wives, and it spoiled the afternoon for me. So charming to look at too. They say he dangled his third wife out of a fifth-storey window by the wrists, but I don't really believe that. He doesn't look strong enough, for one thing. Looks as if he had chest trouble as a child – that peaky look and thin wrists. Not strong enough to dangle anyone. Certainly not out of a fifth-storey . . .'

The gentle monologue went on all through the pudding course; and Robert withdrew his attention and thought about The Franchise. He came to the surface as they rose from table and moved into the sitting-room for coffee.

'It is the most becoming garment, if maids would only realize it,' she was saying.

'What is?'

'An apron. She was a maid in the palace, you know, and wore one of those silly bits of muslin – so becoming. Did those people at The Franchise have a maid, by the way? No? Well, I am not surprised. They starved the last one, you know. Gave her –'

'Oh, Aunt *Lin*!'

'I assure you. For breakfast she got the crusts they cut off the toast. And when they had milk pudding . . .'

Robert did not hear what enormity was born of the milk pudding. In spite of his good dinner he was suddenly tired and depressed. If kind, silly Aunt Lin saw no harm in repeating those absurd stories, what would the real gossips of Milford achieve with the stuff of a real scandal?

'And talking of maids – the brown sugar is finished, dear, so you will have to have lump for tonight – talking of maids, the Carley's little maid has got herself into trouble.'

'You mean someone else has got her into trouble.'

'Yes. Arthur Wallis, the potman at the White Hart.'

'What, Wallis *again*!'

'Yes, it really is getting past a joke, isn't it? I can't think why the man doesn't get married. It would be much cheaper.'

But Robert was not listening. He was back in the drawing-room at The Franchise being gently mocked for his legal intolerance of a generalization. Back in the shabby room with the unpolished furniture, where things lay about on chairs and no one bothered to tidy them away.

And where, now he came to think of it, no one ran round after him with an ash-tray.

5

IT was more than a week later that Mr Heseltine put his thin, small, grey head round Robert's door to say that Inspector Hallam was in the office and would like to see him for a moment.

The room on the opposite side of the hall, where Mr Heseltine lorded it over the clerks, was always referred to as 'the office', although both Robert's room and the little one behind it used by Nevil Bennet were, in spite of their carpets and their mahogany, plainly offices too. There was an official waiting-room behind 'the office', a small room corresponding to young Bennet's, but it had never been popular with the Blair, Hayward, and Bennet clients. Callers stepped into the office to announce themselves and usually stayed there gossiping until such time as Robert was free to see them. The little 'waiting-room' had long ago been appropriated by Miss Tuff for writing Robert's letters in, away from the distraction of visitors and from the office-boy's sniffings.

When Mr Heseltine had gone away to fetch the Inspector, Robert noticed with surprise that he was apprehensive as he had not been apprehensive since in the days of his youth he approached a list of examination results pinned on a board. Was his life so placid that a stranger's dilemma should stir it to that extent? Or was it that the Sharpes had been so constantly in his thoughts for the last week that they had ceased to be strangers?

He braced himself for whatever Hallam was going to say; but what emerged from Hallam's careful phrases was that Scotland Yard had let them understand that no proceedings would be taken on the present evidence. Blair noticed the 'present evidence' and gauged its meaning accurately. They were not dropping the case – did the Yard ever drop a case? – they were merely sitting quiet.

The thought of Scotland Yard sitting quiet was not a particularly reassuring one in the circumstances.

'I take it that they lack corroborative evidence,' he said.

'They couldn't trace the lorry driver who gave her the lift,' Hallam said.

'That wouldn't surprise them.'

'No,' Hallam agreed; 'no driver is going to risk the sack by confessing he gave anyone a lift. Especially a girl. Transport bosses are strict about that. And when it is the case of a girl in trouble of some kind and when it's the police that are doing the asking, no man in his right sense is going to own up to even having seen her.' He took the cigarette that Robert offered him. 'They needed that lorry driver,' he said; 'or someone like him,' he added.

'Yes,' Robert said, reflectively. 'What did you make of her, Hallam?'

'The girl? I don't know. Nice kid. Seemed quite genuine. Might have been one of my own.'

This, Blair realized, was a very good sample of what they would be up against if it ever came to a case. To every man of good feeling the girl in the witness-box would look like his own daughter. Not because she was a waif, but for the very good reason that she wasn't. The decent school coat, the mousy hair, the unmade-up young face with its appealing hollow below the cheek-bone, the wide-set, candid eyes – it was a prosecuting counsel's dream of a victim.

'Just like any other girl of her age,' Hallam said, still considering it. 'Nothing against her.'

'So you don't judge people by the colour of their eyes,' Robert said idly, his mind still on the girl.

'Ho! Don't I!' said Hallam surprisingly. 'Believe me, there's a particular shade of baby blue that condemns a man, as far as I'm concerned, before he has opened his mouth. Plausible liars every one of them.' He paused to pull at his cigarette. 'Given to murder, too, come to think of it – though I haven't met many killers.'

'You alarm me,' Robert said. 'In the future I shall give baby-blue eyes a wide berth.'

Hallam grinned. 'As long as you keep your pocket-book shut you needn't worry. All Baby-blue's lies are for money. He only murders when he gets too entangled in his lies. The real murderer's mark is not the colour of the eyes but their setting.'

'Setting?'

'Yes. They are set differently. The two eyes, I mean. They look as if they belonged to different faces.'

'I thought you hadn't met many.'

'No; but I've read all the case histories and studied the photographs. I've always been surprised that no book on murder mentions it, it happens so often. The inequality of setting, I mean.'

'So it's entirely your own theory.'

'The result of my own observation, yes. You ought to have a go at it sometimes. Fascinating. I've got to the stage where I look for it now.'

'In the street, you mean?'

'No, not quite as bad as that. But in each new murder case. I wait for the photograph, and when it comes I think: "There! What did I tell you?"'

'And when the photograph comes and the eyes are of a mathematical identity?'

'Then it is nearly always what one might call an accidental murder – the kind of murder that might happen to anyone given the circumstances.'

'And when you turn up a photograph of the reverend vicar of Nether Dumbleton, who is being given a presentation by his grateful parishioners to mark his fiftieth year of devoted service, and you note that his eyes are wildly unequal in setting, what conclusion do you come to?'

'That his wife satisfies him, his children obey him, his stipend is sufficient for his needs, he has no politics, he gets on with the local big-wigs, and he is allowed to have the kind of services he wants. In fact, he has never had the slightest need to murder anyone.'

'It seems to me that you are having your cake and eating it very nicely.'

'Huh!' Hallam said disgustedly. 'Just wasting good police observation on a legal mind. I'd have thought,' he added, moving to go, 'that a lawyer would be glad of some free tips about judging perfect strangers.'

'All you are doing,' Robert pointed out, 'is corrupting an innocent mind. I shall never be able to inspect a new client from now on without my subconscious registering the colour of his eyes and the symmetry of their setting.'

'Well, that's something. It's about time you knew some of the facts of life.'

'Thank you for coming to tell me about The Franchise affair,' Robert said, returning to sobriety.

'The telephone in this town,' Hallam said, 'is about as private as the radio.'

'Anyhow, thank you. I must let the Sharpes know at once.'

As Hallam took his leave, Robert lifted the telephone receiver.

He could not, as Hallam said, talk freely over the telephone, but he would say that he was coming out to see them immediately and that the news was good. That would take the present weight off their minds. It would also – he glanced at his watch – be time for Mrs Sharpe's daily rest, so perhaps he would have a hope of avoiding the old dragon. And also a hope of a tête-à-tête with Marion Sharpe, of course; though he left that thought unformulated at the back of his mind.

But there was no answer to his call.

With the bored and reluctant aid of the Exchange he rang the number for a solid five minutes, without result. The Sharpes were not at home.

While he was still engaged with the Exchange, Nevil Bennet strolled in, clad in his usual outrageous tweed, a pinkish shirt, and a purple tie. Robert, eyeing him over the receiver, wondered for the hundredth time what was going to become of Blair, Hayward, and Bennet when it at last slipped from his good Blair grasp into the hands of this young sprig of the Bennets. That the boy had brains he knew, but brains wouldn't take him far in Milford. Milford expected a man to stop being undergraduate when he reached graduate age. But there was no sign of Nevil's acceptance of the world outside his coterie. He was still actively, if unconsciously, *épate*-ing that world – as his clothes bore witness.

It was not that Robert had any desire to see the boy in customary suits of solemn black. His own suit was a grey tweed; and his country clientele would look doubtfully on 'town' clothes. ('That awful little man with the striped suits,' Marion

45

Sharpe had said of a town-clad lawyer, in that unguarded moment on the telephone.) But there were tweeds and tweeds, and Nevil Bennet's were the second kind. Quite outrageously the second kind.

'Robert,' Nevil said, as Robert gave it up and laid down the receiver, 'I've finished the papers on the Calthorpe transfer, and I thought I would run into Larborough this afternoon if you haven't anything you want me to do.'

'Can't you talk to her on the telephone?' Robert asked – Nevil being engaged, in the casual modern fashion, to the Bishop of Larborough's third daughter.

'Oh, it isn't Rosemary. She is in London for a week.'

'A protest meeting at the Albert Hall, I suppose,' said Robert, who was feeling disgruntled because of his failure to speak to the Sharpes when he was primed with good news for them.

'No, at the Guildhall,' Nevil said.

'What is it this time? Vivisection?'

'You are frightfully last-century now and then, Robert,' Nevil said with his air of solemn patience. 'No one objects to vivisection nowadays except a few cranks. The protest is against this country's refusal to give shelter to the patriot Kotovich.'

'The said patriot is very badly "wanted" in his own country, I understand.'

'By his enemies ; yes.'

'By the police – for two murders.'

'Executions.'

'You a disciple of John Knox, Nevil?'

'Good God, no. What has that to do with it?'

'*He* believed in self-appointed executioners. The idea has a little "gone out" in this country, I understand. Anyhow, if it's a choice between Rosemary's opinion of Kotovich and the opinion of the Special Branch, I'll take the Special Branch.'

'The Special Branch only do what the Foreign Office tells them. Everyone knows that. But if I stay and explain the ramifications of the Kotovich affair to you, I shall be late for the film.'

'What film?'

'The French film I am going into Larborough to see.'

'I suppose you know that most of those French trifles that

the British intelligentsia bate their breath about are considered very so-so in their own country? However. Do you think you could pause long enough to drop a note into the letter-box of The Franchise as you go by?'

'I might. I always wanted to see what was inside that wall. Who lives there now?'

'An old woman and her daughter.'

'Daughter?' repeated Nevil, automatically pricking his ears.

'Middle-aged daughter.'

'Oh. All right, I'll just get my coat.'

Robert wrote merely that he had tried to talk to them, that he had to go out on business for an hour or so, but that he would ring them up again when he was free, and that Scotland Yard had no case, as the case stood, and acknowledged the fact.

Nevil swept in with a dreadful raglan affair over his arm, snatched up the letter and disappeared with a 'Tell Aunt Lin I may be late. She asked me over to dinner.'

Robert donned his own sober grey hat and walked over to the Rose and Crown to meet his client – an old farmer and the last man in England to suffer from chronic gout. The old man was not yet there, and Robert, usually so placid, so lazily good-natured, was conscious of impatience. The pattern of his life had changed. Up to now it had been an even succession of equal attractions ; he had gone from one thing to another without hurry and without emotion. Now there was a focus of interest, and the rest revolved round it.

He sat down on one of the chintz-covered chairs in the lounge and looked at the dog-eared journals lying on the adjacent coffee table. The only current number was *The Watchman*, the weekly review, and he picked it up reluctantly, thinking yet once more how the dry feel of the paper offended his finger-tips and its serrated edges set his own teeth on edge. It was the usual collection of protests, poems, and pedantry ; the place of honour among the protests was accorded to Nevil's future father-in-law, who spread himself for three-quarters of a column on England's shame in that she refused sanctuary to a fugitive patriot.

The Bishop of Larborough had long ago extended the Christian philosophy to include the belief that the under-dog is always right. He was wildly popular with Balkan revolutionaries, British strike committees, and all the old lags in the local penal establishment. (The sole exception to this last being that chronic recidivist Bandy Brayne, who held the good bishop in vast contempt and reserved his affection for the Governor – to whom a tear in the eye was just a drop of H_2O, and who unpicked his most heartbreaking tales with a swift, unemotional accuracy.) There was *nothing*, said the old lags affectionately, that the old boy would not believe; you could lay it on with a trowel.

Normally Robert found the Bishop mildly amusing, but today he was merely irritated. He tried two poems, neither of which made sense to him, and flung the thing back on the table.

'England in the wrong again?' asked Ben Carley, pausing by his chair and jerking a head at *The Watchman*.

'Hullo, Carley.'

'A Marble Arch for the well-to-do,' the little lawyer said, flicking the paper scornfully with a nicotine-stained finger. 'Have a drink?'

'Thanks, but I'm waiting for old Mr Wynyard. He doesn't move a step more than he need, nowadays.'

'No, poor old boy. The sins of the fathers. Awful to be suffering for port you never drank! I saw your car outside The Franchise the other day.'

'Yes,' said Robert, and wondered a little. It was unlike Ben Carley to be blunt. And if he had seen Robert's car he had also seen the police cars.

'If you know them you'll be able to tell me something I always wanted to know about them. Is the rumour true?'

'Rumour?'

'*Are* they witches?'

'Are they supposed to be?' said Robert lightly.

'There's a strong support for the belief in the countryside, I understand,' Carley said, his bright black eyes resting for a moment on Robert's with intention and then going on to wander over the lounge with their habitual quick interrogation.

Robert understood that the little man was offering him, tacitly, information that he thought ought to be useful to him.

48

'Ah well,' Robert said, 'since entertainment came into the country with the cinema, God bless it, an end has been put to witch-hunting.'

'Don't you believe it. Give these Midland morons a good excuse and they'll witch-hunt with the best. An inbred crowd of degenerates, if you ask me. Here's your old boy. Well, I'll be seeing you.'

It was one of Robert's chief attractions that he was genuinely interested in people and in their troubles, and he listened to old Mr Wynyard's rambling story with a kindness that won the old man's gratitude – and added, although he was unaware of it, a hundred to the sum that stood against his name in the old farmer's will; but as soon as their business was over he made straight for the hotel telephone.

There were far too many people about, and he decided to use the one in the garage over in Sin Lane. The office would be shut by now, and anyhow it was farther away. And if he telephoned from the garage, so his thoughts went as he strode across the street, he would have his car at hand if she – if they asked him to come out and discuss the business further, as they very well might, as they almost certainly would – yes, of course they would want to discuss what they could do to discredit the girl's story, whether there was to be a case or not. He had been so relieved over Hallam's news that he had not yet come round in his mind to considering what –

'Evening, Mr Blair,' Bill Brough said, oozing his large person out of the narrow office door, his round, calm face bland and welcoming. 'Want your car?'

'No, I want to use your telephone first, if I may.'

'Sure. Go ahead.'

Stanley, who was under a car, poked his fawn's face out and asked: 'Know anything?'

'Not a thing, Stan. Haven't had a bet for months.'

'I'm two pounds down on a cow called Bright Promise. That's what comes of putting your faith in horseflesh. Next time you know something –'

'Next time I have a bet I'll tell you. But it will still be horseflesh.'

'As long as it's not a cow –' Stanley said, disappearing under

49

the car again; and Robert moved into the hot, bright little office and picked up the receiver.

It was Marion who answered, and her voice sounded warm and glad.

'You can't imagine what a relief your note was to us. Both my mother and I have been picking oakum for the last week. Do they still pick oakum, by the way?'

'I think not. It is something more constructive nowadays, I understand.'

'Occupational therapy.'

'More or less.'

'I can't think of any compulsory sewing that would improve my character.'

'They would probably find you something more congenial. It is against modern thought to compel a prisoner to do anything that he doesn't want to.'

'That is the first time I have heard you sound tart.'

'Was I tart?'

'Pure angostura.'

Well, she had reached the subject of drink; perhaps now she would suggest his coming out for sherry before dinner.

'What a charming nephew you have, by the way.'

'Nephew?'

'The one who brought the note.'

'He is not my nephew,' Robert said coldly. Why was it so ageing to be avuncular? 'He is my first cousin once removed. But I am glad you liked him.' This would not do; he would have to take the bull by the horns. 'I should like to see you sometime to discuss what we can do to straighten things out. To make things safer –' He waited.

'Yes, of course. Perhaps we could look in at your office one morning when we are shopping? What kind of thing could we do, do you think?'

'Some kind of private inquiry, perhaps. I can't very well discuss it over the telephone.'

'No, of course you can't. How would it do if we came in on Friday morning? That is our weekly shopping day. Or is Friday a busy day for you?'

50

'No, Friday would be quite convenient,' Robert said, swallowing down his disappointment. 'About noon?'

'Yes, that would do very well. Twelve o'clock the day after tomorrow at your office. Good-bye, and thank you again for your support and help.'

She rang off firmly and cleanly, without all the usual preliminary twitterings that Robert had come to expect from women.

'Shall I run her out for you?' Bill Brough asked as he came out into the dim daylight of the garage.

'What? Oh, the car. No, I shan't need it tonight, thanks.'

He set off on his normal evening walk down the High Street, trying hard not to feel snubbed. He had not been anxious to go to The Franchise in the first instance and had made his reluctance pretty plain ; she was quite naturally avoiding a repetition of the circumstances. That he had identified himself with their interests was a mere business affair, to be resolved in an office, impersonally. They would not again involve him further than that.

Ah well, he thought, flinging himself down in his favourite chair by the wood fire in the sitting-room and opening the evening paper (printed that morning in London), when they came to the office on Friday he could do something to put the affair on a more personal basis, to wipe out the memory of that first unhappy refusal.

The quiet of the old house soothed him. Christina had been closeted in her room for two days in prayer and meditation, and Aunt Lin was in the kitchen preparing dinner. There was a gay letter from Lettice, his only sister, who had driven a truck for several years of bloody war, fallen in love with a tall, silent Canadian, and was now raising five blond brats in Saskatchewan. 'Come out soon, Robin dear,' she finished, 'before the brats grow up and before the moss grows *right* round you. You know how *bad* Aunt Lin is for you!' He could hear her saying it. She and Aunt Lin had never seen eye to eye.

He was smiling, relaxed and reminiscent, when both his quiet and his peace were shattered by the interruption of Nevil.

'Why didn't you *tell* me she was like that!' Nevil demanded.

'Who?'

'The Sharpe woman! Why didn't you tell me?'

'I didn't expect you would meet her,' Robert said. 'All you had to do was drop the letter through the door.'

'There was nothing in the door to drop it through, so I rang, and they had just come back from wherever they were. Anyhow, *she* answered it.'

'I thought she slept in the afternoons.'

'I don't believe she ever sleeps. She doesn't belong to the human family at all. She is all compact of fire and metal.'

'I know she's a very rude old woman, but you have to make allowances. She has had a very hard –'

'*Old?* Who are you talking about?'

'Old Mrs Sharpe, of course.'

'I didn't even see old Mrs Sharpe. I'm talking about Marion.'

'Marion Sharpe? And how did you know her name was Marion?'

'She told me. It does suit her, doesn't it? She couldn't be anything but Marion.'

'You seem to have become remarkably intimate for a doorstep acquaintance.'

'Oh, she gave me tea.'

'Tea! I thought you were in a desperate hurry to see a French film.'

'I'm never in a desperate hurry to do anything when a woman like Marion Sharpe invites me to tea. Have you noticed her eyes? But of course you have. You're her lawyer. That wonderful shading of grey into hazel. And the way her eyebrows lie above them, like the brush-mark of a painter genius. Winged eyebrows, they are. I made a poem about them on the way home. Do you want to hear it?'

'No,' Robert said firmly. 'Did you enjoy your film?'

'Oh, I didn't go.'

'You didn't *go*!'

'I told you I had tea with Marion instead.'

'You mean you have been at The Franchise *the whole afternoon*!'

'I suppose I have,' Nevil said dreamily, 'but, by God, it didn't seem more than seven minutes.'

'And what happened to your thirst for French cinema?'

'But Marion *is* French film. Even you must see that!' Robert winced at the 'even you'. 'Why bother with the shadow, when you can be with the reality? Reality. That is her great quality, isn't it? I've never met anyone as real as Marion is.'

'Not even Rosemary?' Robert was in the state known to Aunt Lin as 'put out'.

'Oh, Rosemary is a darling and I'm going to marry her, but that is quite a different thing.'

'Is it?' said Robert, with deceptive meekness.

'Of course. People don't marry women like Marion Sharpe, any more than they marry winds and clouds. Any more than they marry Joan of Arc. It's positively blasphemous to consider marriage in relation to a woman like that. She spoke very nicely of you, by the way.'

'That was very kind of her.'

The tone was so dry that even Nevil caught the flavour of it.

'Don't you like her?' he asked, pausing to look at his cousin in surprised disbelief.

Robert had ceased for the moment to be kind, lazy, tolerant Robert Blair; he was just a tired man who hadn't yet had his dinner and was suffering from the memory of a frustration and a snubbing.

'As far as I am concerned,' he said, 'Marion Sharpe is just a skinny woman of forty who lives with a rude old mother in an ugly old house, and needs legal advice on occasion, like anyone else.'

But even as the words came out he wanted to stop them, as if they were a betrayal of a friend.

'No, probably she *isn't* your cup of tea,' Nevil said tolerantly. 'You have always preferred them a little stupid and blonde, haven't you?' This was said without malice, as one stating a dullish fact.

'I can't imagine why you should think that.'

'All the women you nearly married were that type.'

'I have never "nearly married" anyone,' Robert said stiffly.

'That's what you think. You'll never know how nearly Molly Manders landed you.'

'Molly Manders?' Aunt Lin said, coming in flushed from her cooking and bearing the tray with the sherry. 'Such a silly girl. Imagined that you used a baking-board for pancakes. And was always looking at herself in that little pocket mirror of hers.'

'Aunt Lin saved you that time, didn't you, Aunt Lin?'

'I don't know what you are talking about, Nevil dear. Do stop prancing about the hearthrug and put a log on the fire. Did you like your French film, dear?'

'I didn't go. I had tea at The Franchise instead.' He shot a glance at Robert, having learned by now that there was more in Robert's reaction than met the eye.

'With those strange people? What did you talk about?'

'Mountains – Maupassant – hens –'

'*Hens*, dear?'

'Yes; the concentrated evil of a hen's face in a close-up.'

Aunt Lin looked vague. She turned to Robert as to terra firma.

'Had I better call, dear, if you are going to know them? Or ask the vicar's wife to call?'

'I don't think I would commit the vicar's wife to anything so irrevocable,' Robert said dryly.

She looked doubtful for a moment, but household cares obliterated the question in her mind. 'Don't dawdle too long over your sherry or what I have in the oven will be spoiled. Thank goodness, Christina will be down tomorrow. At least I hope so; I have never known her salvation take more than two days. And I don't really think I *will* call on those Franchise people, dear, if it is all the same to you. Apart from being strangers and very odd, they quite frankly terrify me.'

Yes; that was a sample of the reaction he might expect where the Sharpes were concerned. Ben Carley had gone out of his way today to let him know that, if there was police trouble at The Franchise, he wouldn't be able to count on an unprejudiced jury. He must take measures for the protection of the Sharpes. When he saw them on Friday he would suggest a private investigation by a paid agent. The police were overworked – had been overworked for a decade and more – and there was just a chance that one man working at his leisure on one trail might be more successful than the orthodox and official investigation had been.

6

BUT by Friday morning it was too late to take measures for the safety of The Franchise.

Robert had reckoned with the diligence of the police; he had reckoned with the slow spread of whispers; but he had reckoned without the *Ack-Emma*.

The *Ack-Emma* was the latest representative of the tabloid newspaper to enter British journalism from the West. It was run on the principle that two thousand pounds for damages is a cheap price to pay for sales worth half a million. It had blacker headlines, more sensational pictures, and more indiscreet letterpress than any paper printed so far by British presses. Fleet Street had its own name for it – monosyllabic and unprintable – but no protection against it. The Press had always been its own censor, deciding what was and what was not permissible by the principles of its own good sense and good taste. If a 'rogue' publication decided not to conform to those principles then there was no power that could make it conform. In ten years the *Ack-Emma* had passed by half a million the daily net sales of the best-selling newspaper in the country to date. In any suburban railway carriage seven out of ten people bound for work in the morning were reading an *Ack-Emma*.

And it was the *Ack-Emma* that blew The Franchise affair wide open.

Robert had been out early into the country on that Friday morning to see an old woman who was dying and wanted to alter her will. This was a performance she repeated on an average once every three months, and her doctor made no secret of the fact that in his opinion she 'would blow out a hundred candles one day without a second puff'. But of course a lawyer cannot tell a client who summons him urgently at eight-thirty in the morning not to be silly. So Robert had taken some new will forms, fetched his car from the garage, and driven into the country. In spite of his usual tussle with the old tyrant among the pillows – who could never be brought to understand the elementary fact that you cannot give away *four* shares amounting to one-third each – he enjoyed the spring countryside. And he hummed to himself on the way home, looking forward to seeing Marion Sharpe in less than an hour.

He had decided to forgive her for liking Nevil. After all, Nevil had never tried to palm her off on Carley. One must be fair.

He ran the car into the garage, under the noses of the morning lot going out from the livery stable, parked it, and then, remembering that it was past the first of the month, strolled over to the office to pay his bill to Brough, who ran the office side. But it was Stanley who was in the office; thumbing over dockets and invoices with the strong hands that so surprisingly finished off his thin forearms.

'When I was in the Signals,' Stanley said, casting him an absent-minded glance, 'I used to believe that the Quarter-bloke was a crook, but now I'm not so sure.'

'Something missing?' said Robert. 'I just looked in to pay my bill. Bill usually has it ready.'

'I expect it's somewhere around,' Stanley said, still thumbing. 'Have a look.'

Robert, used to the ways of the office, picked up the loose papers discarded by Stanley so as to come on the normal tidy strata of Bill's arrangement below. As he lifted the untidy pile he uncovered a girl's face: a newspaper picture of a girl's face. He did not recognize it at once, but it reminded him of someone and he paused to look at it.

'Got it!' said Stanley in triumph, extracting a sheet of paper from a clip. He swept the remaining loose papers on the desk into a pile and so laid bare to Robert's gaze the whole front page of that morning's *Ack-Emma*.

Cold with shock, Robert stared at it.

Stanley, turning to take the papers he was holding from his grasp, noticed his absorption and approved it.

'Nice little number, that,' he said. 'Reminds me of a bint I had in Egypt. Same far-apart eyes. Nice kid she was. Told the most original lies.'

He went back to his paper-arranging, and Robert went on staring.

said the paper in enormous black letters across the top of the page ; and below it, occupying two-thirds of the page, was the girl's photograph. And then, in smaller but still obtrusive type, below:

IS THIS THE HOUSE?

and below it a photograph of The Franchise.

Across the bottom of the page was the legend:

THE GIRL SAYS YES: WHAT DO THE POLICE SAY?

See inside for the story

He put out his hand and turned over the page.

Yes ; it was all there except the Sharpes' name.

He dropped the page and looked again at that shocking frontispiece. Yesterday The Franchise was a house protected by four high walls; so unobtrusive, so sufficient unto itself that even Milford did not know what it looked like. Now it was there to be stared at on every bookstall, on every newsagent's counter from Penzance to Pentland: it's flat, forbidding front a foil for the innocence of the face above it.

The girl's photograph was a head-and-shoulders affair, and appeared to be a studio portrait. Her hair had an arranged-for-an-occasion look and she was wearing what looked like a party frock. Without her school coat she looked – not less innocent, nor older ; no. He sought for the word that would express it. She looked less – taboo, was it? The school coat had stopped one thinking of her as a woman, just as a nun's habit would. A whole treatise could probably be written, now he came to think of it, on the protective quality of school coats. Protective in both senses: armour and camouflage. Now that the coat was no longer there, she was feminine instead of merely female.

But it was still a pathetically young face, immature and appealing. The candid brow, the wide-set eyes, the beestung lip that gave her mouth the expression of a disappointed child – it made a formidable whole. It would not be only the Bishop of Larborough who would believe a story told by that face.

'May I borrow this paper?' he asked Stanley.

'Take it,' Stanley said. 'We had it for our elevenses. There's nothing in it.'

Robert was surprised. 'Didn't you find this interesting?' he asked, indicating the front page.

Stanley cast a glance at the pictured face. 'Not except that she reminded me of that bint in Egypt, lies and all.'

'So you don't believe that story she told?'

'What do *you* think!' Stanley said, contemptuous.

'Where do you think the girl was, then, all that time?'

'If I remember what I *think* I remember about the Red Sea sadie, I'd say very definitely – oh, but definitely – on the tiles,' Stanley said, and went out to attend to a customer.

Robert picked up the paper and went soberly away. At least one man-in-the-street had not believed the story; but that seemed to be due as much to an old memory as to present cynicism.

And although Stanley had quite obviously read the story without reading the names of the characters concerned or even the place-names, only ten per cent of readers did that (according to the best Mass Observation); the other ninety per cent would have read every word, and would now be discussing the affair with varying degrees of relish.

At his own office he found that Hallam had been trying to reach him by telephone.

'Shut the door and come in, will you?' he said to old Mr Heseltine, who had caught him with the news on his arrival and was now standing in the door of his room. 'And have a look at that.'

He reached for the receiver with one hand and laid the paper under Mr Heseltine's nose with the other.

The old man touched it with his small-boned, fastidious hand, as one seeing a strange exhibit for the first time. 'This is the publication one hears so much about,' he said, and gave his attention to it, as he would to any strange document.

'We are both in a spot, aren't we?' Hallam said, when they were connected, and raked his vocabulary for some epithets suitable to the *Ack-Emma*. 'As if the police hadn't enough to do without having that rag on their tails!' he finished, being naturally absorbed in the police point of view.

'Have you heard from the Yard?'

'Grant was burning the wires at nine this morning. But there's nothing they can do. Just grin and bear it. The police are fair game. Nothing you can do, either, if it comes to that.'

'Not a thing,' Robert said. 'We have a fine free Press.'

Hallam said a few more things about the Press. 'Do your people know?' he asked.

'I shouldn't think so. I'm quite sure they would never normally see the *Ack-Emma* and there hasn't been time for some kind soul to send it to them. But they are due here in about ten minutes, and I'll show it to them then.'

'If it was ever possible for me to be sorry for that old battle-axe,' Hallam said, 'it would be at this minute.'

'How did the *Ack-Emma* get the story? I thought the parents – the girl's guardians, I mean – were very strongly against that kind of publicity.'

'Grant says the girl's brother went off the deep end about the police taking no action and went to the *Ack-Emma* off his own bat. They are strong on the champion act. "The *Ack-Emma* will see right done!" I once knew one of their crusades run into a third day.'

When he hung up Robert thought that if it was a bad break for both sides, it was at least an even break. The police would without doubt redouble their efforts to find corroborative evidence; on the other hand, the publication of the girl's photograph meant for the Sharpes a faint hope that somebody somewhere would recognize it and say: 'This girl could not have been in The Franchise on the date in question because she was at such-and-such a place.'

'A shocking story, Mr Robert,' Mr Heseltine said. 'And if I may say so, a quite shocking publication. Most offensive.'

'That house,' Robert said, 'is The Franchise, where old Mrs Sharpe and her daughter live, and where I went the other day, if you remember, to give them some legal advice.'

'You mean that these people are our clients?'

'Yes.'

'But, Mr Robert, that is not at all in our line.' Robert winced at the dismay in his voice. 'That is quite outside our usual – indeed, quite beyond our normal – we are not competent –'

'We are competent, I hope, to defend any client against a publication like the *Ack-Emma*,' Robert said coldly.

Mr Heseltine eyed the screaming rag on the table. He was obviously facing the difficult choice between a criminal clientele and a disgraceful journal.

'Did you believe the girl's story when you read it?' Robert asked.

'I don't see how she could have made it up,' Mr Heseltine said simply. 'It is such a very circumstantial story, isn't it?'

'It is, indeed. But I saw the girl when she was brought to The Franchise to identify it last week – that was the day I went out so hurriedly just after tea – and I don't believe a word she says. Not a word,' he added, glad to be able to say it loudly and distinctly to himself and to be sure at last that he believed it.

'But how could she have thought of The Franchise at all or known all those things if she wasn't there?'

'I don't know. I haven't the least idea.'

'It is a most unlikely place to pick on, surely – a remote, invisible house like that, on a lonely road, in country that people don't visit very much.'

'I know. I don't know how the job was worked, but that it *is* a job I am certain. It is a choice not between stories but between human beings. I am quite certain that the two Sharpes are incapable of insane conduct like that. Whereas I don't believe the girl incapable of telling a story like that. That is what it amounts to.' He paused for a moment. 'And you'll just have to trust my judgement about it, Timmy,' he added, using his childhood's name for the old clerk.

Whether it was the 'Timmy' or the argument, it was apparent that Mr Heseltine had no further protest to make.

'You'll be able to see the criminals for yourself,' Robert said, 'because I hear their voices in the hall now. You might bring them in, will you?'

Mr Heseltine went dumbly out on his mission, and Robert

60

turned the newspaper over so that the comparatively innocu-
ous GIRL SMUGGLED ABOARD was all that would meet the
visitors' eyes.

Mrs Sharpe, moved by some belated instinct for conven-
tion, had donned a hat in honour of the occasion. It was a
flattish affair of black satin, and the general effect was that
of a doctor of learning. That the effect had not been wasted
was obvious by the relieved look on Mr Heseltine's face. This
was obviously not the kind of client he had expected; it was,
on the other hand, the kind of client he was used to.

'Don't go away,' Robert said to him, as he greeted the visitors; and to the others: 'I want you to meet the oldest member of the firm, Mr Heseltine.'

It suited Mrs Sharpe to be gracious; and exceedingly Victoria Regina was old Mrs Sharpe when she was being gracious. Mr Heseltine was more than relieved; he capitulated.
Robert's first battle was over.

When they were alone Robert noticed that Marion had been
waiting to say something.

'An odd thing happened this morning,' she said. 'We went
to the Anne Boleyn place to have coffee – we quite often do –
and there were two vacant tables, but when Miss Truelove
saw us coming she very hastily tilted the chairs against the
tables and said they were reserved. I might have believed her
if she hadn't looked so embarrassed. You don't think that rumour has begun to get busy already, do you? That she did
that because she has heard some gossip?'

'No,' Robert said sadly; 'because she has read this morning's *Ack-Emma*.' He turned the newspaper front side up. 'I
am sorry to have such bad news for you. You'll just have to
shut your teeth and take it, as small boys say. I don't suppose
you have ever seen this poisonous rag at close quarters. It's a
pity that the acquaintance should begin on so personal a basis.'

'Oh no!' Marion said, in passionate protest as her eye fell
on the picture of The Franchise.

And then there was unbroken silence while the two women
absorbed the contents of the inner page.

'I take it,' Mrs Sharpe said at last; 'that we have no redress
against this sort of thing?'

'None,' Robert said. 'All the statements are perfectly true. And it is all statement and not comment. Even if it were comment – and I've no doubt the comment will come – there has been no charge so the case is not *sub judice*. They are free to comment if they please.'

'The whole thing is one huge implied comment,' Marion said, 'that the police failed to do their duty. What do they think we did? Bribed them?'

'I think the suggestion is that the humble victim has less pull with the police than the wicked rich.'

'Rich,' repeated Marion, her voice curdling with bitterness.

'Anyone who has more than six chimneys is rich. Now, if you are not too shocked to think, consider. We *know* that the girl was never at The Franchise, that she could not – ' But Marion interrupted him.

'Do *you* know it?' she asked.

'Yes,' Robert said.

Her challenging eyes lost their challenge and her glance dropped.

'Thank you,' she said quietly.

'If the girl was never there, how could she have seen the house? ... She did see it somehow. It is too unlikely for belief that she could be merely repeating a description that someone gave her ... How could she see it? Naturally, I mean.'

'You could see it, I suppose, from the top deck of a bus,' Marion said. 'But there are no doubledecker buses on the Milford route. Or from on top of a load of hay; but it is the wrong time of the year for hay.'

'It may be the wrong time for hay,' croaked Mrs Sharpe, 'but there is no season for lorry-loads. I have seen lorries loaded with goods as high as any hay waggon.'

'Yes,' Marion said. 'Suppose the lift the girl got was not in a car, but on a lorry.'

'There is only one thing against that. If a girl was given a lift on a lorry she would be in the cabin even if it meant sitting on someone's knee. They wouldn't perch her up on top of the load. Especially as it was a rainy evening, you may remember ... No one ever came to The Franchise to ask the way or to sell something or to mend something – someone that the girl could have been with, even in the background?'

But no; they were both sure that no one had come, within the time the girl had been on holiday.

'Then we take it for granted that what she learned about The Franchise she learned from being high enough on one occasion to see over the wall. We shall probably never know when or how, and we probably could not prove it if we did know. So our whole efforts will have to be devoted to proving not that she wasn't at The Franchise but that she *was* somewhere else!'

'And what chance is there of that?' Mrs Sharpe asked.

'A better chance than before this was published,' Robert said, indicating the front page of the *Ack-Emma*. 'Indeed, it is the one bright spot in the bad business. *We* could not have published the girl's photograph in the hope of information about her whereabouts during that month. But now that *they* have published it – her own people, I mean – the same benefit should come to us. They have broadcast the story – and that is our bad luck; but they have also broadcast the photograph – and if we have any good luck at all someone somewhere will observe that the story and the photograph do not fit. That at the material time, as given in the story, the subject of the photograph could not possibly have been in the stated place, because they personally know her to have been elsewhere.'

Marion's face lost a little of its bleak look and even Mrs Sharpe's thin back looked less rigid. What had seemed a disaster might be, after all, the means of their salvation.

'And what can we do in the way of private investigation?' Mrs Sharpe asked. 'You realize, I expect, that we have very little money; and I take it that a private inquiry is a spendthrift business.'

'It does usually run away with more than one had bargained for, because it is difficult to budget for. But to begin with I am going myself to see the various people involved and find out, if possible, on what lines any inquiry should be based. Find out what she was *likely* to do.'

'Will they tell you that?'

'Oh no. They are probably unaware themselves of her

tendencies. But if they talk about her at all a picture must emerge. At least I hope so.'

There was a few moments' silence.

'You are extraordinarily kind, Mr Blair.'

Victoria Regina had come back to Mrs Sharpe's manner, but there was a hint of something else. Almost of surprise: as if kindness was not one of the things she had normally met with in life, nor expected. Her stiffly gracious acknowledgement was as eloquent as if she had said: 'You know that we are poor and that we may never be able to pay you adequately, and we are not at all the kind of people that you would choose to represent, but you are going out of your way to do us the best service in your power, and we are grateful.'

'When do you go?' Marion asked.

'Directly after lunch.'

'Today!'

'The sooner the better.'

'Then we won't keep you,' Mrs Sharpe said, rising. She stood for a moment looking down at the paper where it lay spread on the table. 'We enjoyed the privacy of The Franchise a great deal,' she said.

When he had seen them out of the door and into their car, he called Nevil into his room and picked up the receiver to talk to Aunt Lin about packing a bag.

'I suppose you don't see the *Ack-Emma* ever?' he asked Nevil.

'I take it that the question is rhetorical,' Nevil said.

'Have a look at this morning's. Hullo, Aunt Lin.'

'Does someone want to sue them for something? It will be sound money for us, if so. They practically always settle out of court. They have a special fund for the –' Nevil's voice died away. He had seen the front page that was staring up at him from the table.

Robert stole a look at him over the telephone and observed with satisfaction the naked shock on his cousin's bright young features. The youth of today, he understood, considered themselves shock-proof; it was good to know that, faced with an ordinary slab of real life, they reacted like any other human being.

'Be an angel, Aunt Lin, and pack a bag for me, will you? Just for overnight . . .'

Nevil had torn the paper open and was now reading the story.

'Just London and back, I expect, but I'm not sure. Anyhow, just the little case, and just the minimum. Not all the things I *might* need, if you love me. Last time there was a bottle of digestion powder weighing nearly a pound, and when in heck did I ever need a digestive powder! . . . All right, then, I *will* have ulcers . . . Yes, I'll be in to lunch in about ten minutes.'

'The blasted *swine!*' said the poet and intellectual, falling back in his need on the vernacular.

'Well, what do you make of it?'

'*Make* of it! Of what?'

'The girl's story.'

'Does one have to *make* anything of it? An obvious piece of sensationalism by an unbalanced adolescent?'

'And if I told you that the said adolescent is a very calm, ordinary, well-spoken-of schoolgirl who is anything but sensational?'

'Have you seen her?'

'Yes. That was why I first went to The Franchise last week – to be there when Scotland Yard brought the girl to confront them. Put that in your pipe and smoke it, young Nevil. She may talk hens and Maupassant with you, but it is me she turns to in trouble.'

'To be there on their behalf?'

'Certainly.'

Nevil relaxed suddenly. 'Oh well, that's all right. For a moment I thought you were against her . . . against them. But that's all right. We can join forces to put a spoke in the wheel of this –' he flicked the paper – 'this moppet.' Robert laughed at this typically Nevil choice of epithet. 'What are you going to do about it, Robert?'

Robert told him. 'And will you hold the fort while I am gone.' He saw that Nevil's attention had gone back to the 'moppet'. He moved over to join him and together they considered the young face looking so calmly up at them.

'An attractive face, on the whole,' Robert said. 'What do you make of it?'

'What I should *like* to make of it,' said the aesthete, with slow venom, 'would be a *very nasty mess.*'

7

THE Wynn's home outside Aylesbury was in a countrified
suburb: the kind of district where rows of semi-detached
houses creep along the edge of the still unspoiled fields; self-
conscious and aware that they are intruders or smug and not
caring, according to the character their builders have given
them. The Wynns lived in one of the apologetic rows – a red-
brick string of ramshackle dwellings that set Robert's teeth
on edge, so raw they were, so crude, so hang-dog. But as he
drove slowly up the road looking for the appropriate number,
he was won over by the love that had gone to the decoration
of these regrettable objects. No love had gone to their building; only a reckoning. But to each owner, as he took over,
the bare little house had represented his 'sufficient beauty',
and having found it he served it. The gardens were small
miracles of loveliness, each succeeding one a fresh revelation
of some unsuspected poet's heart.

Nevil really ought to be here to see, Robert thought, slow-
ing down yet once more as a new perfection caught his eye:
there was more poetry here than in a whole twelve months of
his beloved *Watchman*. All his clichés were here: form,
rhythm, colour, total gesture, design, impact ...

Or would Nevil see only a row of suburban gardens – only
Meadowside Lane, Aylesbury, with some Woolworth plants
in the gardens?

Probably.

Number 39 was the one with the plain green grass bordered
by a rockery. It was also distinguished by the fact that its curtains were invisible. No genteel net was stretched across the
window-pane, no cream casement cloth hung at the sides. The
windows were bare to the sun, the air, and the human gaze.
This surprised Robert as much as it probably surprised the
neighbours. It augured a noncomformity that he had not
expected.

He rang the bell, wishing that he did not feel like a bagman. He was a suppliant, and that was a new role for Robert Blair.

Mrs Wynn surprised him even more than her windows did. It was only when he had met her that he realized how complete a picture he had built in his mind of the woman who had adopted and mothered the child Betty Kane: the grey hair, the solid, matronly, comfortable figure, the plain, broad, sensible face; perhaps, even, an apron or one of those flowered overalls that housewives wear. But Mrs Wynn was not at all like that. She was slight and neat and young and modern and dark and pink-cheeked and still pretty, and had a pair of the most intelligent bright brown eyes that Robert had ever seen.

When she saw a stranger she looked defensive and made an involuntary closing movement with the door she was holding; but a second glance seemed to reassure her. Robert explained who he was, and she listened without interrupting him in a way he found quite admirable. Very few of his own clients listened without interrupting, male or female.

'You are under no obligation to talk to me,' he finished, having explained his presence. 'But I hope very much that you won't refuse. I told Inspector Grant that I was going to see you this afternoon, on my clients' behalf.'

'Oh, if the police know about it and don't mind —' She stepped back to let him come past her. 'I expect you have to do your best for those people if you are their lawyer. And we have nothing to hide. But if it is really Betty you want to interview, I'm afraid you can't. We have sent her into the country to friends for the day, to avoid all the fuss. Leslie meant well, but it was a stupid thing to do.'

'Leslie?'

'My son. Sit down, won't you?' She offered him one of the easy chairs in a pleasant, uncluttered sitting-room. 'He was too angry about the police to think clearly — angry about their failure to do anything when it seemed so proved, I mean. He has always been devoted to Betty. Indeed, until he got engaged they were inseparable.'

Robert's ears pricked. This was the kind of thing he had come to hear.

'Engaged?'

'Yes. He got engaged just after the New Year to a very nice girl. We are all delighted.'

'Was Betty delighted?'

'She wasn't jealous, if that's what you mean,' she said, looking at him with her intelligent eyes. 'I expect she missed not coming first with him, as she used to, but she was very nice about it. She *is* a nice girl, Mr Blair. Believe me. I was a schoolmistress before I married – not a very good one: that is why I got married at the first opportunity – and I know a lot about girls. Betty has never given me a moment's anxiety.'

'Yes; I know. Everyone reports excellently of her. Is your son's fiancée a schoolfellow of hers?'

'No, she is a stranger. Her people have come to live near here and he met her at a dance.'

'Does Betty go to dances?'

'Not grown-up dances. She is too young yet.'

'So she had not met the fiancée?'

'To be honest, none of us had. He rather sprang her on us. But we liked her so much we didn't mind.'

'He must be very young to be settling down?'

'Oh, the whole thing is absurd, of course. He is twenty and she is eighteen. But they are very sweet together. And I was very young myself when I married and I have been very happy. The only thing I lacked was a daughter, and Betty filled the gap.'

'What does she want to do when she leaves school?'

'She doesn't know. She has no special talent for anything, as far as I can see. I have a notion that she will marry early.'

'Because of her attractiveness?'

'No, because –' She paused and apparently changed what she had been going to say. 'Girls who have no particular bent fall easily into matrimony.'

He wondered if what she had been going to say had any remote connexion with slate-blue eyes.

'When Betty failed to turn up in time to go back to school, you thought she was playing truant – although she was a well-behaved child?'

'Yes; she was growing bored with school and she had al-

69

ways said – which is quite true – that the first day back at school is a wasted one. So we thought she was just "taking advantage" for once, as they say. "Trying it on" as Leslie said when he heard that she hadn't turned up.'

'I see. Was she wearing school clothes on her holiday?'

For the first time Mrs Wynn looked doubtfully at him, uncertain of his motive in asking.

'No. No, she was wearing her week-end clothes ... You know that when she came back she was wearing only a frock and shoes?'

Robert nodded.

'I find it difficult to imagine women so depraved that they would treat a helpless child like that.'

'If you could meet the women, Mrs Wynn, you would find it still more difficult to imagine.'

'But all the worst criminals look innocent and harmless, don't they?'

Robert let that pass. He wanted to know about the bruises on the girl's body. Were they fresh bruises?

'Oh, quite fresh. Most of them had not begun to "turn" even.'

This surprised Robert a little. 'But there were older bruises as well, I take it.'

'If there were they had faded so much as to be unnoticeable among all the bad new ones.'

'What did the new ones look like? A whipping?'

'Oh no. She had actually been knocked about. Even her poor little face. One jaw was swollen and there was a big bruise on the other temple.'

'The police say that she grew hysterical when it was suggested that she should tell them her story.'

'That was when she was still ill. Once we had got the story out of her and she had had a long rest, it was easy enough to persuade her to repeat it to the police.'

'I know you will answer this frankly, Mrs Wynn. Has there never been any suspicion in your mind that Betty's story might not be true? Even a momentary suspicion?'

'Not even a momentary one. Why should there be? She has always been a truthful child. Even if she hadn't, how could she invent a long, circumstantial story like that without being found out? The police asked her all the questions they wanted to; there was never any suggestion of accepting her statement as it stood.'

'When she first told her story to you, did she tell it all in a piece?'

'Oh no; it was spread over a day or two: the outline first, and then filling in the details as she remembered them. Things like the window in the attic being round.'

'Her days of coma had not blurred her memory.'

'I don't think they would in any case. I mean, with Betty's kind of brain. She has a photographic memory.'

Has she indeed! thought Robert, both ears erect and wide open.

'Even as a small child she could look at the page of a book – a child's book, of course – and repeat most of the contents from the picture in her mind. And when we played the Kim game – you know, the objects on the tray – we had to put Betty out of the game because she invariably won. Oh no, she would remember what she saw.'

Well, there was another game in which the cry was 'Growing warm!', Robert remembered.

'You say she was always a truthful child – and everyone supports you in that – but did she never indulge in romanticizing her own life, as children sometimes do?'

'Never,' said Mrs Wynn firmly. The idea seemed faintly to amuse her. 'She couldn't,' she added. 'Unless it was the real thing it was no use to Betty. Even playing dolls' tea-parties, she would never imagine the things on the plates, as most children are quite happy to do; there had to be a real thing there, even if it was only a little cube of bread. Usually it was something nicer, of course; it was a good way to wangle an extra and she was always a little greedy.'

Robert admired the detachment with which she considered her longed-for and much-loved daughter. The remains of a schoolmistress's cynicism? So much more valuable, anyhow, for a child than a blind love. It was a pity that her intelligence and devotion had been so ill-rewarded.

'I don't want to keep on at a subject that must be unpleasant for you,' Robert said. 'But perhaps you could tell me something about the parents.'

'Her parents?' Mrs Wynn asked, surprised.

'Yes. Did you know them well? What were they like?'

'We didn't know them at all. We never even saw them.'

'But you had Betty for – what was it … nine months? – before her parents were killed, hadn't you?'

'Yes; but her mother wrote shortly after Betty came to us and said that to come to see her would only upset the child and make her unhappy, and that the best thing for everyone would be to leave her to us until such time as she could go back to London. She said, would I talk to Betty about her at least once every day.'

Robert's heart contracted with pity for this unknown dead woman who had been willing to tear her own heart out for her only child. What treasure of love and care had been poured out in front of Betty Kane, child evacuee!

'Did she settle down easily when she came? Or did she cry for her mother?'

'She cried because she didn't like the food. I don't remember her ever crying for her mother. She fell in love with Leslie the first night – she was just a baby, you know – and I think her interest in him blotted out any grief she might have felt. And he, being four years older, was just the right age to feel protective. He still does – that is why we are in this mess today.'

'How did this *Ack-Emma* affair happen? I know it was your son who went to the paper, but did you eventually come round to his –'

'Good heavens, no,' Mrs Wynn said indignantly. 'It was all over before we could do anything about it. My husband and I were out when Leslie and the reporter came – they sent a man back with him when they heard his story, to get it first-hand from Betty – and when –'

'And Betty gave it quite willingly?'

'I don't know how willingly. I wasn't there. My husband and I knew nothing about it until this morning, when Leslie laid an *Ack-Emma* under our noses. A little defiantly, I may add. He is not feeling too good about it now that it is done.

72

The *Ack-Emma*, I should like to assure you, Mr Blair, is not normally my son's choice. If he had not been worked-up –'

'I know. I know exactly how it happened. And that tell-us-your-troubles-and-we'll-see-right-done is very insidious stuff.' He rose. 'You have been very kind indeed, Mrs Wynn, and I am exceedingly grateful to you.'

His tone was evidently more heartfelt than she had expected and she looked doubtfully at him. What have I said to help you? she seemed to be asking, half-dismayed.

He asked where Betty's parents had lived in London and she told him. 'There is nothing there now,' she added. 'Just the open space. It is to be part of some new building scheme, so they have done nothing to it so far.'

On the doorstep he ran into Leslie.

Leslie was an extraordinarily good-looking young man who seemed to be entirely unaware of the fact – a trait that endeared him to Robert, who was in no mood to look kindly on him. Robert had pictured him as the bull-in-a-china-shop type; but on the contrary he was a rather delicate, kind-looking boy with shy, earnest eyes and untidy, soft hair. He glared at Robert with frank enmity when his mother presented him and had explained his business there; but, as his mother had said, there was a shade of defiance in the glare. Leslie was obviously not very happy with his own conscience this evening.

'No one is going to beat my sister and get away with it,' he said fiercely when Robert had mildly deplored his action.

'I sympathize with your point of view,' Robert said, 'but I personally would rather be beaten nightly for a fortnight than have my photograph on the front page of the *Ack-Emma*. Especially if I was a young girl.'

'If you had been beaten every night for a fortnight and no one did anything about it, you might be very glad to have your photograph published in any rag if it got you justice,' Leslie observed pertinently, and brushed past them into the house.

Mrs Wynn turned to Robert with a small, apologetic smile; and Robert, taking advantage of her softened moment, said: 'Mrs Wynn, if it ever occurs to you that anything in that story of Betty's does not ring true, I hope you won't decide that sleeping dogs are best left.'

'Don't pin your faith to that hope, Mr Blair.'

'You would let sleeping dogs lie and the innocent suffer?'

'Oh no; I didn't mean that. I meant the hope of my doubting Betty's story. If I believed her at the beginning I am not likely to doubt her later.'

'One never knows. Some day it may occur to you that this or that does not "fit". You have a naturally analytical mind; it may present you with a piece of subconscious when you least expect it. Something that has puzzled you deep down may refuse to be pushed down any more.'

She had walked to the gate with him, and as he spoke the last sentence he turned to take farewell of her. To his surprise something moved behind her eyes at that light remark of his.

So she wasn't certain, after all. Somewhere, in the story, in the circumstances, there was some small thing that left a question in that sober, analytical mind of hers. What was it?

And then, with what he always remembered afterwards as the only perfect sample of telepathic communication in his experience, he paused as he was stepping into his car and said: 'Had she anything in her pockets when she came home?'

'She had only one pocket: the one in her dress.'

'And was there anything in it?'

There was the faintest tightening of the muscles round her mouth. 'Just a lipstick,' she said evenly.

'A lipstick! She is a little young for that, isn't she?'

'My dear Mr Blair, they start experimenting with lipstick at the age of ten. As a wet-day amusement it has taken the place of dressing-up in mother's things.'

'Yes, probably; Woolworth is a great benefactor.'

She smiled and said good-bye again, and moved towards the house as he drove away.

What puzzled her about the lipstick? Robert wondered, as he turned from the uneven surface of Meadowside Lane on to the black, smooth surface of the main Aylesbury–London road. Was it just the fact that the fiends at The Franchise should have left it with the girl? Was that what she found odd?

How amazing that the worry in her subconscious mind had communicated itself so instantly to him! He had not known that he was going to say that sentence about the girl's pockets until he heard himself saying it. It would never have occurred to him, left to himself, to wonder what was in the pocket of her frock. It would not occur to him that the frock might have a pocket at all.

So there was a lipstick. And its presence was something that puzzled Mrs Wynn.

Well; that was a straw that could be added to the little heap he had collected. To the fact that the girl had a photographic memory; to the fact that her nose had been put out of joint without warning only a month or two ago; to the fact that she was bored with school; to the fact that she liked 'reality'.

To the fact – above all – that no one in that household, not even detatched, sensible Mrs Wynn, knew what went on in Betty Kane's mind. It was quite unbelievable that a girl of fifteen who had been the centre of a young man's world could see herself supplanted overnight without reacting violently to the situation. But Betty had been 'very nice about it.'

Robert found this heartening. It was proof that that candid young face was no guide at all to the person who was Betty Kane.

8

ROBERT had decided to kill a great many birds with one stone by spending the night in London.

To begin with, he wanted to have his hand held. And in the circumstances no one would hold his hand to better purpose than his old school friend Kevin Macdermott. What Kevin did not know about crime was probably not so anyhow. And as a well-known defending counsel his knowledge of human nature was extensive, varied, and peculiar.

At the moment the betting was evens whether Macdermott would die of high blood-pressure before he was sixty or grace the Woolsack when he was seventy. Robert hoped the latter. He was very fond of Kevin.

They had first gravitated towards each other at school because they were both 'going in for law', but they had become and remained friends because they were complementary. To the Irishman, Robert's equanimity was amusing, provocative, and – when he was tired – restful. To Robert, Kevin's Celt flamboyance was exotic and fascinating. It was typical that Robert's ambition was to go back to the little country town and continue life as it was; while Kevin's was to alter everything that was alterable in the law and to make as much noise as possible in the doing of it.

So far Kevin had not altered much – though he had done his best where some judges' rulings were concerned – but he had made considerable noise in his effortless, slightly malicious fashion. Already the presence of Kevin Macdermott in a case added fifty per cent to its newspaper value – and a good deal more than that to its cost.

He had married – advantageously but happily – had a pleasant house near Weybridge and three hardy sons, lean and dark and lively like their father. For town purposes he kept a small flat in St Paul's Churchyard, where, as he pointed out, he 'could afford to look down on Queen Anne'. And whenever Robert was in town – which was not oftener than Robert could help – they dined together, either at the flat or at the latest place where Kevin had found good claret. Outside the law Kevin's interests were show hacks, claret, and the livelier films of Warner Brothers.

Kevin was to be at some Bar dinner tonight, so his secretary had said when Robert had tried to reach him from Milford; but he would be delighted to have a legitimate excuse for dodging the speeches, so would Robert go along to St Paul's Churchyard after dinner and wait for him.

That was a good thing; if Kevin came from a dinner he would be relaxed and prepared to settle down for the evening – not restless and with three-quarters of his mind still back in the court-room, as he sometimes was.

Meanwhile he would ring up Grant at Scotland Yard and see if he could spare him some minutes tomorrow morning. He must get it clear in his mind how he stood in relation with Scotland Yard: fellow sufferers, but on opposite sides of the fence.

At the Fortescue, the Edwardian old place in Jermyn Street where he had stayed ever since he was first allowed to go to London on his own, they greeted him like a nephew and gave him 'the room he had last time': a dim comfortable box with a shoulder-high bed and a buttoned-plush settee; and brought him up a tray on which reposed an outsize brown kitchen teapot, a Georgian silver cream jug, about a pound of sugar lumps in a sixpenny glass dish, a Dresden cup with flowers and little castles, a red-and-gold Worcester plate made for 'their Maj's' William IV and his Queen, and a much buckled kitchen knife with a stained brown handle. Both the tea and the tray refreshed Robert. He went out into the evening streets feeling vaguely hopeful.

His search for the truth about Betty Kane brought him, only half consciously, to the vacant space where that block of flats had been: the spot where both her parents had died in one shattering burst of high explosive. It was a bare, neat space, waiting its appointed part in some plan. Nothing was there to show that a building had ever stood on the spot. Round about, the unharmed houses stood with blank, smug faces, like mentally deficient children too idiotic to have understood the meaning of a disaster. It had passed them by and that was all they knew or cared about.

On the opposite side of the wide street a row of small shops still stood as they had obviously stood for fifty years or more. Robert crossed to them and went into the tobacconist's to buy cigarettes; a tobacconist-and-newsagent knows everything.

'Were you here when that happened?' Robert asked, leaning his head towards the door.

'When what happened?' asked the rosy little man, so used to the blank space that he had long ago become unaware of it. 'Oh, the incident? No, I was out on duty. Warden, I was.'

Robert said that he had meant was he here in business at the time.

Oh yes; yes, certainly he had the business then; and for long before it. Brought up in the neighbourhood, he was, and succeeded his father in the business.

'You would know the local people well, then. Do you remember the couple who were caretakers of the block of flats, by any chance?'

'The Kanes? Of course I do. Why shouldn't I remember them? They were in and out of this place all day. He for his paper in the morning and then her for her cigarettes shortly after; and then back for his evening paper and her back for the third time probably for cigarettes again; and then he and I used to have a pint at the local when my boy had finished his lessons and would take over for me here. You knew them, sir?'

'No. But I met someone the other day who spoke of them. How was the whole place wrecked?'

The little pink man sucked his teeth with a derisive sound.

'Jerry-built. That's what it was. Just jerry-built. The bomb fell in the area there – that's how the Kanes were killed, they were down in their basement feeling fairly safe – and the whole thing just settled down like a house of cards. Shocking.' He straightened the edge of a pile of evening papers. 'It was just her bad luck that the only evening in weeks that she was at home with her husband, a bomb had to come.' He seemed to find a sardonic pleasure in the thought.

'Where was she usually, then?' Robert asked. 'Did she work somewhere in the evenings?'

'Work!' said the little man with vast scorn. 'Her!' And then, recollecting: 'Oh, I'm sorry, I'm sure. I forgot for the minute that they might be friends of –'

Robert hastened to assure him that his interest in the Kanes was purely academic. Someone had remembered them as caretakers of the block of flats, that was all. If Mrs Kane was not out working in the evenings, what was she out doing?

'Having a good time, of course. Oh yes, people managed to have a good time even then – if they wanted it enough and looked hard enough for it. Kane, he wanted her to go away to the country with that little girl of theirs, but would she? Not her! Three days of the country would kill her, she said. She didn't even go to see the little thing when they evacuated her. The authorities, that is. With the rest of the children. It's my opinion she was tickled to death to have the child off her hands so that she could go dancing at nights.'

'Whom did she go dancing with?'

'Officers,' the little man said succinctly. 'A lot more exciting than watching the grass grow. I don't say there was any actual harm in it, mind you,' he said hastily. 'She's dead and I wouldn't like to pin anything on her that she isn't here to unpin, if you take my meaning. But she was a bad mother and a bad wife, that's flat; and no one ever said anything to the contrary.'

'Was she pretty?' Robert asked, thinking of the good emotion he had wasted on Betty's mother.

'In a sulky sort of way, yes. She sort of smouldered. You wondered what she would be like when she was lit up. Excited, I mean, not tight. I never saw her tight. She didn't get her excitement that way.'

'And her husband?'

'Ah, he was all right, Bert Kane was. Deserved better luck than that woman. One of the best, Bert was. Terribly fond of the little girl. Spoiled her, of course. She had only to want something and he got it for her; but she was a nice kid, for all that. Demure; butter wouldn't melt in her little mouth. Yes, Bert deserved better out of life than a good-time wife and a cupboard-love kid. One of the best, Bert was ...' He looked over the roadway at the empty space reflectively. 'It took them the best part of a week to find him,' he said.

Robert paid for his cigarettes and went out into the street both saddened and relieved. Sad for Bert Kane, who had deserved better; but glad that Betty Kane's mother was not the woman he had pictured. All the way to London his mind had grieved for that dead woman: the woman who had broken her heart for her child's good. It had seemed to him unbearable that the child she had so greatly loved should be Betty Kane. But now he was free of that grief. Betty Kane's mother was exactly the mother he would have chosen for her if he were God. And she on her part looked very like being her mother's daughter.

'A cupboard-love kid.' Well, well. And what was it Mrs Wynn had said? 'She cried because she didn't like the food, but I don't remember her crying for her mother.' Nor for that father who so devotedly spoiled her, apparently.

When he got back to the hotel he took his copy of the *Ack-Emma* from his dispatch case, and over his solitary dinner at the Fortescue considered at his leisure the story on page two. From its poster-simplicity opening –

On a night in April a girl came back to her home clad in nothing but a frock and shoes. She had left home, a bright, happy schoolgirl with not a ...

to its final fanfare of sobs it was of its kind a small masterpiece. It did perfectly what it set out to do. And that was to appeal to the greatest number of readers with one and the same story. To those who wanted sex interest it offered the girl's lack of clothes, to the sentimentalist her youth and charm, to the partisan her helpless condition, to the sadist the details of her beatings, to the sufferer from class-hatred a description of the big white house behind its high walls, and to the warm-hearted British public in general the impression that the police had been if not 'nobbled' then at least lax, and that Right had not been Done.

Yes, it was clever.

Of course the story was a gift for them – which is why they had sent a man back immediately with young Leslie Wynn. But Robert felt that, when really on their mettle, the *Ack-Emma* could probably make a good story of a broken connecting-rod.

80

It must be a dreary business catering exclusively for the human failings. He turned the pages over, observing how consistently each story was used to appeal to the regrettable in the reader. Even GAVE AWAY A MILLION, he noticed, was the story of a disgraceful old man unloading on his income-tax and not of a boy who had climbed out of a slum by his own courage and enterprise.

With a slight nausea he put the thing back in his case and took the case with him to St Paul's Churchyard. There he found the 'daily' woman waiting for him with her hat on. Mr Macdermott's secretary had telephoned to say that a friend of his was coming and that he was to be given the run of the house and left alone in it without scruple; she had stayed merely to let him in; she would now leave him to it; there was whisky on the little table by the fire and there was another bottle in the cupboard, but it might, if you asked her, be wise not to remind Mr Macdermott about it or he would stay up too late, and she had great trouble getting him up in the morning.

'It's not the whisky,' Blair said, smiling at her, 'it's the Irish in him. All the Irish hate getting up.'

This gave her pause on the doorstep; evidently struck by this new idea.

'I wouldn't wonder,' she said. 'My old man's the same, and he's Irish. It's not whisky with him; just original sin. At least, that's what I always thought. But perhaps it's just his misfortune in being a Murphy.'

It was a pleasant little place, warm and friendly, and peaceful now that the roar of the city traffic was still. He poured himself a drink; went to the window to look down on Queen Anne; paused a moment to note once more how lightly the great bulk of the church floated on its base – so proportioned, so balanced, that it looked as if one could take it up on a palm and dangle it there; and then sat down and, for the first time since he had gone out that morning to see a maddening old woman who was changing her will again, relaxed.

He was half asleep when he heard Kevin's key in the lock and his host was in the room before he could move.

Macdermott tweaked his neck in an evil pinch as he passed

behind him to the decanters on the table. 'It's beginning, old boy,' he said, 'it's beginning.'

'What is?' Robert asked.

'The thickening of that handsome neck of yours.'

Robert rubbed his neck lazily where it stung. 'I do begin to notice draughts on the back of it, now you come to mention it,' he said.

'Christ, Robert! Does nothing distress you?' Kevin said, his eyes pale and bright and mocking under their black brows. 'Even the imminent prospect of losing those good looks of yours?'

'I'm a little distressed at the moment, but it isn't my looks.'

'Well, what with Blair, Hayward, and Bennet, it can't be bankruptcy; so I suppose it's a woman.'

'Yes, but not the way you mean.'

'Thinking of getting married? You ought to, Rob.'

'You said that before.'

'You want an heir for Blair, Hayward, and Bennet, don't you?' The calm certainty of Blair, Hayward, and Bennet had always pricked Kevin into small gibes, Robert remembered.

'There is no guarantee that it wouldn't be a girl. Anyhow, Nevil is taking care of that.'

'The only thing that young woman of Nevil's will ever give birth to is a gramophone record. She was gracing a platform again the other day, I hear. If she had to earn the money for her train fares she mightn't be so willing to dash about the country being the Vocal Minority.' He sat down with his drink. 'I needn't ask if you are up on business. Sometimes you really ought to come up and see this town. I suppose you dash off again tomorrow after a ten a.m. interview with someone's solicitors.'

'No,' Robert said. 'With Scotland Yard.'

Kevin paused with his glass half-way to his mouth. 'Robert, you're slipping,' he said. 'What has the Yard to do with your Ivory Tower?'

'That's just it,' Robert said equably, ignoring this additional flick at his Milford security. 'It's there on the doorstep and I don't quite know how to deal with it. I want to listen to some-one being intelligent about the situation. I don't know why I

82

should unload it on you. You must be sick of problems. But you always did do my algebra for me.'

'And you always reckoned the stocks and shares ones, if I remember rightly. I was always a fool about stocks. I still owe you something for saving me from a bad investment. Two bad investments,' he added.

'Two?'

'Tamara and Topeka Tin.'

'I remember saving you from Topeka Tin, but I had nothing whatever to do with your breaking with Tamara.'

'Oh, hadn't you, indeed! My good Robert, if you could have seen your face when I introduced you to her. Oh no, not that way. Quite the contrary. The instantaneous *kindness* of your expression, that blasted English mask of courtesy and good breeding – it said everything. I saw myself going through life introducing Tamara to people and watching their faces being well-bred about it. It cured me of her in record time. I have never ceased being grateful to you. So produce what is in the dispatch case.'

Nothing escaped Kevin, Robert thought, taking out his own copy of Betty Kane's statement to the police.

'This is a very short statement. I wish you would read it and tell me how it strikes you.'

He watched the impact on Kevin, without preliminaries to dull the edge of it.

Macdermott took it, read the first paragraph in one swift eye movement, and said: 'This is the *Ack-Emma*'s protégée, I take it.'

'I had no idea that you ever saw the *Ack-Emma*,' Robert said, surprised.

'God love you, I feed on the *Ack-Emma*. No crime, no *causes célèbres*: no *causes célèbres*, no Kevin Macdermott. Or only a piece of him.' He lapsed into utter silence. For four minutes his absorption was so complete that Robert felt alone in the room, as if his host had gone away. 'Humph!' he said, coming out of it.

'Well!'

'I take it that your clients are the two women in the case, and not this girl?'

'Of course.'

'Now you tell me your end,' Kevin said, and listened.

Robert gave him the whole story. His reluctant visit; his growing partisanship as it became clear that it was a choice between Betty Kane and the two women; Scotland Yard's decision not to move on the available evidence; and Leslie Wynn's rash visit to the offices of the *Ack-Emma*.

'So tonight,' Macdermott said, 'the Yard is moving heaven and earth to find corroborative evidence that will back up the girl's story.'

'I suppose so,' said Robert, depressed. 'But what I want to know is: do you or do you not believe the girl's story?'

'I never believe anyone's story,' Kevin pointed out with gentle malice. 'What you want to know is: do I find the girl's story believable? And of course I do.'

'You do!'

'I do. Why not?'

'But it's an absurd story,' Robert said, more hotly than he had intended.

'There is nothing absurd about it. Women who live lonely lives do insane things – especially if they are poor gentlewomen. Only the other day an elderly woman was found to have kept her sister chained up to a bed in a room no bigger than a good-sized cupboard. She had kept her like that for three years, and had fed her on the crusts and potato skins and other scraps that she didn't want herself. She said, when it was discovered, that their money was going down too fast and this was her way of making ends meet. She had quite a good bank balance actually, but it was the fear induced by insecurity that had sent her crazy. That is a much more unbelievable – and from your point of view absurd – story than the girl's.'

'Is it? It seems to me just an ordinary tale of insanity.'

'Only because you know it happened. I mean, that someone had actually seen the thing. Suppose, on the contrary, that the rumour had merely gone round; that the crazy sister had heard it and released her victim before any investigation could be made; that the investigators found only two old ladies living an apparently normal life except for the invalidish nature of one of them. What then? Would you have believed the "chained-up" tale? Or would you, more likely, have called it an "absurd story"?'

Robert sank a little deeper into his depression.

'Here are two lonely and badly dowered women saddled with a big house in the country, one of them too old to do much household work and the other loathing it. What is the most likely form for their mild insanity to take? The capture of a girl to be servant to them, of course.'

Damn Kevin and his counsel's mind. He had thought that he had wanted Kevin's opinion, but what he had wanted was Kevin's backing for his own opinion.

'The girl they capture happens to be a blameless schoolgirl conveniently far from home. It is their bad luck that she is so blameless, because since she had never been caught out in a lie to date, everyone is going to take her word against theirs. If I were the police I would have risked it. It seems to me they are losing their nerve.'

He shot an amused glance at Robert, sunk in his chair, glooming down his long legs at the fire. He sat for a moment or two enjoying his friend's discomfiture.

'Of course,' he said at length, 'they may have remembered a parallel case, where everyone believed the girl's heart-rending story and were very thoroughly led up the garden.'

'A parallel!' Robert said, folding his legs and sitting up. 'When?'

'Seventeen-something. I forget the exact date.'

'Oh,' said Robert, dashed again.

'I don't know what is "Oh" about it,' Macdermott said mildly. 'The nature of alibis has not changed much in two centuries.'

'Alibis?'

'If the parallel case is any guide the girl's story is an alibi.'

'Then you believe – I mean, you find it believable that the girl's story is all nonsense?'

'A complete invention from beginning to end.'

'Kevin, you are maddening. You said you found it believable.'

'So I do. I also find it believable that it is a tissue of lies. I am not briefed for either side. I can make a very good case out

85

for either, at the shortest notice. On the whole I should prefer to be counsel for the young woman from Aylesbury. She would be wonderful in the witness-box, and from what you tell me neither of the Sharpes would be much help, visually, to a counsel.'

He got up to help himself to more whisky, holding out his other hand for Robert's glass. But Robert was in no mood for conviviality. He shook his head without lifting his gaze from the fire. He was tired and beginning to be out of temper with Kevin. He had been wrong to come. When a man had been a counsel in the criminal courts as long as Kevin had, his mind had only points of view, not convictions any more. He would wait until Kevin had half-finished the glass he was sitting down with, and then make a movement to go. It would be good to put his head on a pillow and forget that he was responsible for other people's problems. Or rather, for the solution of them.

'I wonder what she was doing all that month,' Kevin said conversationally, taking a large gulp of practically neat whisky.

Robert's mouth opened to say: 'Then you *do* believe the girl is a fake!' but he stopped himself in time. He rebelled against dancing any more this evening to Kevin's piping.

'If you drink so much whisky on top of claret, what *you* will be doing for a month is a cure, my lad,' he said. And to his surprise Kevin lay back and laughed like a schoolboy.

'Oh, Rob, I love you,' he said delightedly. 'You are the very essence of England. Everything we admire and envy in you. You sit there so mild, so polite, and let people bait you until they conclude that you are an old tabby and they can do what they like with you, and then just when they are beginning to preen themselves they go that short step too far and wham! out comes that business-like paw with the glove off!' He picked Robert's glass out of his hand without a by-your-leave and rose to fill it and Robert let him. He was feeling better.

9

THE London–Larborough road was a black, straight ribbon in the sunshine, giving off diamond sparks as the crowded traffic caught the light and lost it again. Pretty soon both the air and the roads would be so full that no one could move in comfort and everyone would have to go back to the railways for quick travel. Progress, that was.

Kevin had pointed out last night that, what with present ease of communications, it was quite on the cards that Betty Kane had spent her month's vacation in Sydney, N.S.W. It was a daunting thought. She could be anywhere from Kamchatka to Peru, and all he, Blair, had to do was a little thing like proving she wasn't in a house on the Larborough–Milford road. If it were not a sunny morning, and if he were not sorry for Scotland Yard, and if he didn't have Kevin to hold his hand, and if he were not doing pretty well on his own so far, he might have felt depressed.

Feeling sorry for Scotland Yard was the last thing he had anticipated. But sorry he was. All Scotland Yard's energies were devoted to proving the Sharpes guilty and Betty Kane's story true – for the very good reason that they believed the Sharpes to be guilty. But what each one of them ached in his private soul to do was to push Betty Kane down the *Ack-Emma*'s throat; and they could only do that by proving her story nonsense. Yes, a really prize state of frustration existed in those large, calm bodies at the Yard.

Grant had been charming in his quiet, reasonable way – it had been rather like going to see a doctor, now he came to think of it – and had quite willingly agreed that Robert should be told about any letters that the *Ack-Emma* might provoke.

'Don't pin your hopes too firmly to that, will you?' he had said in friendly warning. 'For one letter that the Yard gets that has any worth it gets five thousand that are nonsense. Letter-writing is the natural outlet of the "odds". The busybodies, the idle, the perverted, the cranks, the feel-it-my-duties –'

'*Pro Bono Publico* –'

'He and *Civis*,' Grant said with a smile. 'Also the plain depraved. They all write letters. It's their *safe* outlet, you see.
They can be as interfering, as long-winded, as obscene, as pom-
pous, as one-idea'd as they like on paper, and no one can kick
them for it. So they write. My God, how they write!'

'But there is a chance –'

'Oh yes. There is a chance. And all these letters will have to
be weeded out, however silly they are. Anything of importance
will be passed on to you, I promise. But I do remind you that
the ordinary intelligent citizen writes only one time in five
thousand. He doesn't like what he thinks of as "poking his
nose in" – which is why he sits silent in a railway carriage and
scandalizes the Americans, who still have a hick interest in
other folk – and anyhow he's a busy man, full of his own
affairs, and sitting down to write a letter to the police about
something that doesn't concern him is against all his instincts.'

So Robert had come away pleased with the Yard and sorry
for them. At least he, Robert, had a straight row to hoe. He
wouldn't be glancing aside every now and then wishing it was
the next row he was hoeing. And moreover he had Kevin's approval of the row he had chosen.

'I mean it,' Kevin had said, 'when I say that if I were the
police I should almost have risked it. They have a good enough
case. And a nice little conviction is always a hitch up the ladder
of promotion for someone. Unfortunately – or fortunately for
the citizen – the man who decides whether there is a case or not
is the chap higher up, and he's not interested in any subordin-
ate's speedy promotion. Amazing that wisdom should be the
by-product of office procedure.'

Robert, mellow with whisky, had let the cynicism flow past
him.

'But let them just get one spot of corroboration and they'll
have a warrant at the door of The Franchise quicker than you
can lift a telephone receiver.'

'They won't get any corroboration,' said the mellow Robert.
'Why should they? How could they? What we want to do is to
disprove the girl's story ourselves, so that it doesn't damn the
Sharpes' lives for as long as they live. Once I have seen the aunt
and uncle tomorrow we may have enough general knowledge

about the girl to justify a start on our own investigation.'

Now he was speeding down the black shining Larborough road on the way to seeing Betty's relations in Mainshill – the people she had stayed with on that memorable holiday. A Mr and Mrs Tilsit, they were. Tilsit, 93 Cherrill Street, Mainshill, Larborough – and the husband was travelling agent for a firm of brush-makers in Larborough and they had no children. That was all Robert knew about them.

He paused for a moment as he turned off the main road in Mainshill. This was the corner where Betty had waited for her bus. Or said she waited. Over there on the other side, it must have been. There was no side turning on that side, nothing but the long stretch of unbroken pavement as far as one could see in either direction. A busy enough road at this time of day, but empty enough, Robert supposed, in the doldrum hour of the late afternoon.

Cherrill Street was one long series of angular bay windows in dirty red brick, their forward surface almost scraping the low red-brick wall that hemmed them in from the pavement. The sour soil on either side of the window that did duty for a garden had none of the virtues of the new-turned earth of Meadowside Lane, Aylesbury; it grew only thin London pride, weedy wallflowers, and moth-eaten forget-me-nots. The same housewife's pride obtained in Cherrill Street as in Aylesbury, of course, and the same crisp curtains hung at the windows; but if there were poets in Cherrill Street they found other outlets for their souls than gardens.

When he had rung unavailingly and then knocked at 93 – indistinguishable from the others, as far as he could see, except by its painted numerals – a woman flung up the bedroom window next door, leaned out and said: 'You looking for Mrs Tilsit?'

Robert said that he was.

'She's gone to get her groceries. The shop at the corner.'

'Oh, thanks. If that's all, I'll wait.'

'Shouldn't wait if you want to see her soon. Should go and fetch her.'

'Oh. Is she going somewhere else?'

'No, just the grocer's; it's the only shop round here. But she takes half a morning deciding between two brands of wheat flakes. You take one packet up right firm and put it in her bag and she'll be quite pleased.'

Robert thanked her and began to walk away to the end of the street, when she hailed him again.

'Shouldn't leave your car. Take it with you.'

'But it's quite a little way, isn't it?'

'Maybe, but it's Saturday.'

'Saturday?'

'School's out.'

'Oh, I see. But there's nothing in it – ' 'to steal,' he was going to say but amended it to: 'Nothing in it that's movable.'

'Movable! Huh! that's good. We had window-boxes once. Mrs Laverty over the way had a gate. Mrs Biddows had two fine wooden clothes-posts and eighteen yards of clothes-rope. They all thought they weren't movable. You leave your car there for ten minutes, you'll be lucky to find the chassis!'

So Robert got obediently into the car and drove down to the grocer's. And as he drove he remembered something, and the memory puzzled him. This was where Betty Kane had been so happy. This rather dreary, rather grimy street – one of a warren of streets very like itself. So happy that she had written to say that she was staying on for the rest of her holidays.

What had she found here that was so desirable?

He was still wondering as he walked into the grocer's and prepared to spot Mrs Tilsit among the morning customers. But there was no need for any guesswork. There was only one woman in the shop, and one glance at the grocer's patient face and the cardboard packet in the woman's either hand made it plain that she was Mrs Tilsit.

'Can I get you something, sir?' the grocer said, detaching himself for a moment from the woman's ponderings – it wasn't wheat flakes this morning, it was powdered soap – and moving towards Robert.

'No, thank you,' Robert said. 'I am just waiting for this lady.'

'For me?' the woman said. 'If it's the gas, then –'

Robert said hastily that he wasn't the gas.

'I *have* a vacuum cleaner and it's going fine,' she offered, and prepared to go back to her problem.

Robert said that he had his car outside and would wait until she had finished, and was beating a hasty retreat; but she said: 'A car! Oh. Well, you can drive me back, can't you, and save me carrying all those things. How much, Mr Carr, please?'

Mr Carr, who had taken a packet of soap-flakes from her during her interest in Robert and wedged it into her shopping-bag, took her money, gave her change, wished her a thankful good-day, and cast a pitiful glance at Robert as he followed the woman out to his car.

Robert had known that it was too much to hope for another woman with Mrs Wynn's detachment and intelligence, but his heart sank as he considered Mrs Tilsit. Mrs Tilsit was one of those women whose minds are always on something else. They chat brightly with you, they agree with you, they admire what you are wearing, and they offer advice, but their real attention is concentrated on what to do with the fish or what Florrie told them about Minnie's eldest or where they have left the laundry book or even just what a bad filling that is in your right front tooth – anything, everything except the subject in hand.

She seemed impressed with the appearance of Robert's car and asked him in to have a cup of tea – there being apparently no hour of the day when a cup of tea was not a possible article of diet. Robert felt that he could not drink with her – even a cup of tea – without making plain his position of opposing counsel, so to speak. He did his best, but it was doubtful if she understood; her mind was so plainly already deciding whether to offer him the Rich Tea or the Mixed Fancy biscuits with his tea. Mention of her niece made none of the expected stir in her emotions.

'A most extraordinary thing, that was, wasn't it?' she said. 'Taking her away and beating her. What good did they think that was going to do them? Sit down, Mr Blayne, come in and sit down. I'll just – '

A bloodcurdling scream echoed through the house. An urgent, high-pitched, desperate screaming that went on and on, without even a pause for breath.

Mrs Tilsit humped her parcels in a movement of exasperation. She leaned near enough to Robert to put her mouth within shouting distance of his ear. 'My kettle,' she yelled. 'I'll be right back.'

Robert sat down, and again considered the surroundings and wondered why Betty Kane had found them so good. Mrs Wynn's front room had been a living-room: a sitting-room warm with human occupation and human traffic. But this was clearly a 'best' room, kept for visitors who were not intimate enough to be admitted to the back regions; the real life of the house was in the poky room at the back. Either kitchen or kitchen-sitting-room. And yet Betty Kane had elected to stay. Had she found a friend? A girl-next-door? A boy-next-door?

Mrs Tilsit came back in what seemed like two minutes, bearing a tray with tea. Robert wondered a little at this promptness of action until he saw the tray's contents. Mrs Tilsit had not waited to make a decision; she had brought them both: Thin Wine and Sweet Shortbread. At least, he thought, watching her pour, this woman explained one of the oddities in the affair: the fact that when the Wynns had writtten to have Betty sent home at once, her aunt had not flown to a telegraph office to break the news that Betty had left for home nearly a fortnight ago. The Betty who had gone a fortnight previously would be much less real in Mrs Tilsit's mind than the jelly that was cooling on the back window sill.

'I wasn't worried about her,' Mrs Tilsit said, as if in echo to his thoughts. 'When they wrote from Aylesbury about her, I knew she would turn up. When Mr Tilsit came home he was quite upset about it – he goes away for a week or ten days at a time, you know: he's agent for Weekses – carried on like a mad thing, he did; but I just said you wait and she'll turn up all right, and she did. Well, nearly all right.'

'She said she enjoyed her holiday here enormously.'

'I suppose she did,' she said vaguely, not looking gratified, as Robert had expected. He glanced at her and realized that her mind was already on something else. The strength of his tea, if one was to judge by the direction of her eye.

'How did she pass her time? Did she make friends?'

'Oh, no; she was in Larborough most of the time.'

'Larborough!'

'Oh, well, when I say most of the time, I do her an injustice.

She helped in the house in the mornings, but in a house this size and me used to doing everything myself there isn't much to do. And she was here on holiday, wasn't she, poor thing, after all that school work? What good all that book work is to a young girl I don't know. Mrs Harrop's daughter over the way could hardly write her name, but she married the third son of a lord. Or perhaps it was the son of a third son,' she said, looking doubtful. 'I forget for the minute. She – '

'How did she spend her time in Larborough? Betty, I mean.'

'Pictures, mostly.'

'Pictures? Oh, the cinema, I see.'

'You can do that from morning till night, if you're given that way, in Larborough. The big ones open at half past ten and they mostly change mid-week and there's about forty of them, so you can just go from one to another till it's time to go home.'

'Is that what Betty did?'

'Oh no. She's quite sensible, Betty is. She used to go in to the morning round because you get in cheaper before noon, and then she'd go bus-riding.'

'Bus-riding. Where?'

'Oh, anywhere the fancy took her. Have another of these biscuits, Mr Bain; they're fresh from the tin. She went to see the castle at Norton one day. Norton's the county town, you know. Everyone imagines Larborough is because it's so big, but Norton's always been – '

'Did she not come home to lunch, then?'

'What? Oh, Betty. No, she'd have coffee lunch somewhere. We always have our real meal at night anyhow, you see, with Mr Tilsit being out all day, so there was always a meal waiting when she came home. It's always been my pride to have a good nourishing, sit-down meal ready for my – '

'What time would that be? Six?'

'No, Mr Tilsit doesn't usually manage home before half past seven.'

'And I suppose Betty was home long before then?'

'Mostly she was. She was late once because she went to an afternoon show at the pictures, but Mr Tilsit he created about it – though I'm sure he had no need to. What harm can you come to at the pictures? And after that she was always home before him. When he was here, that is. She wasn't so careful when he was away.'

So the girl had been her own mistress for a good fortnight. Free to come and go without question and limited only by the amount of holiday money in her pocket. It was an innocent-sounding fortnight, and in the case of most girls of her age it undoubtedly would have been that. The cinema in the morning or window-gazing; a coffee lunch; a bus-ride into the country in the afternoon – a blissful holiday for an adolescent; the first taste of unsupervised freedom.

But Betty Kane was no normal adolescent. She was the girl who had told that long and circumstantial story to the police without a tremor. The girl with four weeks of her life un-accounted for. The girl that someone had ended by beating un-mercifully. How, then, had Betty Kane spent her unsupervised freedom?

'Did she go to Milford on the bus, do you know?'

'No, *they* asked me that, of course, but I couldn't say yes or not.'

'They?'

'The police.'

Yes, of course; he had forgotten for the moment that the police would have checked Betty Kane's every sentence to the limit of their power.

'You're not police, I think you said.'

'No,' Robert said yet once again; 'I'm a lawyer. I represent the two women who are supposed to have detained Betty.'

'Oh yes. You told me. I suppose they have to have a lawyer like anyone else, poor things. To ask questions for them. I hope I'm telling you the things you want to know, Mr Blayne.'

He had another cup of tea in the hope that sooner or later she would tell him something he wanted to know. But it was mere repetition now.

'Did the police know that Betty was away on her own all day?' he asked.

She really thought about that. 'That I can't remember,' she said. 'They asked me how she passed her time and I said that mostly she went to pictures or bus-riding, and they said did I go with her and I said – well, I'll have to admit I told a white lie

94

about it and said that I did now and then. I didn't want them to think that Betty went to places alone. Though of course there was no harm in it.'

What a mind!

'Did she have letters while she was here?' he asked as he was taking his leave.

'Just from home. Oh yes, I would know. I always took the letters in. In any case, they wouldn't have written to her, would they?'

'Who?'

'Those women who kidnapped her.'

It was with a feeling of escape that Robert drove in to Larborough. He wondered if Mr Tilsit had always been away 'ten days at a time' from his home or if he had got the travelling job as an alternative to flight or suicide.

In Larborough Blair sought out the main garage of the Larborough and District Motor Services. He knocked at the door of the small office that guarded one side of the entrance and went in. A man in a bus inspector's uniform was going through papers on the desk. He glanced up at Robert and without asking his business continued his own affairs.

Robert said that he wanted to see someone who would know about the Milford bus service.

'Time-table on the wall outside,' the man said without looking up.

'I don't want to know about times. I know them. I live in Milford. I want to know if you ever run a double-decker bus on that route.'

There was silence for a long time: a silence expertly calculated to end at the point where Robert was about to open his mouth again.

'No,' said the man.

'Never?' Robert asked.

This time there was no answer at all. The inspector made it plain that he was finished with him.

'Listen,' Robert said; 'this is important. I am a partner in a firm of solicitors in Milford and I –'

The man turned on him. 'I don't care if you are the Shah of Persia. There are *no double-decker buses on the Milford run!*

And what do *you* want?' he added as a small mechanic appeared behind Robert in the doorway.

The mechanic hesitated, as if the business he had come on had been upset by a newer interest. But he pulled himself together and began to state his business. 'It's about those spares for Norton. Shall I –'

As Robert was edging past him out of the office he felt a tug on his coat and realized that the little mechanic wanted him to linger until he could talk to him. Robert went out and bent over his own car, and presently the mechanic appeared at his elbow.

'You asking about double-decker buses? I couldn't contradict him straight out, you know ; in the mood he's in now it'd be as much as my job's worth. You want to *use* a double-decker, or just to know if they ever run at all? Because, you can't *get* a double-decker on that route, not to travel in, because the buses on that run are all –'

'I know, I know. They are single-decks. What I wanted to know was whether there *ever* are two-deck buses on the Milford route.'

'Well, there are not supposed to be, you understand, but once or twice this year we've had to use a double-decker when one of the old single ones broke down unexpected. Sooner or later they'll be all double-deck, but there isn't enough traffic on the Milford run to justify a double, so all the old crocks of singles eventually land on that route and a few more like it. And so – '

'You're a great help. Would it be possible to find out exactly when a double-decker did run on that route?'

'Oh, certainly,' the mechanic said, with a shade of bitterness. 'In this firm it's recorded every time you spit. But the records are in there' – he tilted his head to indicate the office – 'and as long as *he's* there there's nothing doing.'

Robert asked at what hour there would be something doing.

'Well, he goes off at the same time as me – six. But I could wait a few minutes and look up the schedules when he's gone if it's very important to you.'

Robert did not know how he was going to wait through the hours till six o'clock, but six o'clock it would have to be.

96

'Righto. I'll meet you in the Bell – that's the pub at the end of the street – about a quarter past six. That do?'

That would do perfectly, Robert said. Perfectly.

And he went away to see what he could bribe the lounge waiter at the Midland into giving him out of hours.

10

'I SUPPOSE you know what you're doing, dear,' Aunt Lin said, 'but I can't help thinking it's very odd of you to defend people like that.'

'I am not "defending" them,' Robert said patiently. 'I am representing them. And there is no evidence whatever that they are "people like that".'

'There is the girl's statement, Robert. She couldn't just have made all that up.'

'Oh, couldn't she?'

'What advantage would it be to her to tell a lot of lies?' She was standing in his doorway passing her prayer-book from one hand to the other as she put on her white gloves. 'What else could she have been doing if she wasn't at The Franchise?'

Robert bit back a 'You'd be surprised!' It was always best with Aunt Lin to take the line of least resistance.

She smoothed her gloves into place. 'If it's just that you're being noble, Robert dear, I must say you are just being wrongheaded. And do you have to go out to the *house*? Surely they could come to the office tomorrow. There's no hurry, is there? It isn't as if someone was going to arrest them on the spot.'

'It was my suggestion that I should go out to The Franchise. If someone accused *you* of stealing things off Woolworth's counter and you couldn't disprove it, I don't suppose you would enjoy walking down Milford High Street in broad daylight.'

'I mightn't like it, but I should most certainly do it – and give Mr Hensell a piece of my mind.'

'Who is Mr Hensell?'

'The manager. Couldn't you come to church with me first and then go out to The Franchise? It's such a long time since you've been, dear.'

'If you stand there much longer you'll be late for the first time in ten years. You go and pray that my judgement may be perfected.'

'I shall most certainly pray for you, dear. I always do. I

shall also put up a little one for myself. All this is going to be very difficult for me.'

'For you?'

'Now that you're acting for those people I shan't be able to talk about it to anyone. It is quite maddening, dear, to sit silent and hear everyone telling for gospel truth things you know for a fact are wrong. It's like wanting to be sick and having to postpone it. Oh dear, the bells have stopped, haven't they? I'll just have to slip into the Bracketts' pew. They won't mind. You won't stay to lunch at that place, will you, dear?'

'I don't suppose that I shall be invited.'

But his welcome at The Franchise was so warm that he felt that he might very well be invited after all. He would say no, of course; not because Aunt Lin's chicken was waiting, but because Marion Sharpe would have to do the washing-up afterwards. When there was no one there they probably ate off trays. Or in the kitchen, for all anyone knew.

'I am sorry we refused to answer the telephone last night,' Marion said, apologizing again. 'But after the fourth or fifth time it really was too much. And we didn't expect you to have news so soon. After all, you had only set out on Friday afternoon.'

'Your telephone callers: were they male or female?'

'One male and four female, as far as I remember. When you rang this morning I thought it was beginning again, but they seem to be late sleepers. Or perhaps they don't really get evil-minded much before evening. We certainly provided the Saturday evening's entertainment for the country youths. They congregated in a group inside the gate and cat-called. Then Nevil found a bar of wood in the out-house –'

'Nevil?'

'Yes, your nephew – I mean, your cousin. He came to pay what he called a visit of condolence, which was very nice of him. And he found a bar that could be wedged in the gateway to keep the thing shut; we have no key for it, you see. But of course that didn't stop them for long. They hoisted each other up on the wall and sat there in a row being offensive until it was time for them to go to their beds.'

'Lack of education,' old Mrs Sharpe said thoughtfully, 'is an extraordinary handicap when one is being offensive. They had no resource at all.'

'Neither have parrots,' Robert said. 'But they can be provocative enough. We must see what police protection we can claim. Meanwhile I can tell you something pleasanter about that wall. I know how the girl saw over it.' He told them about his visit to Mrs Tilsit and his discovery that the girl amused herself by bus-riding (or said she did) and his subsequent visit to the Larborough and District Motor Services garage.

'In the fortnight that the girl was at Mainshill there were two breakdowns of single-deck buses due to go out on the Milford run; and each time a double-decker had to be substituted. There are only three services each way daily, you know. And each time the breakdown happened to the bus due to go out on the midday service. So there were at least two occasions in that fortnight when she could have seen the house, the courtyard, you two, and the car, all together.'

'But could anyone passing on top of a bus take in so much?'

'Have you ever travelled on the upper deck of a country bus? Even when the bus is going at a steady thirty-five, the pace seems funereal. What you can see is so much farther away and you can see it so much longer. Down below, the hedges brush the window and the pace seems good because things are closer. That is one thing. The other is that she has a photographic memory.' And he told them what Mrs Wynn had said.

'Do we tell the police this?' Mrs Sharpe asked.

'No. It doesn't prove anything; just solves the problem of how she knew about you. When she needed an alibi she remembered you, and risked your not being able to prove that you were somewhere else. When you bring your car to the door, by the way, which side of the car is nearest the door?'

'Whether I bring it round from the garage or in from the road the off-side is next to the door, because it's easier to get out of.'

'Yes; so that the near side, with the darker paint on the front wheel, would be facing the gate,' Robert said conclusively. 'That is the picture she saw. The grass and the divided path, the car at the door with the odd wheel, two women – both individual – the round attic window in the roof. She had only to look at the picture in her mind and describe it. The day she was using the picture for – the day she was supposed to have been kidnapped – was more than a month away, and it was a thousand to one against your being able to say what you had done or where you had been on that day.'

'And I take it,' Mrs Sharpe said, 'that the odds are very much greater against our being able to say what she has done or where she has been in that month?'

'The odds are against us, yes. As my friend Kevin Macdermott pointed out the other night, there is nothing to hinder her having been in Sydney, N.S.W. But somehow I am far more hopeful today than I was on Friday morning. We know so much more about the girl now.' He told them of his interviews in Aylesbury and Mainshill.

'But if the police inquiries didn't unearth what she was doing that month – '

'The police inquiries were devoted to checking her statement. They didn't start, as we do, with the premise that her statement is untrue from beginning to end. They checked it and it checked. They had no particular reason to doubt it. She had a blameless reputation, and when they inquired from her aunt how she had spent her holiday time they found that it had consisted of innocent visits to the cinema and country bus-rides.'

'And what do *you* think it consisted of?' Mrs Sharpe asked.

'I think she met someone in Larborough. That, anyhow, is the obvious explanation. It's from that supposition that I think any inquiry of ours should start.'

'And what do we do about engaging an agent?' asked Mrs Sharpe. 'Do you know of one?'

'Well,' Robert said, hesitating, 'it had crossed my mind that you might let me pursue my own inquiries a little farther before we engage a professional. I know that – '

'Mr Blair,' the old woman said, interrupting him, 'you have been called into this unpleasant case without warning, and it cannot have been very willingly ; and you have been very kind in doing your best for us. But we cannot expect you to turn yourself into a private inquiry agent on our behalf. We are not rich – indeed, we have very little to live on – but as long as we have any money at all we shall pay for what services are proper.

And it is not proper that you should turn yourself into a – what is it? – a Sexton Blake for our benefit.'

'It may not be proper, but it is very much to my taste. Believe me, Mrs Sharpe, I hadn't planned it with any conscious thought of saving your pocket. Coming home in the car last night, very pleased with what I had done so far, I realized how much I should hate giving up the search to someone else. It had become a personal hunt. Please don't discourage me from – '

'If Mr Blair is willing to carry on a little longer,' Marion interrupted, 'I think we should thank him heartily and accept. I know just how he feels. I wish I could go hunting myself.'

'There will no doubt come a time when I shall have to turn it over to a proper inquiry agent whether I want to or not. If the trail leads far from Larborough, for instance. I have too many other commitments to follow it far. But as long as the search is on our doorsteps I do want to be the one to pursue it.'

'How had you planned to pursue it?' Marion asked, interested.

'Well, I had thought of beginning with the coffee-lunch places. In Larborough, I mean. For one thing, there can't be so many of them. And for another, we do know that, at any rate at the beginning, that was the kind of lunch she had.'

'Why do you say "at the beginning"?' Marion asked.

'Once she had met the hypothetical X, she may have lunched anywhere. But up till then she paid for her own lunches and they were "coffee" ones. A girl of that age prefers a bun lunch anyhow, even if she has money for a two-course meal. So I concentrate on the coffee-places. I flourish the *Ack-Emma* at the waitresses and find out as tactfully as a country lawyer knows how whether they have ever seen the girl in their place. Does that sound like sense to you?'

'Very good sense,' Marion said.

Robert turned to Mrs Sharpe. 'But if you think you will be better served by a professional – and that is more than possible – then I shall bow out with – '

'I don't think we could be better served by anyone,' Mrs Sharpe said. 'I have expressed my appreciation already of the trouble you have gone to on our behalf. If it would really please you to run down this – this – '

'Moppet,' supplied Robert happily.

'Mopsy,' Mrs Sharpe amended, 'then we can only agree and be grateful. But it seems to me likely to be a very long run.'

'Why long?'

'There is a big gap, it seems to me, between meeting a hypothetical X in Larborough and walking into a house near Aylesbury wearing nothing but a frock and shoes and well and truly beaten. Marion, there is still some of the Amontillado, I think.'

In the silence that succeeded Marion's departure to fetch the sherry the quiet of the old house became apparent. There were no trees in the courtyard to make small noises in the wind and no birds to chatter. The silence was as absolute as the midnight silence of a small town. Was it peaceful, Robert wondered, after the crowded life of a boarding-house? Or was it lonely and a little frightening?

They had valued its privacy, old Mrs Sharpe had said in his office on Friday morning. But was it a good life shut in behind the high walls in the perpetual silence?

'It seems to me,' Mrs Sharpe said, 'that the girl took a great risk in choosing The Franchise, knowing nothing of the household or its circumstances.'

'Of course she took a risk,' Robert said. 'She had to. But I don't think it was as big a gamble as you think.'

'No?'

'No. What you are saying is that for all the girl knew there might be a large household of young people and three maid-servants at The Franchise.'

'Yes.'

'But I think she knew quite well that there was no such thing.'

'How could she?'

'Either she gossiped with the bus-conductor or – and I think this is more likely – she overheard comment from her fellow-passengers. You know the kind of thing: "There are the Sharpes. Fancy living alone in a big house like that, just the two of them. And no maids willing to stay alone in a lonely place so far from shops and the pictures – " and so on. It is very much a "local" bus, that Larborough–Milford one. And it is a lonely route, with no wayside cottages and no village other than Ham Green. The Franchise is the only spot of human interest for miles. It would be more than human nature is capable of to pass the combined interest of the house, the owners, and their car without comment of some kind.'

'I see. Yes, that makes sense.'

'I wish, in a way, it *had* been through chatting with the conductor that she learned about you. That way, he would be more likely to remember her. The girl says she was never in Milford and doesn't know where it is. If a conductor remembered her, we could at least shake her story to that extent.'

'If I know anything of the young person she would open those childlike eyes of hers and say: "Oh, was that Milford? I just got on a bus and went to the terminus and back".'

'Yes. It wouldn't take us very far. But if I fail to pick up the girl's trail in Larborough, I'll try her picture on the local conductors. I do wish she was a more memorable creature.'

The silence fell round them again while they contemplated the un-memorable nature of Betty Kane.

They were sitting in the drawing-room, facing the window, looking out on the green square of the courtyard and faded pink of the brick wall. And as they looked the gate was pushed open and a small group of seven or eight people appeared and stood at gaze. Entirely at their ease they were: pointing out to each other the salient points of interest – the favourite being apparently the round window in the roof. If last night The Franchise had provided the country youth with its Saturday-evening entertainment, it was now, so it would seem, providing Sunday-morning interest for Larborough. Certainly a couple of cars were waiting for them outside the gate, since the women of the party wore silly little shoes and indoor frocks.

Robert glanced across at Mrs Sharpe, but except for a tightening of her always grim mouth she had not moved.

'Our public,' she said at last, witheringly.

'Shall I go and move them on?' Robert said. 'It's my fault for not putting back the wooden bar you left off for me.'

'Let them be,' she said. 'They will go presently. This is what royalty puts up with daily; we can support it for a few moments.'

But the visitors showed no signs of going. Indeed, one group moved round the house to inspect the out-buildings; and the rest were still there when Marion came back with the sherry. Robert apologized again for not having put up the bar. He was feeling small and inadequate. It went against the grain to stay there quietly and watch strangers prowling round as if they owned the place or were contemplating buying it. But if he went out and asked them to move on and they refused to, what power had he to make them go? And how would he look in the Sharpes's eyes if he had to beat a retreat to the house and leave these people in possession?

The group of explorers came back from their tour round the house and reported with laughter and gesticulation what they had seen. He heard Marion say something under her breath and wondered if she were cursing. She looked like a woman who would have a very fine line in curses. She had put down the sherry tray and had apparently forgotten about it; it was no moment for hospitality. He longed to do something decisive and spectacular to please her, just as he had longed to rescue his lady-love from burning buildings when he was fifteen. But, alas, there was no surmounting the fact that he was forty-odd and had learned that it is wiser to wait for the fire-escape.

And while he hesitated, angry with himself and with those crude human creatures outside, the fire-escape arrived in the person of a tall young man in a regrettable tweed suit.

'Nevil,' breathed Marion, watching the picture.

Nevil surveyed the group with his most insufferable air of superiority, and it seemed that they wilted slightly, but they were evidently determined to stand their ground. Indeed, the male with the sports-jacket and the pin-striped trousers was clearly preparing to make an issue of it.

Nevil looked at them silently for a further few seconds and then fished in his inner pocket for something. At the first movement of his hand a strange difference came over the group. The outer members of it detached themselves and faded unobtrusively through the gate; the nearer ones lost their air of bravado and became placatory. Finally the sports-jacket made small rejecting movements of surrender and joined the retreat through the gate.

Nevil banged the gate to behind them, levered the wooden bar into place, and strolled up the path to the door, wiping his hands fastidiously on a really shocking handkerchief. And Marion ran out to the door to meet him.

'Nevil!' Robert heard her say. 'How did you do it?'

'Do what?' Nevil asked.

'Get rid of those creatures.'

'Oh, I just asked their names and addresses,' Nevil said. 'You've no idea how discreet people become if you take out a notebook and ask for their name and address. It's the modern equivalent to: "Fly, all is discovered." They don't wait to ask your credentials in case you may actually have some. Hello, Robert. Good morning, Mrs Sharpe. I'm actually on my way to Larborough, but I saw the gates open and those two frightful cars outside so I stopped to investigate. I didn't know Robert was here.'

This quite innocent implication that of course Robert was capable of dealing equally well with the situation was the unkindest cut of all. Robert could have brained him.

'Well, now that you are here and have so expertly rid us of the nuisance you must stay and drink a glass of sherry,' Mrs Sharpe said.

'Could I come in and drink it on my way home in the evening?' Nevil said. 'You see, I'm on my way to lunch with my prospective father-in-law, and it being Sunday there is a ritual. One must be there for the warming-up exercises.'

'But of course come in on your way home,' Marion said. 'We shall be delighted. How shall we know it is you? For the gate, I mean.' She was pouring sherry and handing it to Robert.

'Do you know morse?'

'Yes, but don't tell me you do.'

'Why not?'

'You look a most unlikely morse addict.'

'Oh, when I was fourteen I was going to sea, and I acquired in the heat of my ambition a lot of incidental idiocies. Morse was one of them. I shall hoot the initials of your beautiful name on the horn, when I come. Two longs and three shorts. I must fly. The thought of talking to you tonight will support me through luncheon at the Palace.'

'Won't Rosemary be any support?' Robert asked, overcome by his baser self.

'I shouldn't think so. On Sundays Rosemary is a daughter in her father's house. It is a role that does not become her. *Au revoir,* Mrs Sharpe. Don't let Robert drink all the sherry.'

'And when,' Robert heard Marion ask as she went with him to the door, 'did you decide not to go to sea?'

'When I was fifteen. I took up ballooning instead.'

'Theoretical, I suppose.'

'Well, I gassed about gases.'

Why did they sound so friendly, so at ease, Robert wondered. As if they had known each other a long time. Why did she like that light-weight Nevil?

'And when you were sixteen?'

If she knew how many things Nevil had taken up and dropped in his time she might not be so pleased to be the latest of them.

'Is the sherry too dry for you, Mr Blair?' Mrs Sharpe asked.

'No, oh no, thank you, it is excellent.' Was it possible that he had been looking sour? Perish the thought.

He made a cautious glance at the old lady and thought that she was looking faintly amused. And old Mrs Sharpe being amused was no comfortable sight.

'I think I had better go before Miss Sharpe bars the gate behind Nevil,' he said. 'Otherwise she will have to come to the gate again with me.'

'But won't you stay and have lunch with us? There is no ritual about it at The Franchise.'

But Robert made his excuses. He didn't like the Robert Blair he was becoming. Petty and childish and inadequate. He would go back and have ordinary Sunday lunch with Aunt Lin and be again Robert Blair of Blair, Hayward, and Bennet, equable and tolerant and at peace with his world.

Nevil had gone by the time he reached the gate, in a flurry of sound that shattered the Sabbath quiet, and Marion was about to close the gate.

'I can't think that the Bishop approves of his future son-in-law's means of transport,' she said, looking after the roaring object as it streaked down the road.

'Exhausting,' Robert said, still caustic.

She smiled at him. 'I think that is the first witty pun I have ever heard anyone make,' she said. 'I hoped you would stay for lunch, but in a way I'm rather relieved that you aren't.'

'Are you indeed?'

'I made a "shape", but it didn't stand up. I'm a very bad cook. I do faithfully what it says in the book, but it hardly ever works out. Indeed, I'm surprised to death when it does. So you will be better off with your Aunt Lin's apple tart.'

And Robert suddenly and illogically wished that he was staying, to share the 'shape' that had not stood up and to be gently mocked by her along with her cooking.

'I'll let you know tomorrow night how I get on in Larborough,' he said matter-of-factly. Since he was not on hens-and-Maupassant terms with her, he would keep the conversation to practicalities. 'And I'll ring up Inspector Hallam and see if one of their men can give a look round The Franchise once or twice a day – just to show the uniform, so to speak, and to discourage idlers.'

'You are very kind, Mr Blair,' she said. 'I can't imagine what it would be without you to lean on.'

Well, if he couldn't be young and a poet, he could be a crutch. A dull thing, a thing resorted to only in emergencies; but useful, useful.

11

By half past ten on Monday morning he was sitting in front of a steaming cup of coffee in the Karena. He began with the Karena because when one thinks of coffee at all one thinks of a Karena, with the smell of the roasting coffee downstairs in the shop and the liquid version waiting upstairs among the little tables. And if he was going to have a surfeit of coffee he might as well have some good stuff while he could still taste it.

He was holding the *Ack-Emma* in his hand with the girl's photograph open to the gaze of the waitresses as they passed, hoping vaguely that his interest in it might cause one of them to say: 'That girl used to come in here every morning.' To his surprise the paper was gently removed from his grasp, and he looked up to see his waitress regarding him with a kind smile.

'That is last Friday's,' she said. 'Here.' And she proffered that morning's *Ack-Emma*.

He thanked her and said that while he would be glad to see this morning's paper he would like to keep the Friday one. Did this girl, this girl on the front page of Friday's ever come in here for coffee?

'Oh no, we'd have remembered her if she did. We were all discussing that case on Friday. Imagine beating her half to death like that.'

'Then you think they did?'

She looked puzzled. 'The paper says they did.'

'No, the paper reports what the girl said.'

She obviously did not follow that. This was the democracy we deified.

'They wouldn't print a story like that if it wasn't true. It would be as much as their life's worth. You a detective?'

'Part time,' Robert said.

'How much do you get an hour for that?'

'Not nearly enough.'

'No, I suppose not. Haven't got a union, I suppose. You don't get your rights in this world unless you have a union.'

'Too true,' said Robert. 'Let me have my bill, will you?'

'Your check, yes.'

At the Palace, the biggest and newest of the cinemas, the restaurant occupied the floor behind the balcony, and had carpets so deep that one tripped on them and lighting so subdued that all the cloths looked dirty. A bored houri with gilt hair, an uneven hem to her skirt, and a wad of chewing-gum in her right jaw took his order without ever glancing at him, and fifteen minutes later put down a cup of washy liquid in front of him without letting her eyes stray even approximately in his direction. Since in the fifteen minutes Robert had discovered that the never-look-at-customers technique was universal – presumably they were all going to be film-stars the year after next and could not be expected to take any interest in a provincial clientele – he paid for the untasted liquid and left.

At the Castle, the other big cinema, the restaurant did not open until afternoon.

At the Violet – royal purple everywhere and yellow curtains – no one had seen her. Robert, casting subtleties aside, asked them bluntly.

Upstairs at Griffon and Waldron's, the big store, it was rush hour and the waitress said: 'Don't *bother* me!' The manageress, looking at him with absent-minded suspicion, said: 'We never give information about our customers.'

At the Old Oak – small and dark and friendly – the elderly waitresses discussed the case interestedly with him. 'Poor love,' they said. 'What an experience for her! Such a nice face, too. Just a baby. Poor love.'

At the Alençon – cream paint and old-rose couches against the walls – they made it plain that they had never heard of the *Ack-Emma* and could not possibly have a client whose photograph appeared in such a publication.

At the Heave Ho – marine frescoes and waitresses in bell-bottomed trousers – the attendants gave it as their unanimous opinion that any girl who took a lift should expect to have to walk home.

At the Primrose – old polished tables with raffia mats and thin, unprofessional waitresses in flowered smocks – they discussed the social implications of lack of domestic service and the vagaries of the adolescent mind.

At the Tea-Pot there was no table to be had and no waitress willing to attend to him, but a second glance at the fly-blown place made him sure that, with the others to choose from, Betty Kane would not have come here.

At half past twelve he staggered into the lounge of the Midland and called for strong waters. As far as he knew he had covered all the likely eating-places in the centre of Larborough and in not one of them had anyone remembered seeing the girl. What was worse, everyone agreed that if she had been there they would have remembered her. They had pointed out, when Robert was sceptical of that, that a large proportion of their customers on any one day were regulars, so that the casuals stood out from the rest and were noted and remembered automatically.

As Albert, the tubby little lounge waiter, set his drink in front of him, Robert asked, more out of habit than volition: 'I suppose you've never seen this girl in your place, Albert?'

Albert looked at the front page of the *Ack-Emma* and shook his head. 'No, sir. Not that I recollect. Looks a little young, sir, if I may say so, for the lounge of the Midland.'

'She mightn't look so young with a hat on,' Robert said, considering it.

'A hat,' Albert paused. 'Now, wait a minute. A *hat*.' Albert laid his little tray down and picked up the paper to consider it. 'Yes, of course – that's the girl in the green hat!'

'You mean she came in here for coffee?'

'No, for tea.'

'Tea!'

'Yes, of course, that's the girl. Fancy me not seeing that, and we had that paper in the pantry last Friday and chewed the rag over it for hours! Of course it's some time ago now, isn't it? About six weeks or so, it must be. She always came early – just about three, when we start serving teas.'

So that is what she did. Fool that he was not to have seen that. She went into the morning round at the cinema in time to pay the cheaper price – just before noon, that was – and came out about three, and had tea, not coffee. But why the Midland, where the tea was the usual dowdy and expensive hotel exhibit, when she could wallow in cakes elsewhere?

'I noticed her because she always came alone. The first time she came I thought she was waiting for relations. That's the kind of kid she looked. You know: nice plain clothes and no airs.'

'Can you remember what she wore?'

'Oh yes. She always wore the same things. A green hat and a frock to match it under a pale grey coat. But she never met any-one. And then one day she picked up the man at the next table. You could have knocked me over with a feather.'

'You mean he picked her up.'

'Don't you believe it! He hadn't even thought of her when he sat down there. I tell you, sir, she didn't look that sort. You'd expect an aunt or a mother to appear at any moment and say: "So sorry to have kept you waiting, darling." She just wouldn't occur to any man as a possible. Oh no; it was the kid's doing. And as neat a piece of business, let me tell you, sir, as if she had spent a lifetime at it. Goodness, and to think that I didn't spot her again without her hat!' He gazed in wonder at the pictured face.

'What was the man like? Did you know him?'

'No, he wasn't one of our regulars. Dark, youngish; business gent, I should say. I remember being a little surprised at her taste, so I don't think he could have been up to much, now I come to think of it.'

'You wouldn't know him again, then.'

'I might, sir, I might. But not to swear to. You – er – plan-ning any swearing to, sir?'

Robert had known Albert for nearly twenty years and had always found him of an excellent discretion. 'It's like this, Albert,' he said. 'These people are my clients.' He tapped the photograph of the The Franchise, and Albert gave vent to a low whistle.

'A tough spot for you, Mr Blair.'

'Yes, as you say: a tough spot. But mostly for them. It is quite unbelievably tough for them. The girl comes out of the blue one day accompanied by the police, to whom she has told this fantastic story. Until then neither of the two women has ever set eyes on her. The police are very discreet and decide that they haven't enough evidence to make it a good case. Then the

Ack-Emma hears about it and makes capital out of it, and the story is all over Britain. The Franchise is wide open, of course. The police can't spare men to afford constant protection, so you can imagine the lives these women are leading. My young cousin, who looked in before dinner last night, says that from lunch-time on crowds of cars arrived from Larborough, and people stood on roofs or hoisted themselves up on the wall to stare or take photographs. Nevil got in because he arrived at the same time as the policeman on the evening beat, but as soon as they left the cars were swarming again. The telephone went continually until they asked the Exchange not to put through any more calls.'

'Have the police dropped it for good, then?'

'No; but they can't do anything to help *us*. What they are looking for is corroboration of the girl's story.'

'Well, that's not very likely, is it? For them to get, I mean.'

'No. But you see the spot we are in. Unless we can find out where the girl was during the weeks she says she was at The Franchise, the Sharpes will be in the position of being permanently convicted of a thing they haven't even been accused of!'

'Well, if it's the girl in the green hat – and I'm sure it is, sir – I'd say she was what is known as "out on the tiles", sir. A very cool customer she was for a girl that age. Butter wouldn't melt in her mouth.'

'Butter wouldn't melt in her little mouth,' the tobacconist had said of the child Betty. And 'on the tiles' was Stanley's verdict on the pictured face that was so like 'the bint he had had in Egypt.'

And the worldly little waiter had used both phrases in his estimate of her – the demure girl in the 'good' clothes who had come every day by herself to sit in the hotel lounge.

'Perhaps it was just a childish desire to be "grand",' the nice side of him prompted; but his common sense refused it. She could have been grand at the Alençon, and eaten well, and seen smart clothes at the same time.

He went in to have lunch, and then spent a large part of the afternoon trying to reach Mrs Wynn on the telephone. Mrs Tilsit had no telephone and he had no intention of involving himself in a Tilsit conversation again if he could help it. When he failed he remembered that Scotland Yard would most certainly, in that painstaking way of theirs, have a description of the clothes the girl was wearing when she went missing. And in less than seven minutes, he had it. A green felt hat, a green wool frock to match, a pale grey cloth coat with large grey buttons, fawn-grey rayon stockings and black court shoes with medium heels.

Well, at last he had it, that setting-off place; that starting-point for inquiry. Jubilation filled him. He sat down in the lounge on his way out and wrote a note to tell Kevin Macdermott that the young woman from Aylesbury was not such an attractive brief as she had been on Friday night; and to let him know, of course – between the lines – that Blair, Hayward, and Bennet could get get a move on when it was necessary.

'Did she ever come back?' he asked Albert, who was hovering. 'I mean, after she had "got her man".'

'I don't remember ever seeing either of them again, sir.'

Well, the hypothetical X had ceased to be hypothetical. He had become plain X. He, Robert, could go back tonight to The Franchise in triumph. He had put forward a theory, and the theory had proved fact, and it was he who had proved it a fact. It was depressing, of course, that the letters received so far by Scotland Yard had all been merely anonymous revilings of the Yard for their 'softness' to the 'rich', and not claims to have seen Betty Kane. It was depressing that practically everyone he had interviewed that morning believed the girl's story without question; was, indeed, surprised and at a loss if asked to consider any other point of view. 'The paper said so.' But these were small things compared to the satisfaction of having arrived at that starting-point; of having unearthed X. He didn't believe that fate could be so cruel as to show that Betty Kane parted with her acquaintance on the steps of the Midland and never saw him again. There *had* to be an extension of that incident in the lounge. The history of the following weeks demanded it.

But how did one follow up a young, dark business gent who had tea in the lounge of the Midland about six weeks previously? Young, dark business gents were the Midland's clientele; and as far as Blair could see all as like as two peas, anyhow. He was very much afraid that this was where he bowed out and handed over to a professional bloodhound. He had no photograph this time to help him, no knowledge of X's character or habits, as he had had in the case of the girl. It would be a long process of small inquiries – a job for an expert. All he could do at the moment, so far as he could see, was to get a list of residents at the Midland for the period in question.

For that he went to the manager, a Frenchman who showed great delight and understanding in this *sub rosa* proceeding, was exquisitely sympathetic about the outraged ladies at The Franchise, and comfortingly cynical about smooth-faced young girls in good clothes who looked as if butter wouldn't melt in their mouths. He sent an underling to copy the entries from the great ledger and entertained Robert to a *sirop* from his own cupboard. Robert had never subscribed to the French taste for small sweet mouthfuls of unidentifiable liquids drunk at odd times, but he swallowed the thing gratefully and pocketed the list the underling brought as one pockets a passport. Its actual value was probably nil, but it gave him a nice feeling to have it. And if he had to turn over the business to a professional, the professional would have somewhere to start his burrowing. X had probably never stayed at the Midland in his life; he had probably just walked in for tea one day. On the other hand, his name might be among that list in his pocket – that horribly long list.

As he drove home he decided that he would not stop at The Franchise. It was unfair to bring Marion to the gate just to give her news that could be told over the telephone. He would tell the Exchange who he was and the fact that the call was official, and they would answer it. Perhaps by tomorrow the first flood of interest in the house would have subsided and it would be safe to unbar the gate again. Though he doubted it. Today's *Ack-Emma* had not been calculated to have an appeasing effect on the mob mind. True, there were no further front-page headlines; the Franchise affair had removed itself to the correspondence page. But the letters the *Ack-Emma* had chosen to print there – and two thirds of them were about the Franchise affair – were not likely to prove oil on troubled waters. They were so much paraffin on a fire that was going quite nicely anyhow.

Threading his way out of the Larborough traffic, the silly phrases came back to him; and he marvelled all over again at the venom that these unknown women had roused in the writers' minds. Rage and hatred spilled over on to the paper; malice ran unchecked through the largely illiterate sentences. It was an amazing exhibition. And one of the oddities of it was that the dearest wish of so many of those indignant protesters against violence was to flog the said women within an inch of their lives. Those who did not want to flog the women wanted to reform the police. One writer suggested that a fund should be opened for the poor young victim of police inefficiency and bias. Another suggested that every man of good will should write to his Member of Parliament about it and make their lives a misery until something was done about this miscarriage of justice. Still another asked if anyone had noticed Betty Kane's marked resemblance to Saint Bernadette.

There was every sign, if today's correspondence page of the *Ack-Emma* was any criterion, of the birth of a Betty Kane cult. He hoped that its corollary would not be a Franchise vendetta.

As he neared the unhappy house he grew anxious, wondering if Monday too had provided its quota of sightseers. It was a lovely evening, the low sun slanting great golden swathes of light over the spring fields; an evening to tempt even Larborough out to the Midland dullness of Milford; it would be a miracle if, after the correspondence in the *Ack-Emma,* The Franchise was not the Mecca of an evening pilgrimage. But when he came within sight of it he found the long stretch of road deserted; and as he came nearer he saw why. At the gate of The Franchise, solid and immobile and immaculate in the evening light, was the dark-blue-and-silver figure of a police-man.

Delighted that Hallam had been so generous with his scanty force, Robert slowed down to exchange greetings; but the greeting died on his lips. Along the full length of the tall brick wall, in letters nearly six feet high, was splashed a slogan. 'FASCISTS!' screamed the large white capitals. And again on the farther side of the gate: 'FASCISTS!'

'Move along, please,' the Force said, approaching the staring Robert with slow, polite menace. 'No stopping here.'

Robert got slowly out of the car.

'Oh, Mr Blair. Didn't recognize you, sir. Sorry.'

'Is it whitewash?'

'No, sir; best quality paint.'

'Great heavens!'

'Some people never grow out of it.'

'Out of what?'

'Writing things on walls. There's one thing: they might have written something worse.'

'They wrote the worst insult they knew,' said Robert wryly. 'I suppose you haven't got the culprits?'

'No, sir. I just came along on my evening beat to clear away the usual gapers – oh yes, there were dozens of them – and found it like that when I arrived. Two men in a car, if all reports are true.'

'Do the Sharpes know about it?'

'Yes, I had to get in to telephone. We have a code now, us and The Franchise people. I tie my handkerchief on the end of my truncheon and wave it over the top of the gate when I want to speak to them. Do you want to go in, sir?'

'No. No, on the whole I think not. I'll get the Post Office to let me through on the telephone. No need to bring them to the gate. If this is going to continue they must get keys for the gate so that I can have a duplicate.'

'Looks as though it's going to continue all right, sir. Did you see today's *Ack-Emma*?'

'I did.'

'Strewth!' said the Force, losing his equanimity at the thought of the *Ack-Emma*. 'You would think to listen to them we were nothing but a collection of itching palms! It's a holy wonder we're not, come to that. It would suit them better to agitate for more pay for us instead of slandering us right and left.'

'You're in very good company, if it's any consolation to you,' Robert said. 'There can't be anything established, respectable, or praiseworthy that they haven't slandered at some time or other. I'll send someone either tonight or first thing in the morning to do something about this – obscenity. Are you staying here?'

'The sergeant said when I telephoned that I was to stay till dark.'

'No one overnight?'

'No, sir. No spare men for that. Anyhow, they'll be all right once the light's gone. People go home, especially the Larborough lot. They don't like the country once it gets dark.'

Robert, who remembered how silent the lonely house could be, felt doubtful. Two women alone in that big, quiet house after dark, with hatred and violence just outside the wall – it was not a comfortable thought. The gate was barred, but if people could hoist themselves on to the wall for the purpose of sitting there and shouting insults, they could just as easily drop down the other side in the dark.

'Don't worry, sir,' the Force said, watching his face. 'Nothing's going to happen to them. This is England, after all.'

'So is *Ack-Emma* England,' Robert reminded him. But he got back into the car again. After all, it *was* England, and the English countryside at that – famed for minding its own business. It was no country hand that had splashed that 'FASCISTS!' on the wall. It was doubtful if the country had ever heard the term. The country, when it wanted insults, used older, Saxon words.

The Force was no doubt right; once the dark came everyone would go home.

12

As Robert turned his car into the garage in Sin Lane and came to a halt, Stanley, who was shrugging off his overalls outside the office door, glanced at his face and said: 'Down the drain again?'

'It isn't a bet,' Robert said, 'it's human nature.'

'You start to be sorry about human nature and you won't have time for anything else. You been trying to reform someone?'

'No, I've been trying to get someone to take some paint off a wall.'

'Oh, work!' Stanley's tone indicated that even to expect someone to do a job of work these days was being optimistic to the point of folly.

'I've been trying to get someone to wipe a slogan off the walls of The Franchise, but everyone is extraordinarily busy all of a sudden.'

Stanley stopped his wriggling. 'A slogan,' he said. 'What kind of slogan?' And Bill, hearing the exchange, oozed himself through the narrow office door to listen.

Robert told them. 'In best quality white paint, so the policeman on the beat assures me.'

Bill whistled. Stanley said nothing; he was standing with his overalls shrugged down to his waist and concertinaed about his legs.

'Who've you tried?' Bill asked.

Robert told them. 'None of them can do anything tonight, and tomorrow morning, it seems, all their men are going out early on important jobs.'

'It's not to be believed,' Bill said. 'Don't tell me they're afraid of reprisals!'

'No, to do them justice I don't think it's that. I think, although they would never say so to me, that they think those women at The Franchise deserve it.' There was silence for a moment.

'When I was in the Signals,' Stanley said, beginning in a

leisurely fashion to pull up his overalls and get into the top half again, 'I was given a free tour of Italy. Nearly a year it took. And I escaped the malaria and the Ities and the Partisans and the Yank transport, and most of the other little nuisances. But I got a phobia. I took a great dislike to slogans on walls.'

'What'll we get it off with?' Bill asked.

'What's the good of owning the best-equipped and most modern garage in Milford if we haven't something to take off a spot of paint?' Stanley said, zipping up his front.

'Will you really try to do something about it?' Robert asked, surprised and pleased.

Bill smiled his slow, expansive smile. 'The Signals, the R.E.M.E., and a couple of brooms. What more do you want?' he said.

'Bless you,' Robert said. 'Bless you both. I have only one ambition tonight: to get that slogan off the wall before breakfast tomorrow. I'll come along and help.'

'Not in that Savile Row suit, you won't,' Stanley said. 'And we haven't a spare suit of –'

'I'll get something old on and come out after you.'

'Look,' Stanley said patiently, 'we don't need any help for a little job like that. If we did we'd take Harry.' Harry was the garage boy. 'You haven't eaten yet and we have, and I've heard it said that Miss Bennet doesn't like her good meals spoiled. I suppose you don't mind if the wall looks smeary? We're just good-intentioned garage hands, not decorators.'

The shops were shut as he walked down the High Street to his home at number 10, and he looked at the place as a stranger walking through on a Sunday night. He had been so far from Milford during his day in Larborough that he felt that he had been away for years. The comfortable quiet of Number 10 – different from the dead silence of The Franchise – welcomed and soothed him. A faint smell of roasting apples escaped from the kitchen. The firelight flickered on the wall of the sitting-room, seen through its half-open door. Warmth and security and comfort rose up in a gentle tide and lapped over him.

Guilty at being the owner of this waiting peace, he picked up the telephone to talk to Marion.

'Oh, *you* – how nice!' she said, when at last he had persuaded the Post Office that his intentions were honourable; and the warmth in her voice catching him unawares – his mind being still on white paint – caught him under the heart and left him breathless for a moment. 'I'm so glad. I was wondering how we were going to talk to you; but I might have known that you would manage it. I suppose you just say you're Robert Blair and the Post Office gives you the freedom of the place.'

How like her, he thought. The genuine gratitude of 'I might have known that you would manage'; and then the faint amusement in the sentence that followed.

'I suppose you've seen our wall decoration?'

Robert said yes, but that no one ever would again, because by the time the sun rose it would have gone.

'Tomorrow!'

'The two men who own my garage have decided to obliterate it tonight.'

'But – could seven maids with seven mops –?'

'I don't know; but if Stanley and Bill have set their minds on it, obliterated it will be. They were brought up in a school that doesn't tolerate frustrations.'

'What school is that?'

'The British Army. And I have more good news for you: I have established the fact that X exists. She had tea with him one day. Picked him up at the Midland, in the lounge.'

'Picked him up? But she is just a child, and so – Oh, well, she told that story, of course. After that anything is possible. How did you find that out?'

He told her.

'You've had a bad day at The Franchise, haven't you?' he said, when he had finished the saga of the coffee shops.

'Yes, I feel dirty all over. What was worse than the audience and the wall was the post. The postman gave it to the police to take in. It is not often that the police can be accused of disseminating obscene literature.'

'Yes, I imagined it must have been pretty bad. That was only to be expected.'

'Well, we have so few letters that we have decided that in future we shall burn everything without opening them, unless

121

we recognize the writing. So don't use typescript if you write to us.'

'But do you know my handwriting?'

'Oh yes, you wrote us a note, you remember. The one Nevil brought that afternoon. Nice handwriting.'

'Have you seen Nevil today?'

'No, but one of the letters was from him. At least, it wasn't a letter.'

'A document of some kind?'

'No, a poem.'

'Oh. Did you understand it?'

'No, but it made quite a nice sound.'

'So do bicycle bells.'

He thought she laughed a little. 'It is nice to have poems made to one's eyebrows,' she said. 'But still nicer to have one's wall made clean. I do thank you for that – you and what's-their -names – Bill and Stanley. If you want to be very kind perhaps you would bring or send us some food tomorrow?'

'Food!' he said, horrified that he had not thought of that before; that was what happened when you lived a life where Aunt Lin put everything down in front of you, all but put the stuff in your mouth: you lost the capacity for imagination. 'Yes, of course. I forgot that you would not be able to shop.'

'It isn't only that. The grocer's van that calls on Monday didn't come today. Or perhaps,' she added hastily, 'it came and just couldn't call our attention. Anyhow, we should be so grateful for some things. Have you got a pencil there?'

She gave him a list of things and then asked: 'We didn't see today's *Ack-Emma*. What there anything about us?'

'Some letters on the correspondence page, that is all.'

'All anti, I suppose.'

'I'm afraid so. I shall bring a copy out tomorrow morning when I bring the groceries, and you can see it for yourselves.'

'I'm afraid we are taking up a great deal of your time.'

'This has become a personal matter with me,' he said.

'Personal?' She sounded doubtful.

'The one ambition of my life is to discredit Betty Kane.'

'Oh; oh, I see.' Her voice sounded half relieved, half –

could it be? – disappointed. 'Well, we shall look forward to seeing you tomorrow.'

But she was to see him long before that.

He went to bed early, but lay awake, rehearsing a telephone conversation that he planned to have with Kevin Macdermott; considering different approaches to the problem of X; wondering if Marion was asleep, in that silent old house, or lying awake listening for sounds.

His bedroom was over the street, and about midnight he heard a car drive up and stop, and presently through the open window he heard Bill's cautious call – not much more than a throaty whisper. 'Mr Blair! Hey, Mr Blair!'

He was at the window almost before the second utterance of his name.

'Thank goodness,' whispered Bill. 'I was afraid the light might be Miss Bennet's.'

'No, she sleeps at the back. What is it?'

'There's trouble at The Franchise. I've got to go for the police because the wire is cut. But I thought you'd want to be called, so I–'

'What kind of trouble?'

'Hooligans. I'll come in for you on my way back. In about four minutes.'

'Is Stanley with them?' Robert asked, as Bill's great bulk merged with the car again.

'Yes, Stan's having his head bound up. Back in a minute.' And the car fled away up the dark, silent High Street.

Before Robert had got his clothes on he heard a soft 'sshush' go past his window, and realized that the police were already on their way. No screaming sirens in the night, no roaring exhausts; with no more sound than a summer wind makes among the leaves the law was going about its business. As he opened the front door, cautiously so as not to wake Aunt Lin (nothing but the last trump was likely to wake Christina), Bill brought his car to a standstill at the pavement.

'Now tell me,' Robert said, as they moved away.

'Well, we finished that little job by the light of the head-lamps – not very professional, it isn't, but a lot better than it was when we got there – and then we switched off the heads

123

and began to put away our things. Sort of leisurely like: there was no hurry and it was a nice night. We'd just lit a cigarette and were thinking of pushing off when there was a crash of glass from the house. No one had got in on our side while we were there, so we knew it must be round the sides or the back. Stan reached into the car and took out his torch – mine was lying on the seat because we'd been using it – and said: "You go round that way and I'll go the other and we'll nip them between us." '

'Can you get round?'

'Well, it was no end of a business. It's hedge up to the wall end. I wouldn't like to have done it in ordinary clothes, but in overalls you just push hard and hope for the best. It's all right for Stan; he's slim. But short of lying on the hedge till it falls down there's no way through for me. Anyhow, we got through, one on each side, and through the one at the back corners, and met in the middle of the back without seeing a soul. Then we heard more crashing of glass and realized that they were making a night of it. Stan said: "Hoist me up, and I'll give you a hand after me." Well, a hand would be no good to me, but it happens that the field level at the back comes fairly high up the wall – in fact, I think it was probably cut away to build the wall – so that we got over fairly easily. Stan said had I anything to hit with besides my torch and I said yes, I had a spanner. Stan said: "Forget your bloody spanner and use your ham fist; it's bigger." '

'What was he going to use?'

'The old rugby tackle, so he said. Stan used to be quite a good stand-off half. Anyhow, we went on in the dark towards the sound of the crashing glass. It seemed as if they were just having a breaking tour round the house. We caught up with them near the front corner again, and switched on our torches. I think there were seven of them. Far more than we had expected, anyhow. We switched off at once, before they could see that we were only two, and grabbed the nearest. Stan said: "You take that one, sergeant," and I thought at the time he was giving me my rank out of old habit, but I realize now he was bluffing them we were police. Anyhow, some of them beat it, because though there was a mix-up there couldn't have been anything like seven of them in it. Then, quite suddenly it seemed, there was quiet – we'd been making a lot of noise – and I realized that we were letting them get away, and Stan said from somewhere on the ground: "Grab one, Bill, before they get over the wall!" And I went after them with my torch on. The last of them was just being helped over, and I grabbed his legs and hung on. But he kicked like a mule, and what with the torch in my hand he slipped from my hands like a trout and was over before I could grab him again. That finished me, because from inside that wall at the back is even higher than it is at the front of the house. So I went back to Stan. He was still sitting on the ground. Someone had hit him a wallop over the head with what he said was a bottle, and he was looking very cheap. And then Miss Sharpe came out to the top of the front steps and said was someone hurt? She could see us in the torchlight. So we got Stan in – the old lady was there and the house was lit by this time – and I went to the phone, but Miss Sharpe said: "That's no use. It's dead. We tried to call the police when they first arrived." So I said I'd go and fetch them. And I said I'd better fetch you too. But Miss Sharpe said no, you'd had a very hard day and I wasn't to disturb you. But I thought you ought to be in on it.'

'Quite right, Bill, I ought.'

The gate was wide open as they drew up, the police car at the door, most of the front rooms lit, and the curtains waving gently in the night wind at the wrecked windows. In the drawing-room which the Sharpes evidently used as a living-room – Stanley was having a cut above his eye-brow attended to by Marion, a sergeant of police was taking notes, and his henchman was laying out exhibits. The exhibits seemed to consist of half bricks, bottles, and pieces of paper with writing on them.

'Oh, Bill, I told you not to,' Marion said as she looked up and saw Robert.

Robert noted how efficiently she was dealing with Stanley's injury – the woman who found cooking beyond her. He greeted the sergeant and bent to look at the exhibits. There was a large array of missiles, but only four messages, which read, respectively: 'Get out!' 'Get out or we'll make you!' 'Foreign bitches!' and 'This is only a sample!'

'Well, we've collected them all, I think,' the sergeant said. 'Now we'll go and search the garden for footprints or whatever clues there may be.' He glanced professionally at the soles that Bill and Stanley held up at his request and went out with his aide to the garden, as Mrs Sharpe came in with a steaming jug and cups.

'Ah, Mr Blair,' she said. 'You still find us stimulating?'

She was fully dressed – in contrast to Marion, who was looking quite human and un-Joan-of-Arc in an old dressing-gown – and apparently unmoved by these proceedings, and he wondered what kind of occasion would find Mrs Sharpe at a disadvantage.

Bill appeared with sticks from the kitchen and lighted the dead fire, Mrs Sharpe poured the hot liquid – it was coffee and Robert refused it, having seen enough coffee lately to lose interest in it – and the colour began to come back to Stan's face. By the time the policeman came back from the garden the room had acquired a family-party air, in spite of the waving curtains and the non-existent windows. Neither Stanley nor Bill, Robert noticed, appeared to find the Sharpes odd or difficult; on the contrary, they seemed relaxed and at home. Perhaps it was that the Sharpes took them for granted; accepting this invasion of strangers as if it were an everyday occurrence. Anyhow, Bill came and went on his ploys as if he had lived in the house for years; and Stanley put out his cup for a second helping without waiting to be asked. Involuntarily, Robert thought that Aunt Lin in their place would have been kind and fussy and they would have sat on the edge of the chairs and remembered their dirty overalls.

Perhaps it was the same taking-for-granted that had attracted Nevil.

'Do you plan to stay on here, ma'am?' the sergeant asked as they came in again.

'Certainly,' Mrs Sharpe said, pouring coffee for them.

'No,' Robert said. 'You mustn't, you really must not. I'll find you a quiet hotel in Larborough, where –'

'I never heard anything more absurd. Of course we are going to stay here. What do a few broken windows matter?'

'It may not stop at broken windows,' the sergeant said. 'And

126

you're a great responsibility to us as long as you are here, a responsibility we haven't really got the force to deal with.'

'I'm truly sorry we are a nuisance to you, sergeant. We wouldn't have flung bricks at our windows if we could help it, believe me. But this is our home and here we are staying. Quite apart from any questions of ethics, how much of our home would be left to come back to if it was left empty? I take it if you are too short of men to guard human beings, you certainly have no men to guard empty property?'

The sergeant looked slightly abashed, as people so often did when Mrs Sharpe dealt with them. 'Well, there is that, ma'am,' he acknowledged, with reluctance.

'And that, I think, disposes of any question of our leaving The Franchise. Sugar, sergeant?'

Robert returned to the subject when the police had taken their departure, and Bill had fetched a brush and shovel from the kitchen and was sweeping up the broken glass in room after room. Again he urged the wisdom of a hotel in Larborough, but neither his emotion nor his common sense was behind the words. He would not have gone if he had been in the Sharpes' place and he could not expect them to; and in addition he acknowledged the wisdom of Mrs Sharpe's view about the fate of the house left empty.

'What you want is a lodger,' said Stanley, who had been refused permission to sweep up glass because he was classed as walking-wounded. 'A lodger with a pistol. What d'you say I come and sleep here of nights? No meals; just sleeping night watchman. They all sleep anyhow, night watchmen do.'

It was evident by their expressions that both the Sharpes appreciated the fact that this was an open declaration of allegiance in what amounted to a local war; but they did not embarrass him with thanks.

'Haven't you got a wife?' Marion asked.

'Not of my own,' Stanley said demurely.

'Your wife – if you had one – might support your sleeping here,' Mrs Sharpe pointed out, 'but I doubt if your business would, Mr – er – Mr Peters.'

'My business?'

'I imagine that if your customers found that you had become night watchman at The Franchise they would take their custom elsewhere.'

'Not them,' Stanley said comfortably. 'There's nowhere else to take it. Lynch is drunk five nights out of seven and Biggins wouldn't know how to put on a bicycle chain. Anyhow, I don't let my customers tell me what I do in my spare time.'

And when Bill returned, he backed Stanley up. Bill was a much married man and it was not contemplated that he should ever sleep anywhere except at home. But that Stanley should sleep at The Franchise seemed to both of them a natural solution of the problem.

Robert was mightily relieved.

'Well,' Marion said, 'if you are going to be our guest at nights you might as well begin now. I am sure that head feels like a very painful turnip. I'll go and make up a bed. Do you prefer a south view?'

'Yes,' said Stanley gravely. 'Well away from kitchen and wireless noises.'

'I'll do what I can.'

It was arranged that Bill should slip a note into the door of Stanley's lodgings to say that he would be in for lunch as usual. 'She won't worry about me,' Stanley said, referring to his landlady. 'I've been out for nights before now.' He caught Marion's eye, and added: 'Ferrying cars for customers – you can do it in half the time at night.'

They tacked down the curtains in all the ground-floor rooms to provide some protection for their contents if it rained before morning, and Robert promised to get glaziers out at the earliest possible moment – deciding privately to go to a Larborough firm and not risk another series of polite rebuffs in Milford.

'And I shall also do something about a key for the gate, so that I can have a duplicate,' he said, as Marion came out with them to bar the gate, 'and save you from being gate-keeper as well as everything else.'

She put out her hand, to Bill first. 'I shall never forget what you three have done for us. When I remember tonight it won't be these clods that I shall remember' – she tilted her head to the windowless house – 'but you three.'

128

'Those clods were local, I suppose you know,' Bill said as they drove home through the quiet spring night.

'Yes,' Robert agreed. 'I realized that. They had no car, for one thing. And "Foreign bitches!" smells of the conservative country, just as "Fascists!" smells of the progressive town.'

Bill said some things about progress.

'I was wrong to let myself be persuaded yesterday evening. The man on the beat was so sure that "everyone would go home when it grew dark" that I let myself believe it. But I should have remembered a warning I got about witch-hunts.'

Bill was not listening. 'It's a funny thing how unsafe you feel in a house without windows,' he said. 'Take a house with the back blown clean off and not a door that will shut: you can live quite happily in a front room provided it still has windows. But without windows even a whole undamaged house feels unsafe.'

Which was not an observation that provided Robert with any comfort.

13

'I WONDER if you would mind calling for the fish, dear,' Aunt Lin said on the telephone on Tuesday afternoon. 'Nevil is coming to dinner, and so we are going to have an extra course of what we were going to have for breakfast. I really don't see why we should have anything extra just for Nevil, but Christina says that it will keep him from making what she calls "inroads" on the tart that is going to do again on her night out tomorrow. So if you wouldn't mind, dear.'

He was not looking forward greatly to an extra hour or two of Nevil's society, but he was feeling so pleased with himself that he was in a better humour to support it than usual. He had arranged with a Larborough firm for the replacement of The Franchise windows; he had miraculously unearthed a key that fitted The Franchise gate – and there would be two duplicates in existence by tomorrow; and he had personally taken out the groceries – together with an offering of the best flowers that Milford could supply. His welcome at The Franchise had been such that he had almost ceased to regret the lack of light exchanges on Nevil's lines. There were, after all, other things than getting to Christian-name terms in the first half-hour.

In the lunch hour he had rung up Kevin Macdermott and arranged with his secretary that when Kevin was free in the evening he would call him at 10 High Street. Things were getting out of hand and he wanted Kevin's advice.

He had refused three invitations to golf, his excuse to his astounded cronies being that he had 'no time to chase a piece of gutta-percha round a golf-course'.

He had gone to see an important client who had been trying to interview him since the previous Friday and who had been provoked into asking him on the telephone if 'he still worked for Blair, Hayward, and Bennet'.

He had got through his arrears of work with a mutely reproachful Mr Heseltine, who, although he had allied himself on the Sharpe side, still obviously felt that The Franchise affair was not one for a firm like theirs to be mixed up in.

And he had been given tea by Miss Tuff out of the blue-patterned china on the lacquer tray covered by the fair white cloth and accompanied by two digestive biscuits on a plate.

It was lying on his desk now, the tea-tray, just as it had been a fortnight ago when the telephone had rung and he had lifted the receiver to hear Marion Sharpe's voice for the first time. Two short weeks ago. He had sat looking at it in its patch of sunlight, feeling uneasy about his comfortable life and conscious of time slipping past him. But today the digestive biscuits held no reproach for him, because he had stepped outside the routine they typified. He was on calling terms with Scotland Yard; he was agent for a pair of scandalous women; he had become an amateur sleuth; and he had been witness of mob violence. His whole world looked different. Even the people he met looked different. The dark, skinny woman he used to see sometimes shopping in the High Street, for instance, had turned into Marion.

Well, one result of stepping out of a routined life was, of course, that you couldn't put on your hat and stroll home at four o'clock of an afternoon. He pushed the tea-tray out of his way and went to work, and it was half-past six before he looked at the clock again and seven before he opened the door of Number 10.

The sitting-room door was ajar as usual – like many doors in old houses, it swung a little if left off the latch – and he could hear Nevil's voice in the room beyond.

'On the contrary, I think you are being extremely silly,' Nevil was saying.

Robert recognized the tone at once. It was the cold rage with which a four-year-old Nevil had told a guest: 'I am extremely sorry that I asked you to my party.' Nevil must be very angry indeed about something.

With his coat half off Robert paused to listen.

'You are interfering in something you know nothing whatever about; you can hardly claim that is an intelligent proceeding.'

There was no other voice, so he must be talking to someone on the telephone – probably keeping Kevin from getting through, the young idiot.

'I am not infatuated with anyone. I never *have* been infatuated with anyone. It is you who are infatuated – with ideas. You are being extremely silly as I said before ... You are taking the part of an unbalanced adolescent in a case you know nothing about ; I should have thought that was sufficient evidence of infatuation ... You can tell your father from me that there is nothing Christian about it, just unwarranted interference. I'm not sure it isn't incitement to violence ... Yes, last night ... No, all their windows broken and things painted on their walls ... If he is so interested in justice he might do something about that. But your lot are never interested in justice, are they? Only injustice ... What do I mean by your lot? Just what I say. You and all your crowd, who are for ever adopting good-for-nothings and championing them against the world. You wouldn't put out a finger to keep a hard-working little man from going down the drain, but let an old lag lack the price of a meal and your sobs can be heard in Antarctica. You make me sick ... Yes, I said you make me sick ... Cat-sick. Sick to my stomach. I retch !'

And the bang of the receiver on its rest indicated that the poet had said his say.

Robert hung up his coat in the cupboard and went in. Nevil, with a face like thunder, was pouring himself out a stiff whisky.

'I'll have one too,' Robert said .'I couldn't help overhearing,' he added. 'That wasn't Rosemary, by any chance?'

'Who else? Is there anyone else in Britain capable of an ineffable silliness like that?'

'Like what?'

'Oh, didn't you hear that bit? She has taken up the cause of the persecuted Betty Kane.' Nevil gulped some whisky, and glared at Robert as if Robert were responsible.

'Well, I don't suppose her stepping on the *Ack-Emma* bandwagon will have much effect one way or another.'

'The *Ack-Emma*! It isn't the *Ack-Emma*; it's *The Watchman*. That mental deficient she calls father has written a letter about it for Friday's issue. Yes, you may well look squeamish. As if we weren't coping with enough without that highfalutin' nugget of perverted sentimentality putting in its sixpence-worth !'

Remembering that *The Watchman* was the only paper ever to have published any of Nevil's poems, Robert thought this showed slight ingratitude. But he approved the description.

'Perhaps they won't print it,' he said, less in hope than looking for comfort.

'You know very well they will print anything he chooses to send them. Whose money saved them just when they were going down for the third time? The Bishop's, of course.'

'His wife's, you mean.' The Bishop had married one of the two grand-daughters of Cowan's Cranberry Sauce.

'All right, his wife's. And the Bishop has *The Watchman* for a lay pulpit. And there isn't anything too silly for him to say in it or too unlikely for them to print. Do you remember that girl who went round shooting taxi-drivers in cold blood for a profit of about seven-and-eleven a time? That girl was just his meat. He sobbed himself practically into a coma about her. He wrote a long heart-breaking letter about her in *The Watchman*, pointing out how under-privileged she had been and how she had won a scholarship to a secondary school and hadn't been able to "take it up" because her people were too poor to provide her with books or proper clothes, and so she had gone to blind-alley jobs and then to bad company – and so, it was inferred, to shooting taxi-drivers, though he didn't actually mention that little matter. Well, all the *Watchman* readers *lahved* that, of course; it was just their cup of tea. All criminals according to the *Watchman* readers are frustrated angels. And then the Chairman of the Board of Governors of the school – the school she was supposed to have won a scholarship to – wrote to point out that, so far from winning anything was she, her name was 159th out of two hundred competitors; and that someone as interested in education as the Bishop was should have known that no one was prevented from accepting a scholarship through lack of money, since in needy cases books and money grants were forthcoming automatically. Well, you would have thought that that would shake him, wouldn't you? But not a bit. They printed the Chairman's letter on a back page in small print; and in the very next issue the old boy was sobbing over some other case that he knew nothing about. And on Friday, so help me, he'll be sobbing over Betty Kane.'

133

'I wonder – if I went over to see him tomorrow –'

'It goes to press tomorrow.'

'Yes, so it does. Perhaps if I telephoned –'

'If you think that anyone or anything will make his lordship keep back a finished composition from the public gaze, you're being naïve.'

The telephone rang.

'If that's Rosemary, I'm in China,' Nevil said.

But it was Kevin Macdermott.

'Well, sleuth,' said Kevin. 'My congratulations. But next time don't waste an afternoon trying to ring up civilians in Aylesbury when you can get the same information from Scotland Yard by return.'

Robert said that he was still sufficiently civilian not to think in terms of Scotland Yard at all, but that he was learning – rapidly.

He sketched the happenings of last night for Kevin's benefit, and said: 'I can't afford to be leisurely about it any more. Something must be done as quickly as possible to clear them of this thing.'

'You want me to give you the name of a private agent, is that it?'

'Yes, I suppose it has come to that. But I did wonder –'

'Wonder what?' Kevin asked, as he hesitated.

'Well, I did think of going to Grant at the Yard and saying quite frankly that I had found out how she could have known about the Sharpes and about the house; and that she had met a man in Larborough and that I had a witness of the meeting.'

'So that they could do what?'

'So that they could investigate the girl's movements during that month instead of us.'

'And you think they would?'

'Of course. Why not?'

'Because it wouldn't be worth their while. All they would do when they found out that she was not trustworthy would be to drop the case thankfully into oblivion. She has not sworn to anything, so they could not prosecute her for perjury.'

'They could proceed against her for having misled them.'

'Yes, but it wouldn't be worth their while. It won't be easy to unearth her movements for that month, we may be sure. And on top of all that unnecessary investigation they would have the job of preparing and presenting a case. It's highly unlikely that an overworked department, with serious cases flooding in at their doors, are going to all that bother when they could quietly drop the thing on the spot.'

'But it's supposed to be a department of justice. It leaves the Sharpes –'

'No, a department of the law. Justice begins in court. As you very well know. Besides, Rob, you haven't brought them any proof of anything. You don't know that she ever went to Milford. And the fact that she picked up a man at the Midland and had tea with him doesn't do anything to disprove her story that she was picked up by the Sharpes. In fact, the only leg you have to stand on is Alec Ramsden, 5 Spring Gardens, Fulham, South West.'

'Who is he?'

'Your private sleuth. And a very good one, take it from me. He has a flock of tame operators at call, so if he is busy himself he can supply you with a fairly good substitute. Tell him I gave you his name and he won't palm off a dud on you. Not that he would, anyhow. He's the salt of the earth. Pensioned from the Force because of a wound "received in the course of duty". He'll do you proud. I must go. If there's anything else I can do just give me a ring some time. I wish I had time to come down and see The Franchise and your witches for myself. They grow on me. Good-bye.'

Robert laid down the receiver, picked it up again, asked for Information, and obtained the telephone number of Alec Ramsden. There was no answer and he sent a telegram saying that he, Robert Blair, needed some work done urgently and that Kevin Macdermott had said that Ramsden was the man to do it.

'Robert,' said Aunt Lin, coming in pink and indignant, 'did you know that you left the fish on the hall table and it has soaked through to the mahogany and Christina was waiting for it?'

'Is the gravamen of the charge the mahogany or keeping Christina waiting?'

'Really, Robert, I hardly know what's come over you. Since you got involved in this Franchise affair you've changed entirely. A fortnight ago you would never have dreamed of putting a parcel of fish down on polished mahogany and forgetting all about it. And if you had you would be sorry about it and apologize.'

'I do apologize, Aunt Lin; I am truly contrite. But it is not often I am saddled with a responsibility as serious as the present one and you must forgive me if I am a little jaded.'

'I don't think you are jaded at all. On the contrary, I have never seen you so pleased with yourself. I think you are positively *relishing* this sordid affair. Only this morning Miss Truelove at the Anne Boleyn was condoling with me on your being mixed up in it.'

'Was she indeed? Well, I condole with Miss Truelove's sister.'

'Condole about what?'

'On having a sister like Miss Truelove. You *are* having a bad time, aren't you, Aunt Lin?'

'Don't be sarcastic, dear. It is not pleasant for anyone in the town to see the notoriety that has overtaken it. It has always been a quiet and dignified little place.'

'I don't like Milford as much as I did a fortnight ago,' Robert said reflectively, 'so I'll save my tears.'

'No less than four separate charabancs arrived from Larborough at one time or another today, having come for nothing but to inspect The Franchise *en route*.'

'And who catered for them?' Robert asked, knowing that coach traffic was not welcomed in Milford.

'No one. They were simply furious.'

'That will larn them to go poking their noses. There is nothing Larborough minds about as much as its stomach.'

'The vicar's wife insists on being Christian about it, but I think that that is the wrong point of view.'

'Christian?'

'Yes – "reserving our judgement", you know. That is merely feebleness, not Christianity. Of course I don't discuss the case, Robert dear; even with her. I am the soul of discretion.

But of course she knows how I feel and I know how she feels, so discussion is hardly necessary.'

What was clearly a snort came from Nevil where he was sunk in an easy chair.

'Did you say something, Nevil dear?'

The nursery tone clearly intimidated Nevil. 'No, Aunt Lin,' he said meekly.

But he was not going to escape so easily; the snort had only too clearly been a snort. 'I don't grudge you the drink, dear, but is that your *third* whisky? There is a Traminer for dinner, and you won't taste it at all after that strong stuff. You mustn't get into bad habits if you are going to marry a bishop's daughter.'

'I am not going to marry Rosemary.'

Miss Bennet stared, aghast. 'Not!'

'I would as soon marry a Public Assistance Board.'

'But, Nevil!'

'I would as soon marry a radio set.' Robert remembered Kevin's remark about Rosemary giving birth to nothing but a gramophone record. 'I would as soon marry a crocodile.' Since Rosemary was very pretty Robert supposed that 'crocodile' had something to do with tears. 'I would as soon marry a soap-box.' Marble Arch, Robert supposed. 'I would as soon marry the *Ack-Emma*.' That seemed to be final.

'But, Nevil dear, *why*?'

'She is a very silly creature. Almost as silly as *The Watch-man*.'

Robert heroically refrained from mentioning the fact that for the last six years *The Watchman* had been Nevil's bible.

'Oh, come, dear; you've had a tiff; all engaged couples do. It's a good thing to get the give-and-take business on a firm basis before marriage; those couples who never quarrel during their engagement lead surprisingly rowdy lives after marriage; so don't take a small disagreement too seriously. You can ring her up before you go home tonight –'

'It is a quite fundamental disagreement,' Nevil said coldly. 'And there is no prospect whatever of my ringing her up.'

'But, Nevil dear, what –'

The three thin cracked notes of the gong floated through her protest and gave her pause. The drama of broken engagements gave place on the instant to more immediate concerns.

'That is the gong. I think you had better take your drink in with you, dear. Christina likes to serve the soup as soon as she has added the egg, and she is not in a very good mood tonight because of getting the fish so late. Though why that should make any difference to her I can't think. It is only grilled, and that doesn't take any time. It's not as if she had to wipe the fish juice off the mahogany, because I did that myself.'

14

IT further upset Aunt Lin that Robert should have breakfast next morning at 7.45 so that he could go early to the office. It was another sign of the degeneration that The Franchise affair was responsible for. To have early breakfast so that he might catch a train, or set out for a distant meet, or attend a client's funeral was one thing. But to have early breakfast just so that he could arrive at work at an office-boy hour was a very odd proceeding and unbefitting a Blair.

Robert smiled, walking up the sunny High Street still shuttered and quiet. He had always liked the early morning hours, and it was at this hour that Milford looked its best; its pinks and sepias and creams as delicate in the sunlight as a tinted drawing. Spring was merging into summer, and already the warmth of the pavement radiated into the cool air; the pollarded limes were full out. That would mean shorter nights for the lonely women at The Franchise, he remembered thankfully. But perhaps – with any luck – by the time the summer was actually here their vindication would be complete and their home no longer a beleaguered fortress.

Propped against the still closed door of the office was a long, thin grey man who seemed to be all bones and to have no stomach at all.

'Good morning,' Robert said. 'Did you want to see me?'

'No,' said the grey man. 'You wanted to see me.'

'*I* did?'

'At least, so your telegram said. I take it you're Mr Blair?'

'But you can't be here already!' Robert said.

'It's not far,' the man said laconically.

'Come in,' said Robert, trying to live up to Mr Ramsden's standard of economy in comment.

In the office he asked as he unlocked his desk: 'Have you had breakfast?'

'Yes, I had bacon and eggs at the White Hart.'

'I am wonderfully relieved that you could come yourself.'

'I had just finished a case. And Kevin Macdermott has done a lot for me.'

Yes, Kevin, for all his surface malice and his overcrowded life, found the will and the time to help those who deserved help. In which he differed markedly from the Bishop of Larborough, who preferred the undeserving.

'Perhaps the best way would be for you to read this statement,' Robert said, handing Ramsden the copy of Betty Kane's statement to the police, 'and then we can go on with the story from there.'

Ramsden took the typescript, sat down in the visitors' chair – folded up would be a more accurate description of his action – and withdrew himself from Robert's presence very much as Kevin had done in the room in St Paul's Churchyard. Robert, taking out his own work, envied them their power of concentration.

'Yes, Mr Blair?' he said presently; and Robert gave him the rest of the story; the girl's identification of the house and its inmates; Robert's own entrance into the affair; the police decision that they would not proceed on the available evidence; Leslie Wynn's resentment and its result in the *Ack-Emma* publicity; his own interviews with the girl's relations and what they revealed; his discovery that she went bus-riding and that a double-decker did run on the Milford bus-route during the relevant weeks; and his unearthing of X.

'To find out more about X is your job, Mr Ramsden. The lounge-waiter, Albert, knows what he looked like, and this is a list of residents for the period in question. It would be too great luck that he should be staying at the Midland, but one never knows. After that you're on your own. Tell Albert I sent you, by the way. I've known him a long time.'

'Very good. I'll get over to Larborough now. I'll have a photograph of the girl by tomorrow, but perhaps you could lend me your *Ack-Emma* one for today.'

'Certainly. How are you going to get a proper photograph of her?'

'Oh. Ways.'

Robert deduced that Scotland Yard had been given one when the girl was reported missing and that his old colleagues at Headquarters would not be too reluctant to give him a copy; so he left it at that.

'There's just a chance that the conductor of one of those double-decker buses may remember her,' he said as Ramsden was going. 'They are Larborough and District Motor Services buses. The garage is in Victoria Street.'

At half-past nine the staff arrived – one of the first being Nevil; a change in routine which surprised Robert. Nevil was usually the last to arrive and the last to settle down. He would wander in, divest himself of his wrappings in his own small room at the back, wander into 'the office' to say good morning, wander into the 'waiting-room' at the back to say hello to Miss Tuff, and finally wander into Robert's room and stand there thumbing open the bound roll of one of the esoteric periodicals that came for him by post and commenting on the permanently deplorable state of affairs in England. Robert had grown quite used to running through his morning post to a Nevil *obbligato*. But today Nevil came in at the appointed time, went into his own room, shut the door firmly after him, and, if the pulling in and out of drawers was any evidence, settled down to work at once.

Miss Tuff came in with her notebook and her dazzling white peter-pan collar, and Robert's normal day had begun. Miss Tuff had worn peter-pan collars over her dark frock for twenty years and would have looked undressed, almost indecent, without them now. A fresh one went on every morning; the previous day's having been laundered the night before and laid ready for putting on tomorrow. The only break in the routine was on Sundays. Robert had once met Miss Tuff on a Sunday and entirely failed to recognize her because she was wearing a jabot.

Until half past ten Robert worked, and then realized that he had had breakfast at an abnormally early hour and was now in need of more sustenance than an office cup of tea. He would go out and have coffee and a sandwich at the Rose and Crown. You got the best coffee in Milford at the Anne Boleyn, but it was always full of shopping females ('*How* nice to see you, my dear! We *did* miss you so at Ronnie's party! And *have* you heard . . .') and that was an atmosphere he would not face for all the coffee in Brazil. He would go across to the Rose and Crown, and afterwards he would shop a little on behalf of the Franchise people, and after lunch he would go out and break to them gently the bad news about *The Watchman*. He could not do it on the telephone because they had no telephone now. The Larborough firm had come out with ladders and putty and recalcitrant sheets of glass and had replaced the windows without fuss or mess. But they, of course, were private enterprise. The Post Office, being a Government department, had taken the matter of the telephone into avizandum and would move in their own elephantile good time. So Robert planned to spend part of his afternoon telling the Sharpes the news he could not tell them by telephone.

It was still early for mid-morning snacks, and the chintz and old oak of the Rose and Crown lounge was deserted except for Ben Carley, who was sitting by the gate-legged table at the window reading the *Ack-Emma*. Carley had never been Robert's cup-of-tea – any more than, he suspected, he was Carley's – but they had the bond of their profession (one of the strongest in human nature), and in a small place like Milford that made them very nearly bosom friends. So Robert sat down as a matter of course at Carley's table; remembering as he did so that he still owed Carley gratitude for that unheeded warning of his about the feeling in the countryside.

Carley lowered the *Ack-Emma* and regarded him with the too-lively dark eyes that were so alien in this English Midland serenity. 'It seems to be dying down,' he said. 'Only one letter today ; just to keep something in the kitty.'

'The *Ack-Emma*, yes. But *The Watchman* is beginning a campaign of its own on Friday.'

'*The Watchman!* What's *it* doing climbing into the *Ack-Emma*'s bed?'

'It wouldn't be the first time,' Robert said.

'No, I suppose not,' Carley said, considering it. 'Two sides of the same penny, when you come to think of it. Oh, well. That needn't worry you. The total circulation of *The Watchman* is about twenty thousand. If that.'

'Perhaps. But practically every one of those twenty thousand has a second cousin in the permanent Civil Service in this country.'

'So what? Has anyone ever known the permanent Civil Service to move a finger in any cause whatever outside their normal routine?'

'No, but they pass the buck. And sooner or later the buck drops into – into a – a –'

'A fertile spot,' Carley offered, mixing the metaphor deliberately.

'Yes. Sooner or later some busybody or sentimentalist or egoist, with not enough to do, thinks that something should be done about this and begins to pull strings. And a string pulled in the Civil Service has the same effect as a string pulled in a peepshow. A whole series of figures is yanked into action, willy-nilly. Gerald obliges Tony, and Reggie obliges Gerald, and so on, to incalculable ends.'

Carley was silent a moment. 'It's a pity,' he said. 'Just when the *Ack-Emma* was losing way. Another two days and they would have dropped it for good. In fact, they're two days over their normal schedule, as it is. I have never known them carry a subject longer than three issues. The response must have been terrific to warrant that amount of space.'

'Yes,' Robert agreed gloomily.

'Of course, it was a gift for them. The beating of kidnapped girls is growing very rare. As a change of fare it was beyond price. When you have only three or four dishes, like the *Ack-Emma,* it's difficult to keep the customers' palates properly tickled. A tit-bit like The Franchise affair must have put up their circulation by thousands in the Larborough district alone.'

'Their circulation will slack off ; it's just a tide. But what I have to deal with is what's left on the beach.'

'A particularly smelly beach, let me say,' Carley observed. 'Do you know that fat blonde with the mauve powder and the uplift brassière who runs that sports-wear shop next to the Anne Boleyn? She's one of the things on your beach.'

'How?'

'She lived at the same boarding-house in London as the Sharpes, it seems ; and she has a lovely story as to how Marion

143

Sharpe once beat a dog half to death in a rage. Her clients loved that story. So did the Anne Boleyn customers. She goes there for her morning coffee.' He glanced wryly at the angry flush on Robert's face. 'I needn't tell you that she has a dog of her own. It has never been corrected in its spoiled life, but it is rapidly dying of fatty degeneration through the indiscriminate feeding of morsels whenever the fat blonde is feeling gooey.'

There were moments, Robert thought, when he could very nearly hug Ben Carley, striped suits and all.

'Ah well, it will blow over,' said Carley, with the pliant philosophy of a race long used to lying low and letting the storm blow past.

Robert looked surprised. Forty generations of protesting ancestors were surprised in his sole person. 'I don't see that blowing over is any advantage,' he said. 'It won't help my clients at all.'

'What can you do?'

'Fight, of course.'

'Fight what? You wouldn't get a slander verdict, if that's what you're thinking of.'

'No, I hadn't thought of slander. I propose to find out what the girl was really doing during those weeks.'

Carley looked amused. 'Just like that,' he said, commenting on this simple statement of a tall order.

'It won't be easy and it will probably cost them all they have, but there is no alternative.'

'They could go away from here. Sell the house and settle down somewhere else. A year from now no one outside the Milford district will remember anything about this affair.'

'They would never do that; and I shouldn't advise them to, even if they would. You can't have a tin can tied to your tail and go through life pretending it isn't there. Besides, it is quite unthinkable that that girl should be allowed to get away with her tale. It's a matter of principle.'

'You can pay too high a price for your damned principles. But I wish you luck, anyhow. Are you considering a private inquiry agent? Because if you are I know a very good – '

Robert said that he had got an agent and that he was already at work.

Carley's expressive face conveyed his amused congratulation at this swift action on the part of the conservative Blair, Hayward, and Bennet.

'The Yard had better look to its laurels,' he said. His eyes went to the street beyond the leaded panes of the window and the amusement in them faded to a fixed attention. He stared for a moment or two and then said softly, 'Well, of all the nerve!'

It was an admiring phrase, not an indignant one, and Robert turned to see what was occasioning his admiration.

On the opposite side of the street was the Sharpes' battered old car, its odd front wheel well in evidence. And in the back, enthroned in her usual place and with her usual air of faint protest at this means of transport, was Mrs Sharpe. The car was pulled up outside the grocer's, and Marion was presumably inside shopping. It could have been there only a few moments or Ben Carley would have noticed it before, but already two errand boys had paused to stare, leaning on their bicycles with voluptuous satisfaction in this free spectacle. And even while Robert took in the scene people came to the doors of neighbouring shops as the news flew from mouth to mouth.

'What incredible folly!' Robert said angrily.

'Folly nothing,' said Carley, his eyes on the picture. 'I wish they were clients of mine.'

He fumbled in his pocket for change to pay for his coffee, and Robert fled from the room. He reached the near side of the car just as Marion came out on to the pavement at the other side. 'Mrs Sharpe,' he said sternly, 'this is an extraordinarily silly thing to do. You are only exacerbating –'

'Oh, good morning, Mr Blair,' she said in polite social tones. 'Have you had your morning coffee or would you like to accompany us to the Anne Boleyn?'

'Miss Sharpe!' he said, appealing to Marion, who was putting her packages down on the seat. 'You must know that this is a silly thing to do.'

'I honestly don't know whether it is or not,' she said, 'but it seems to be something that we must do. Perhaps we have grown childish with living too much to ourselves, but we found that neither of us could forget that snub at the Anne Boleyn – that condemnation without trial.'

'We suffer from spiritual indigestion, Mr Blair. And the only cure is a hair of the dog that bit us. To wit, a cup of Miss Truelove's excellent coffee.'

'But it is so unnecessary! So –'

'We feel that at half past ten in the morning there must be a large number of free tables at the Anne Boleyn,' Mrs Sharpe said tartly.

'Don't worry, Mr Blair,' Marion said. 'It is a gesture only. Once we have drunk our token cup of coffee at the Anne Boleyn we shall never darken its doors again.' She burlesqued the phrase in characteristic fashion.

'But it will merely provide Milford with a free –'

Mrs Sharpe caught him up before he could utter the word. 'Milford must get used to us as a spectacle,' she said dryly, 'since we have decided that living entirely within four walls is not something that we can contemplate.'

'But –'

'They will soon grow used to seeing monsters and take us for granted again. If you see a giraffe once a year it remains a spectacle ; if you see it daily it becomes part of the scenery. We propose to become part of the Milford scenery.'

'Very well, you plan to become part of the scenery. But do one thing for me just now.' Already the curtains of the first-floor windows were being drawn aside and faces appearing. 'Give up the Anne Boleyn plan – give it up for today at least – and have your coffee with me at the Rose and Crown.'

'Mr Blair, coffee with you at the Rose and Crown would be delightful, but it would do nothing to relieve my spiritual indigestion, which, in the popular phrase, "is killing me".'

'Miss Sharpe, I appeal to you. You have said that you realize that you are probably being childish, and – well, as a personal obligation to me as your agent, I ask you not to go on with the Anne Boleyn plan.'

'*That* is blackmail,' Mrs Sharpe remarked.

'It is unanswerable, anyhow,' Marion said, smiling faintly at him. 'We seem to be going to have coffee at the Rose and Crown'. She sighed. 'Just when I was all strung up for a gesture!'

'Well, of all the nerve!' came a voice from overhead. It was

Carley's phrase over again, but held none of Carley's admiration; it was loaded with indignation.

'You can't leave the car here,' Robert said. 'Quite apart from the traffic laws, it is practically Exhibit A.'

'Oh, we didn't intend to,' Marion said. 'We were taking it round to the garage so that Stanley can do something technical to its inside with some instrument he has there. He is exceedingly scornful about our car, Stanley is.'

'I dare say. Well, I shall go round with you; and you had better step on it before we are run in for attracting a crowd.'

'Poor Mr Blair,' Marion said, pressing the starter. 'It must be horrid for you not to be part of the landscape any more, after all those years of comfortable merging.'

She said it without malice – indeed, there was genuine sympathy in her voice– but the sentence stuck in his mind and made a small tender place there as they drove round into Sin Lane, avoided five hacks and a pony that were trailing temperamentally out of the livery stable, and came to rest in the dimness of the garage.

Bill came out to meet them, wiping his hands on an oily rag. 'Morning, Mrs Sharpe. Glad to see you out. Morning, Miss Sharpe. That was a neat job you did on Stan's forehead. The edges closed as neat as if they had been stitched. You ought to have been a nurse.'

'Not me. I have no patience with people's fads. But I might have been a surgeon. You can't be very faddy on the operating table.'

Stanley appeared from the back, ignoring the two women, who now ranked as intimates, and took over the car. 'What time do you want this wreck?' he asked.

'An hour do?' Marion asked.

'A year wouldn't do; but I'll do all that can be done in an hour.' His eye went on to Robert. 'Anything for the Guineas?'

'I've had a good tip for Bali Boogie.'

'Nonsense,' old Mrs Sharpe said. 'None of that Hippocras blood were any good when it came to a struggle. Just turned it up.'

The three men stared at her, astonished.

'You are interested in racing?' Robert said, unbelieving.

147

'No; in horseflesh. My brother bred thoroughbreds.' Seeing their faces she gave a dry cackle of laughter, so like a hen's squawk. 'Did you think I went to rest every afternoon with my Bible, Mr Blair? Or perhaps with a book on black magic? No, indeed; I take the racing page of the daily paper. And Stanley would be well advised to save his money on Bali Boogie; if anything in horseflesh ever deserved so obscene a name that animal does.'

'And what instead?' Stanley asked, with his usual economy.

'They say that horse sense is the instinct that keeps horses from betting on men. But if you must do something as silly as betting, then you had better put your money on Kominsky.'

'Kominsky!' Stanley said. 'But it's at sixties!'

'You can, of course, lose your money at a shorter price if you like,' she said dryly. 'Shall we go, Mr Blair?'

'All right,' Stan said. 'Kominsky it is; and you're on to a tenth of my stake.'

They walked back to the Rose and Crown; and as they emerged from the comparative privacy of Sin Lane into the open street Robert had the exposed feeling that being out in a bad air-raid used to give him. All the attention and all the venom in the uneasy night seemed to be concentrated on his shrinking person. So now in the bright early-summer sunlight he crossed the street feeling naked and unprotected. He was ashamed to see how relaxed and seemingly indifferent Marion swung along at his side, and hoped that his self-consciousness was not apparent. He talked as naturally as he could, but he remembered how easily her mind had always read the contents of his, and felt that he was not making a very good job of it.

A solitary waiter was picking up the shilling that Ben Carley had left on the table, but otherwise the lounge was deserted. As they seated themselves round the bowl of wallflowers on the black oak table Marion said: 'You heard that our windows are in again?'

'Yes; P.C. Newsam looked in on his way home last night to tell me. That was smart work.'

'Did you bribe them?' Mrs Sharpe asked.

'No. I just mentioned that it was the work of hooligans. If your missing windows had been the result of blast you would no doubt still be living with the elements. Blast ranks as misfortune and therefore a thing to be put up with. But hooliganism is one of those things that Something Must Be Done About. Hence your new windows. I wish that it was all as easy as replacing windows.'

He was unaware that there had been any change in his voice, but Marion searched his face and said: 'Some new development?'

'I'm afraid there is. I was coming out this afternoon to tell you about it. It appears that just when the *Ack-Emma* is dropping the subject – there is only one letter today and that a mild one – just when the *Ack-Emma* has grown tired of Betty Kane's cause *The Watchman* is going to take it up.'

'Excelsior!' said Marion. '*The Watchman* snatching the torch from the failing hands of the *Ack-Emma* is a charming picture.'

'Climbing into the *Ack-Emma*'s bed,' Ben Carley had called it; but the sentiment was the same.

'Have you spies in *The Watchman* office, Mr Blair?' Mrs Sharpe asked.

'No; it was Nevil who got wind of it. They are going to print a letter from his future father-in-law, the Bishop of Larborough.'

'Hah!' said Mrs Sharpe. 'Toby Byrne.'

'You know him?' asked Robert, thinking that the quality of her tone would peel the varnish off wood if spilt on it.

'He went to school with my nephew – the son of the horse-leech brother. Toby Byrne, indeed. He doesn't change.'

'I gather that you didn't like him.'

'I never knew him. He went home for the holidays once with my nephew, but was never asked back.'

'Oh?'

'He discovered for the first time that stable lads got up at the crack of dawn, and he was horrified. It was slavery, he said; and he went round the lads urging them to stand up for their rights. If they combined, he said, not a horse would go out of the stable before nine o'clock in the morning. The lads used to mimic him for years afterwards; but he was not asked back.'

'Yes; he doesn't change,' agreed Robert. 'He has been using the same technique ever since, on everything from Kaffirs to crèches. The less he knows about a thing the more strongly he feels about it. Nevil was of the opinion that nothing could be done about the proposed letter, since the Bishop had already written it and what the Bishop had written is not to be contemplated as waste-paper. But I couldn't just sit and do nothing about it; so I rang him up after dinner and pointed out as tactfully as I could that he was embracing a very doubtful cause and at the same time doing harm to two possibly innocent people. But I might have saved my breath. He pointed out that *The Watchman* existed for the free expression of opinion and inferred that I was trying to prevent such freedom. I ended up by asking him if he approved of lynching, because he was doing his best to bring one about. That was after I saw it was hopeless and had stopped being tactful.' He took the cup of coffee that Mrs Sharpe had poured out for him. 'He's a sad comedown after his predecessor in the See, who was the terror of every evil-doer in five counties and a scholar to boot.'

'How did Toby Byrne achieve gaiters?' Mrs Sharpe wondered.

'I assume that Cowan's Cranberry Sauce had no inconsiderable part in his translation.'

'Ah, yes. His wife. I forgot. Sugar, Mr Blair?'

'By the way, here are the two duplicate keys to The Franchise gate. I take it that I may keep one. The other you had better give to the police, I think, so that they can look round as they please. I also have to inform you that you now have a private agent in your employ.' And he told them about Alec Ramsden, who appeared on doorsteps at half past eight in the morning.

'No word of anyone recognizing the *Ack-Emma* photograph and writing to Scotland Yard?' Marion asked. 'I had pinned my faith to that.'

'Not so far. But there is still hope.'

'It is five days since the *Ack-Emma* printed it. If anyone was ever going to recognize it they would have by now.'

'You don't make allowances for the discards. That is nearly always the way it happens. Someone spreads open their parcel of chips and says: "Dear me, where did I see that face?" Or someone is using a bundle of newspapers to line drawers in an hotel. Or something like that. Don't lose hope, Miss Sharpe. Between the good Lord and Alec Ramsden, we'll triumph in the end.'

She looked at him soberly. 'You really believe that, don't you?' she said, as one noting a phenomenon.

'I do,' he said.

'You believe in the ultimate triumph of good?'

'Yes.'

'Why?'

'I don't know. I suppose because the other thing is unthinkable. Nothing more positive or more commendable than that.'

'I should have a greater faith in a God who hadn't given Toby Byrne a bishopric,' Mrs Sharpe said. 'When does Toby's letter appear, by the way?'

'On Friday morning.'

'I can hardly wait,' said Mrs Sharpe.

15

ROBERT was less sure about the ultimate triumph of good by Friday afternoon.

It was not the Bishop's letter which shook his faith. Indeed, the events of Friday did much to take the wind out of the Bishop's sails; and if Robert had been told on Wednesday morning that he would bitterly regret anything that served to deflate the Bishop he would not have believed it.

His lordship's letter had not run very true to form. *The Watchman*, he said, had always set its face against violence and was not now, of course, proposing to condone it, but there were occasions when violence was but a symptom of a deep social unrest, resentment, and insecurity. As in the recent Nullahbad case, for instance. (The 'unrest, resentment, and insecurity' in the Nullahbad case lay entirely in the bosoms of two thieves, who could not find the opal bracelet they had come to steal and by the way of reprisal killed the seven sleeping occupants of the bungalow in their beds.) There were undoubtedly times when the proletariat felt themselves helpless to redress a patent wrong, and it was not to be marvelled at that some of the more passionate spirits were moved to personal protest (Robert thought that Bill and Stanley would hardly recognize the louts of Monday night under the guise of 'passionate spirits'; and he held that 'personal protest' was a slight understatement for the entire wrecking of the ground-floor windows of The Franchise.) The people to be blamed for the unrest (*The Watchman* had a passion for euphemism: unrest, under-privileged, backward, unfortunate – where the rest of the world talked about violence, the poor, mentally deficient, and prostitutes; and one of the things that *Ack-Emma* and *The Watchman* had in common, now he thought about it, was the belief that all prostitutes were hearts-of-gold who had taken the wrong turning) – the people to be blamed for the unrest were not those perhaps misguided persons who had demonstrated their resentment so unmistakably, but the powers whose weakness, ineptitude, and lack of zeal had led to the injustice of a dropped case. It was part of the

English heritage that justice should not only be done but that it should be shown to be done ; and the place for that was in open court.

'What good does he think it would do anyone for the police to waste time preparing a case that they were foreordained to lose?' Robert asked Nevil, who was reading the letter over his shoulder.

'It would have done *us* a power of good,' Nevil said. 'He doesn't seem to have thought of that. If the magistrate dismissed the case the suggestion that his poor bruised darling was telling fibs could hardly be avoided, could it? Have you come to the bruises?'

'No.'

The bruises came near the end. The 'poor bruised body' of this young and blameless girl, his lordship said, was a crying indictment of a law that had failed to protect her and now failed to vindicate her. The whole conduct of this case was one that demanded the most searching scrutiny.

'That must be making the Yard very happy this morning,' Robert said.

'This afternoon,' amended Nevil.

'Why this afternoon?'

'No one at the Yard would read a bogus publication like *The Watchman*. They won't see it until someone sends it to them this afternoon.'

But they had seen it, as it turned out. Grant had read it in the train. He had picked it off the bookstall with three others – not because it was his choice but because it was a choice between that and coloured publications with bathing-belle covers.

Robert deserted the office and took the copy of *The Watchman* out to The Franchise together with that morning's *Ack-Emma*, which had quite definitely no further interest in The Franchise affair. Since the final, subdued letter on Wednesday it had ceased to mention the matter. It was a lovely day: the grass in The Franchise courtyard absurdly green, the dirty-white front of the house glorified by the sun into a semblance of grace, the reflected light from the rosy brick wall flooding the shabby drawing-room and giving it a smiling warmth. They had sat there, the three of them, in great contentment. The *Ack-*

Emma had finished its undressing of them in public; the Bishop's letter was not, after all, as bad as it might have been; Alec Ramsden was busy on their behalf in Larborough and would without doubt unearth facts sooner or later that would be their salvation; the summer was here with its bright, short nights; Stanley was proving himself 'a great dear'; they had paid a second short visit to Milford yesterday in pursuance of their design to become part of the scenery, and nothing untoward had happened to them beyond stares, black looks, and a few audible remarks. Altogether, the feeling of the meeting was that it all might be worse.

'How much ice will this cut?' Mrs Sharpe asked Robert, stabbing her skinny index finger at the correspondence page of *The Watchman*.

'Not much, I think. Even among *The Watchman* clique the Bishop is looked at slightly sideways nowadays, I understand. His championship of Mahoney didn't do him any good.'

'Who was Mahoney?' Marion asked.

'Have you forgotten Mahoney? He was the Irish "patriot" who put a bomb in a woman's bicycle basket in a busy English street and blew four people to pieces, including the woman, who was later identified by her wedding ring. The Bishop held that Mahoney were merely misguided, not a murderer; that he was fighting on behalf of a repressed minority – the Irish, believe it or not – and that we should not make him into a martyr. That was a little too much for even *Watchman* stomachs, and since then the Bishop's prestige is not what it was, I hear.'

'Isn't it shocking how one forgets when it doesn't concern oneself!' Marion said. 'Did they hang Mahoney?'

'They did, I am glad to say – much to his own pained surprise. So many of his predecessors had benefited from the plea that we should not make martyrs, that murder had ceased to be reckoned in their minds as one of the dangerous trades. It was rapidly becoming as safe as banking.'

'Talking of banking,' Mrs Sharpe said, 'I think it would be best if our financial position were made clear to you, and for that you should get in touch with old Mr Crowle's solicitors in London, who manage our affairs. I shall write to them explaining that you are to be given full details, so that you may know how much we have to come and go on, and can make corresponding arrangements for the spending of it in defence of our good name. It is not exactly the way we had planned to spend it.'

'Let us be thankful we have it to spend,' Marion said. 'What does a penniless person do in a case like this?'

Robert quite frankly did not know.

He took the address of the Crowle solicitors and went home to lunch with Aunt Lin, feeling happier than he had at any time since he first caught sight of the *Ack-Emma*'s front page on Bill's desk last Friday. He felt as one feels in a bad thunderstorm when the noise ceases to be directly overhead; it will still continue and probably still be very unpleasant, but one can see a future through it, whereas but a moment ago there was nothing but the dreadful 'now'.

Even Aunt Lin seemed to have forgotten The Franchise for a spell and was at her woolly and endearing best – full of the birthday presents she was buying for Lettice's twins in Saskatchewan. She had provided his favourite lunch – cold ham, boiled potatoes, and brown-betty with thick cream – and moment by moment he was finding it more difficult to realize that this was the Friday morning he had dreaded because it would see the beginning of a *Watchman* campaign against them. It seemed to him that the Bishop of Larborough was very much what Lettice's husband used to call a 'a busted flush'. He couldn't imagine now why he had wasted a thought on him.

It was in this mood that he went back to the office. And it was in this mood that he picked up the receiver to answer Hallam's call.

'Mr Blair?' Hallam said. 'I'm at the Rose and Crown. I'm afraid I've got bad news for you. Inspector Grant's here.'

'At the Rose and Crown?'

'Yes. And he's got a warrant.'

Robert's brain stopped functioning. 'A search warrant?' he asked stupidly.

'No ; a warrant to arrest.'

'No!'

'I'm afraid so.'

'But he *can't* have!'

'I expect it's a bit of a shock for you. I admit I hadn't anticipated it myself.'

'You mean he has managed to get a witness – a corroborative
witness?'

'He has two of them. The case is sewn up and tied with
ribbon.'

'I can't believe it.'

'Will you come over or shall we go to you? I expect you'll
want to come out with us.'

'Out where? Oh yes. Yes, of course I shall. I'll come over to
the Rose and Crown now. Where are you? In the lounge?'

'No, in Grant's bedroom. Number five. The one with the
casement window on the street – over the bar.'

'All right. I'm coming straight over. I say!'

'Yes?'

'A warrant for both?'

'Yes. For two.'

'All right. Thank you. I'll be with you in a moment.'

He sat for a moment getting back his breath and trying to
orientate himself. Nevil was out on business, but Nevil was not
much of a moral support at any time. He got up, took his hat,
and went to the door of 'the office'.

'Mr Heseltine, please,' he said, in the polite formula always
used in the presence of the younger staff; and the old man
followed him into the hall and out to the sunlit doorway.

'Timmy,' Robert said, 'we're in trouble. Inspector Grant is
here from Headquarters with a warrant to arrest The Franchise
people.' Even as he said the words he could not believe that the
thing was really happening.

Neither could old Mr Heseltine; that was obvious. He stared,
wordless, his pale old eyes aghast.

'It's a bit of a shock, isn't it, Timmy?' He shouldn't have
hoped for support from the frail old clerk.

But shocked as he was, and frail and old, Mr Heseltine was
nevertheless a law clerk, and the support was forthcoming.
After a lifetime among formulae his mind reacted automatically
to the letter of the situation.

'A warrant,' he said. 'Why a *warrant*?'

'Because they can't arrest anyone without one,' Robert said a trifle impatiently. Was old Timmy getting past his work?

'I don't mean that. I mean, it's a misdemeanour they're accused of, not a felony. They could surely make it a summons, Mr Robert? They don't need to *arrest* them, surely? Not for a misdemeanour.'

Robert had not thought of that. 'A summons to appear,' he said. 'Yes, why not? Of course there's nothing to hinder them arresting them if they want to.'

'But why should they want to? People like the Sharpes wouldn't run away. Nor do any further harm while they are waiting to appear. Who issued the warrant, did they say?'

'No, they didn't say. Many thanks, Timmy; you've been as good as a stiff drink. I must go over to the Rose and Crown now – Inspector Grant is there with Hallam – and face the music. There's no way of warning The Franchise, because they have no telephone. I'll just have to go out there with Grant and Hallam hanging round my neck. And only this morning we were beginning to see daylight, so we thought. You might tell Nevil when he comes in, will you? And stop him doing anything foolish or impulsive.'

'You know very well, Mr Robert, I've never been able to stop Mr Nevil doing anything he wanted to do. Though it has seemed to me that he has been surprisingly sober this last week. In the metaphorical sense, I mean.'

'Long may it last,' Robert said, stepping out into the sunlit street.

It was the dead period of the afternoon at the Rose and Crown and he passed through the hall and up the wide, shallow stairs without meeting anyone, and knocked at the door of Number Five. Grant, calm and polite as always, let him in. Hallam, vaguely unhappy-looking, was leaning against the dressing-table in the window.

'I understand that you hadn't expected this, Mr Blair,' Grant said.

'No, I hadn't. To be frank, it is a great shock to me.'

'Sit down,' Grant said. 'I don't want to hurry you.'

157

'You have new evidence, Inspector Hallam says.'

'Yes; what we think is conclusive evidence.'

'May I know what it is?'

'Certainly. We have a man who saw Betty Kane being picked up by the car at the bus stop –'

'By *a* car,' Robert said.

'Yes, if you like, by *a* car – but its description fits that of the Sharpes'.'

'So do ten thousand others in Britain. And?'

'The girl from the farm, who went once a week to help clean The Franchise, will swear she heard screams coming from the attic.'

'*Went* once a week? Doesn't she go any longer?'

'Not since the Kane affair became common gossip.'

'I see.'

'Not very valuable pieces of evidence in themselves, but very valuable as proof of the girl's story. For instance, she really did miss that Larborough-London coach. Our witness says that it passed him about half a mile down the road. When he came in sight of the bus-stop a few moments later the girl was there waiting. It is a long, straight road, the main London road through Mainshill –'

'I know. I know it.'

'Yes; well, when he was still some way from the girl he saw the car stop by her, saw her get in, and saw her driven away.'

'But not who drove the car?'

'No. It was too far away for that.'

'And this girl from the farm – did she volunteer the information about the screaming?'

'Not to us. She spoke about it to her friends, and we acted on information and found her quite willing to repeat the story on oath.'

'Did she speak about it to her friends before the gossip about Betty Kane's abduction got round?'

'Yes.'

That was unexpected and Robert was rocked back on his heels. If that was really true – that the girl had mentioned screaming before there was any question of the Sharpes being in trouble – then the evidence would be damning. Robert got up and walked restlessly to the window and back. He thought enviously of Ben Carley. Ben wouldn't be hating this as he hated it, feeling inadequate and at a loss. Ben would be in his element, his mind delighting in the problem and in the hope of outwitting established authority. Robert was dimly aware that his own deep-seated respect for established authority was a handicap to him rather than an asset; he needed some of Ben's native belief that authority is there to be circumvented.

'Well, thank you for being so frank,' he said at last. 'Now, I'm not minimizing the crime you are accusing these people of, but it *is* misdemeanour, not felony – so why a warrant? Surely a summons would meet the case perfectly?'

'A summons would be in order certainly,' Grant said smoothly. 'But in cases where the crime is aggravated – and my superiors take a grave view of the present one – a warrant is issued.'

Robert could not help wondering how much the gadfly attentions of the *Ack-Emma* had influenced the calm judgements at the Yard. He caught Grant's eye and knew that Grant had read his thoughts.

'The girl was missing for a whole month – all but a day or two,' Grant said, 'and had been very badly knocked about, very deliberately. It is not a case to be taken lightly.'

'But what do you gain from arrest?' Robert asked, remembering Mr Heseltine's point. 'There is no question of these people not being there to answer the charge. Nor any question of a similar crime being committed by them in the interval. When did you want them to appear, by the way?'

'I planned to bring them up at the police court on Monday.'

'Then I suggest that you serve them with a summons to appear.'

'My superiors have decided on a warrant,' Grant said, without emotion.

'But you could use your judgement. Your superiors can have no knowledge of local conditions, for instance. If The Franchise is left without occupants it will be a wreck in a week. Have your superiors thought of that? And if you arrest these women, you can only keep them in custody until Monday, when I shall ask for bail. It seems a pity to risk hooliganism at The Franchise just for the gesture of arrest. And I know Inspector Hallam has no men to spare for its protection.'

This right-and-left gave them both pause. It was amazing how ingrained the respect for property was in the English soul; the first change in Grant's face had occurred at the mention of the possible wrecking of the house. Robert cast an unexpectantly kind thought to the louts who had provided the precedent, and so weighted his argument with example. As for Hallam, quite apart from his limited force he was not likely to look kindly on the prospect of fresh hooliganism in his district and fresh culprits to track down.

Into the long pause Hallam said tentatively: 'There is something in what Mr Blair says. Feeling in the countryside is very strong and I doubt if they would leave the house untouched if it was empty. Especially if news of the arrest got about.'

It took nearly half an hour to convince Grant, however. For some reason there was a personal element in the affair for Grant, and Robert could not imagine what it could be or why it should be there.

'Well,' the Inspector said at length, 'you don't need me to serve a summons.' It was as if a surgeon was contemptuous at being asked to open a boil, Robert thought, amused and vastly relieved. 'I'll leave that to Hallam and get back to town. But I'll be in court on Monday. I understand that the Assizes are imminent, so if we avoid a remand the case can go straight on to the Assizes. Can you be ready with your defence by Monday, do you think?'

'Inspector, with all the defence my clients have we could be ready by tea-time,' Robert said bitterly.

To his surprise, Grant turned to him with a broader smile than was usual with him; and it was a very kind smile. 'Mr Blair,' he said, 'you have done me out of an arrest this afternoon, but I don't hold it against you. On the contrary, I think your clients are luckier than they deserve in their solicitor. It will be my prayer that they are less lucky in their counsel! Otherwise I may find myself talked into voting them a testimonial.'

So it was not with 'Grant and Hallam hanging round his neck' that Robert went out to The Franchise: not with a

160

warrant at all. He went out in Hallam's familiar car with a summons sticking out of the pocket of it; and he was sick with relief when he thought of the escape they had had and sick with apprehension when he thought of the fix they were in.

'Inspector Grant seemed to have a very personal interest in executing that warrant,' he said to Hallam as they went along. 'Is it that the *Ack-Emma* has been biting him, do you think?'

'Oh no,' Hallam said. 'Grant's as nearly indifferent to that sort of thing as a human being can be.'

'Then why?'

'Well, it's my belief – strictly between ourselves – that he can't forgive them for fooling him. The Sharpes, I mean. He's famous at the Yard for his good judgement of people, you see; and, again between ourselves, he didn't much care for the Kane girl *or* her story; and he liked them even less when he had seen The Franchise people, in spite of all the evidence. Now he thinks the wool was pulled over his eyes and he's not taking it lightly. It would have given him a lot of pleasure, I imagine, to produce that warrant in their drawing-room.'

As they pulled up by The Franchise gate and Robert took out his key, Hallam said: 'If you open both sides I'll drive the car inside, even for the short time. No need to advertise the fact that we're here.' And Robert, pushing open the solid iron leaves, thought that when visiting actresses said 'Your policemen are wonderful' they didn't know the half of it. He got back into the car and Hallam drove up the short straight drive and round the circular path to the door. As Robert got out of the car Marion came round the corner of the house wearing gardening gloves and a very old skirt. Where her hair was blown up from her forehead by the wind it changed from the heavy, dark stuff that it was to a soft smoke. The first summer sun had darkened her skin and she looked more than ever like a gipsy. Coming on Robert unexpectedly she had not time to guard her expression, and the lighting of her whole face as she saw him made his heart turn over.

'How nice!' she said. 'Mother is still resting, but she will be down soon and we can have some tea. I –' Her glance went on to Hallam and her voice died away uncertainly. 'Good afternoon, Inspector.'

'Good afternoon, Miss Sharpe. I'm sorry to break into your mother's rest, but perhaps you would ask her to come down. It's important.'

She paused a moment, and then led the way indoors. 'Yes, certainly. Has there been some – some new development? Come in and sit down.' She led them into the drawing-room that he knew so well by now – the lovely mirror, the dreadful fireplace, the bead-work chair, the good 'pieces', the old pink carpet faded to a dirty grey – and stood there, searching their faces, savouring the new threat in the atmosphere.

'What is it?' she asked Robert.

But Hallam said: 'I think it would be easier if you fetched Mrs Sharpe and I told you both at the same time.'

'Yes. Yes, of course,' she agreed, and turned to go. But there was no need to go. Mrs Sharpe came into the room very much as she had on that previous occasion when Hallam and Robert had been there together: her short strands of white hair standing on end where they had been pushed up by her pillow, her sea-gull's eyes bright and inquiring.

'Only two kinds of people,' she said, 'arrive in noiseless cars: millionaires and the police. Since we have no acquaintances among the former and an ever-widening acquaintance with the latter – I deduced that some of *our* acquaintances had arrived.'

'I'm afraid I'm even less welcome than usual, Mrs Sharpe. I've come to serve a summons on you and Miss Sharpe.'

'A summons?' Marion said, puzzled.

'A summons to appear at the police court on Monday morning to answer a charge of abduction and assault.' It was obvious that Hallam was not happy.

'I don't believe it,' Marion said slowly. 'I don't believe it. You mean you are charging us with this thing?'

'Yes, Miss Sharpe.'

'But how? Why now?' She turned to Robert.

'The police think they have the corroborative evidence they needed,' Robert said.

'What evidence?' Mrs Sharpe asked, reacting for the first time.

'I think the best plan would be for Inspector Hallam to serve

162

you both with the summonses, and we can discuss the situation at greater length when he has gone.'

'You mean, we have to accept them?' Marion said. 'To appear in the public court – my mother too – to answer a – to be accused of a thing like that?'

'I'm afraid there's no alternative.'

She seemed half intimidated by his shortness, half resentful at his lack of championship. And Hallam, as he handed the document to her, seemed to be aware of this last and to resent it in his turn.

'And I think I ought to tell you, in case he doesn't, that but for Mr Blair here it wouldn't be a mere summons, it would be a warrant – and you would be sleeping tonight in a cell instead of in your own beds. Don't bother, Miss Sharpe: I'll let myself out.'

And Robert, watching him go and remembering how Mrs Sharpe had snubbed him on his first appearance in that room, thought that the score was now game all.

'Is that true?' Mrs Sharpe asked.

'Perfectly true,' Robert said; and told them about Grant's arrival to arrest them. 'But it isn't me you have to thank for your escape: it is old Mr Heseltine in the office.' And he described how the old clerk's mind reacted automatically to stimulus of a legal sort.

'And what is this new evidence they think they have?'

'They have it all right,' Robert said dryly. 'There is no thinking about it.' He told them about the girl being picked up on the London road through Mainshill. 'That merely corroborates what we have always suspected: that when she left Cherrill Street, ostensibly on her way home, she was keeping an appointment. But the other piece of evidence is much more serious. You told me once that you had a woman – a girl – from the farm who came in one day a week and cleaned for you.'

'Rose Glyn, yes.'

'I understand that since the gossip got round she doesn't come any more.'

'Since the gossip – you mean the Betty Kane story? Oh, she was sacked before that ever came to light.'

'*Sacked?*' Robert said sharply.

'Yes. Why do you look so surprised? In our experience of domestic workers sacking is not an unexpected occurrence.'

'No; but in this case it might explain a lot. What did you sack her for?'

'Stealing,' said old Mrs Sharpe.

'She had always lifted a shilling or two from a purse if it was left around,' supplemented Marion; 'but because we needed help so badly we turned a blind eye and kept our purses out of her way. Also any small liftable articles, like stockings. And then she took the watch I'd had for twenty years. I had taken it off to wash some things – the soapsuds rise up one's arms, you know – and when I went back to look for it it had gone. I asked her about it, but of course she "hadn't seen it". That was too much. That watch was part of me, as much a part of me as my hair or my fingernails. There was no recovering it, because we had no evidence at all that she had taken it. But after she had gone we talked it over, and next morning we walked over to the farm and just mentioned that we would not be needing her any more. That was Tuesday – she always came on Mondays – and that afternoon after my mother had gone up to rest Inspector Grant arrived with Betty Kane in the car.'

'I see. Was anyone else there when you told the girl at the farm that she was sacked?'

'I don't remember. I don't think so. She doesn't belong to the farm – to Staples, I mean; they are delightful people. She is one of the labourers' daughters. And as far as I remember we met her outside their cottage and just mentioned the thing in passing.'

'How did she take it?'

'She got very pink and flounced a bit.'

'She grew beetroot red and bridled like a turkeycock,' Mrs Sharpe said. 'Why do you ask?'

'Because she will say on oath that when she was working here she heard screams coming from your attic.'

'Will she indeed,' said Mrs Sharpe contemplatively.

'What is much worse, there is evidence that she mentioned the screams before there was any rumour of the Betty Kane trouble.'

This produced a complete silence. Once more Robert was

164

aware how noiseless the house was, how dead. Even the French clock on the mantelpiece was silent. The curtain at the window moved inwards on a gust of air and fell back to its place as soundless as if it were moving in a film.

'That,' said Marion at last, 'is what is known as a facer.'

'Yes. Definitely.'

'A facer for you, too.'

'For us, yes.'

'I don't mean professionally.'

'No? How then?'

'You are faced with the possibility that we have been lying.'

'Really, Marion!' he said impatiently, using her name for the first time and not noticing that he had used it. 'What I am faced with, if anything, is the choice between your words and the word of Rose Glyn's friends.'

But she did not appear to be listening. 'I wish,' she said passionately, 'oh, how I wish that we had one small, just one small piece of evidence on our side! She gets away – that girl gets away with everything, everything. We keep on saying "It is not true", but we have no way of *showing* that it is not true. It is all negative. All inconclusive. All feeble denial. Things combine to back up her lies, but nothing happens to help prove that we are telling the truth. Nothing!'

'Sit down, Marion,' her mother said. 'A tantrum won't improve the situation.'

'I could kill that girl; I could kill her. My God, I could torture her twice a day for a year and then begin again on New Year's day. When I think what she has done to us I – '

'Don't think,' Robert interrupted. 'Think instead of the day when she is discredited in open court. If I know anything of human nature that will hurt Miss Kane a great deal worse than the beating someone gave her.'

'You still believe that that is possible?' Marion said, incredulous.

'Yes. I don't quite know how we shall bring it about. But that we shall bring it about I do believe.'

'With not one tiny piece of evidence for us, not one; and evidence just – just *blossoming* for her?'

'Yes. Even then.'

'Is that just native optimism, Mr Blair,' Mrs Sharpe asked, 'or your innate belief in the triumph of good, or what?'

'I don't know. I think truth has a validity of its own.'

'Dreyfus didn't find it very valid; nor Slater; nor some others of whom there is record,' she said dryly.

'They did in the end.'

'Well, frankly, I don't look forward to a life in prison waiting for truth to demonstrate its validity.'

'I don't believe that it will come to that – prison, I mean. You will have to appear on Monday, and since we have no adequate defence you will no doubt be sent for trial. But we shall ask for bail, and that means that you can go on staying here until the Assizes at Norton. And before that I hope that Alec Ramsden will have picked up the girl's trail. Remember we don't even have to know what she was doing for the rest of the month. All we have to show is that she did something else on the day she says you picked her up. Take away that first bit and her whole story collapses. And it is my ambition to take it away in public.'

'To undress her in public the way the *Ack-Emma* has undressed us? Do you think she would mind?' Marion said. 'Mind as we minded?'

'To have been the heroine of a newspaper sensation, to say nothing of the adored centre of a loving and sympathetic family, and then to be uncovered to the public gaze as a liar, a cheat, and a wanton? I think she would mind. And there is one thing she would mind particularly. One result of her escapade was that she got back Leslie Wynn's attention – the attention she had lost when he became engaged. As long as she is a wronged heroine she is assured of that attention; once we show her up she has lost it for good.'

'I never thought to see the milk of human kindness so curdled in your gentle veins, Mr Blair,' Mrs Sharpe remarked.

'If she had broken out as a result of the boy's engagement – as she very well might – I should have nothing but pity for her. She is at an unstable age and his engagement must have been a shock. But I don't think that had very much to do with it. I think she is her mother's daughter; and was merely setting out a little early on the road her mother took. As selfish, as self-indulgent, as greedy, as plausible as the blood she came of. Now

166

I must go. I said that I would be at home after five o'clock if Ramsden wanted to ring up to report. And I want to ring Kevin Macdermott and get his help about counsel and things.'

'I'm afraid that we – that I, rather – have been rather ungracious about this,' Marion said. 'You have done and are doing so much for us. But it was such a shock. So entirely unexpected and out of the blue. You must forgive me if –'

'There is nothing to forgive. I think you have both taken it very well. Have you got someone in the place of the dishonest and about-to-commit-perjury Rose? You can't have this huge place entirely on your hands.'

'Well, no one in the locality would come, of course. But Stanley – what would we do without Stanley? – Stanley knows a woman in Larborough who might be induced to come out by bus once a week. You know, when the thought of that girl becomes too much for me, I think of Stanley.'

'Yes,' Robert said, smiling. 'The salt of the earth.'

'He is even teaching me how to cook. I know how to turn eggs in the frying pan without breaking them now. "Do you have to go at them as if you were conducting the Philharmonic?" he asked me. And when I asked him how he got so neat-handed he said it was with "cooking in a bivvy two feet square."'

'How are you going to get back to Milford?' Mrs Sharpe asked.

'The afternoon bus from Larborough will pick me up. No word of your telephone being repaired, I suppose?'

Both women took the question as comment, not interrogation. Mrs Sharpe took leave of him in the drawing-room, but Marion walked to the gate with him. As they crossed the circle of grass enclosed by the branching driveway, he remarked: 'It's a good thing you haven't a large family or there would be a worn track across the grass to the door.'

'There is that as it is,' she said, looking at the darker line in the rough grass. 'It is more than human nature can bear to walk round that unnecessary curve.'

Small talk, he was thinking; small talk. Idle words to cover up a stark situation. He had sounded very brave and fine about the validity of truth, but how much was mere sound? What were the odds on Ramsden's turning up evidence in time for the courts on Monday? In time for the Assizes? Long odds against, wasn't it? And he had better grow used to the thought.

At half past five Ramsden rang up to give him the promised report; and it was one of unqualified failure. It was the girl he was looking for, of course, having failed to identify the man as a resident at the Midland and having therefore no information at all about him. But nowhere had he found even a trace of her. His own men had been given duplicates of the photograph and with them had made inquiries at the airports, the railway termini, travel agencies, and the more likely hotels. No one claimed to have seen her. He himself had combed Larborough and was slightly cheered to find that the photograph he had been given was at least recognizable, since it had been readily identified at the places where Betty Kane had actually been. At the two main picture houses, for instance – where, according to the box-office girls' information, she had always been alone – and at the ladies' cloakroom of the bus-station. He had tried the garages, but had drawn blank.

'Yes,' Robert said. 'He picked her up at the bus-stop on the London road through Mainshill – where she would normally have gone to catch her coach home.' And he told Ramsden of the new developments. 'So things really are urgent now. They are being brought up on Monday. If only we could prove what she did that first evening! That would bring her whole story crashing down.'

'What kind of car was it?' Ramsden asked.

Robert described it, and Ramsden sighed audibly over the telephone.

'Yes,' Robert agreed. 'A rough ten thousand of them between London and Carlisle. Well, I'll leave you to it. I want to ring up Kevin Macdermott and tell him our woes.'

Kevin was not in chambers, nor yet at the flat in St Paul's Churchyard, and Robert eventually ran him to earth at his home near Weybridge. He sounded relaxed and amiable, and was instantly attentive when he heard the news that the police had got their evidence. He listened without remark while Robert poured out the story to him.

'So you see, Kevin,' Robert finished, 'we're in a frightful jam.'

'A schoolboy description,' Kevin said, 'but exquisitely accurate. My advice to you is to "give" them the police court and concentrate on the Assizes.'

'Kevin, couldn't you come down for the week-end and let me talk about it to you? It's six years, Aunt Lin was saying yesterday, since you spent a night with us, so you're overdue anyhow. Couldn't you?'

'I promised Sean I'd take him over to Newbury on Sunday to choose a pony.'

'But couldn't you postpone it? I'm sure Sean wouldn't mind if he knew it was in a good cause.'

'Sean,' said his doting parent, 'has never taken the slightest interest in any cause that was not to his own immediate advantage. Being a chip off the old block. If I came would you introduce me to your witches?'

'But of course.'

'And would Christina make me some butter tarts?'

'Assuredly.'

'And could I have the room with the text in wools?'

'Kevin, you'll come?'

'Well, it's a damned dull country, Milford, except in the winter' – this was a reference to hunting, Kevin's only eye for country being from the back of a horse – 'and I was looking forward to a Sunday riding on the downs. But a combination of witches, butter tarts, and a bedroom with a text in wools is no small draw.'

As he was about to hang up Kevin paused and said: 'Oh, I say, Rob?'

'Yes?' Robert said, and waited.

'Have you considered the possibility that the police have the right of it?'

'You mean, that the girl's absurd tale may be true?'

'Yes. Are you keeping that in mind – as a possibility, I mean?'

'If I were I shouldn't – ' Robert began angrily, and then laughed. 'Come down and see them,' he said.

'I come, I come,' Kevin assured him, and hung up.

Robert called the garage, and when Bill answered asked if Stanley was still there.

'It's a wonder you can't hear him from where you are,' Bill said.

'What's wrong?'

'We've just been rescuing that bay pony of Matt Ellis's from our inspection pit. Did you want Stan?'

'Not to speak to. Would you be very kind and ask him to pick up a note for Mrs Sharpe on his way past tonight?'

'Yes, certainly. I say, Mr Blair, is it true that there is fresh trouble coming about The Franchise affair – or shouldn't I ask that?'

Milford! thought Robert. How did they do it? A sort of information-pollen blown on the wind?

'Yes, I'm afraid there is,' he said. 'I expect they'll tell Stanley about it when he goes out tonight. Don't let him forget about the note, will you?'

'No, that's all right.'

He wrote to The Franchise to say that Kevin Macdermott was coming down for Saturday night and could he bring him out to see them on Sunday afternoon before he left to go back to town?

16

'DOES Kevin Macdermott *have* to look like a tout when he comes to the country?' Nevil asked the following evening, as he and Robert waited for the guest to finish his ablutions and come down to dinner.

What Kevin in country clothes actually looked like, Robert considered, was a rather disreputable trainer of jumpers for the smaller meetings; but he refrained from saying that to Nevil. Remembering the clothes that Nevil had startled the country-side with for the last few years, he felt that Nevil was in no position to criticize anyone's taste. Nevil had turned up to din-ner in a chaste dark grey suit of the most irreproachable ortho-doxy, and seemed to think that his new conformity made him free to forget the experimentalism of his immediate past.

'I suppose Christina is in the usual lather of sentiment?'

'A lather of white of egg, as far as I have been able to judge.'

Christina regarded Kevin as 'Satan in person' and adored him. His Satanic qualities came not from his looks – though Kevin did indeed look a little like Satan – but from the fact that he 'defended the wicked for the sake of worldly gain'. And she adored him because he was good-looking and a possibly re-claimable sinner, and because he praised her baking.

'I hope it's a soufflé, then, and not that meringue stuff. Do you think that Macdermott could be lured into coming down to defend them at Norton Assizes?'

'I think he is much too busy for that, even if he were inter-ested. But I'm hoping that one of his dogsbodies will come.'

'Primed by Macdermott?'

'That's the idea.'

'I really don't see why Marion should have to slave to pro-vide Macdermott with lunch. Does he realize that she has to prepare and clear away and wash up every single thing, to say nothing of carting them to and fro a day's journey to that ante-diluvian kitchen?'

'It was Marion's own idea that he should come to lunch with them. I take it that she considers the extra trouble worth while.'

'Oh, you were always crazy about Kevin; and you simply don't know how to begin to appreciate a woman like Marion. It's – it's *obscene* that she should be wasting her vitality on household drudgery, a woman like that. She should be hacking her way through jungles or scaling precipices or ruling a barbarous race or measuring the planets. Ten thousand nit-wit blondes dripping with mink have nothing to do but sit back and have the polish on their predatory nails changed, and Marion carts coal. Coal! *Marion!* And I suppose by the time this case is finished they won't have a penny to pay a maid even if they could get one.'

'Let us hope that by the time this case is finished they are not doing hard labour by order.'

'Robert, it *couldn't* come to that! It's unthinkable.'

'Yes, it's unthinkable. I suppose it is always unbelievable that anyone one knows should go to prison.'

'It's bad enough that they should go into the dock. Marion who never did a cruel or underhand or shabby thing in her life And just because a – Do you know, I had a lovely time the other night, I found a book on torture, and I stayed awake till two o'clock choosing which one I would use on Kane.'

'You should get together with Marion. That is her ambition too.'

'And what would yours be?' There was a faint hint of scorn in the tone, as though it was understood that the mild Robert would have no strong feelings on the subject. 'Or haven't you considered it?'

'I don't need to consider it,' Robert said slowly. 'I'm going to undress her in public.'

'*What?*'

'Not that way. I'm going to strip her of every rag of pretence, in open court, so that everyone will see her for what she is.'

Nevil looked curiously at him for a moment. 'Amen,' he said quietly. 'I didn't know you felt like that about it, Robert.' He was going to add something, but the door opened and Macdermott came in, and the evening had begun.

Eating solidly through Aunt Lin's superb dinner, Robert hoped that it was not going to be a mistake to take Kevin to Sunday lunch at The Franchise. He was desperately anxious that the Sharpes should make a success with Kevin; and there was no denying that Kevin was temperamental and the Sharpes not everyone's cup of tea. Was lunch at The Franchise likely to be an asset to their cause – a lunch cooked by Marion for Kevin, who was a gourmet? When he had first read the invitation – handed in by Stanley this morning – he was glad that they had made the gesture, but misgiving was slowly growing in him. And as one perfection succeeded another in unhurried procession across Aunt Lin's shining mahogany, with Christina's large face hovering in eager benevolence beyond the candle-light, the misgiving swelled until it took entire possession of him. 'Shapes that did not stand up' might fill his breast with a warm, protective affection; but they could hardly be expected to have the same effect on Kevin.

At least Kevin seemed glad to be here, he thought, listening to Macdermott making open love to Aunt Lin, with a word thrown to Christina every now and then to keep her happy and faithful. Dear Heaven, the Irish! Nevil was on his best behaviour, full of earnest attention, with a discreet 'sir' thrown in now and again – often enough to make Kevin feel superior, but not often enough to make him feel old. The subtler English form of flattery, in fact. Aunt Lin was like a girl, pink-cheeked and radiant: absorbing flattery like a sponge, subjecting it to some chemical process, and pouring it out again as charm. Listening to her talk Robert was amused to find that the Sharpes had suffered a sea-change in her mind. By the mere fact of being in danger of imprisonment, they had been promoted from 'these people' to 'poor things'. This had nothing to do with Kevin's presence; it was a combination of native kindness and woolly thinking.

It was odd, Robert thought, looking round the table, that this family party – so gay, so warm, so secure – should be occasioned by the dire need of two helpless women in that dark, silent house set down among the endless fields.

He went to bed with the warm aura of the party still round him, but in his heart a chill anxiety and an ache. Were they asleep out there at The Franchise? How much sleep had they had lately?

He lay long awake and wakened early: listening to the Sunday morning silence, hoping that it would be a good day – The Franchise looked its worst in rain, when its dirty-white became almost grey – and that whatever Marion made for lunch would 'stand up'. Just before eight a car came in from the country and stopped below the window and someone whistled a soft bugle call. A company call, it was – B Company. Stanley presumably. He got up and put his head out of the window.

Stanley, hatless as usual – he had never seen Stanley in any kind of head covering – was sitting in the car regarding him with tolerant benevolence.

'You Sunday snoozers,' said Stanley.

'Did you get me up just to sneer at me?'

'No. I have a message from Miss Sharpe. She says when you come out you're to take Betty Kane's statement with you, and you're on no account to forget it because it's of the first importance. I'll say it's important! She's going round looking as if she had unearthed a million.'

'Looking happy!' Robert said, unbelieving.

'Like a bride. Indeed I haven't seen a woman look like that since my cousin Beulah married her Pole. A face like a scone, Beulah has; and believe me, that day she looked like Venus, Cleopatra, and Helen of Troy rolled into one.'

'Do you know what it is that Miss Sharpe is so happy about?'

'No. I did cast out a few feelers, but she's saving it up, it seems. Anyhow, don't forget the copy of the statement, or the responses won't come right or something. The password's in the statement.'

Stanley proceeded on his way up the street towards Sin Lane and Robert took his towel and went to the bathroom greatly puzzled. While he waited for breakfast he looked out the statement from among the papers in his dispatch case and read it through again with a new attention. What had Marion remembered or discovered that was making her so happy? Betty Kane had slipped somewhere, that was obvious. Marion was radiant and Marion wanted him to bring the Kane statement when he came. That could only mean that somewhere in the statement was proof that Betty Kane was lying.

He reached the end of the statement without finding any likely sentence and began to hunt through it again. What could it be?

That she had said it was raining and that it – perhaps – had not been raining? But that would not have been vital or even important to the credibility of her story. The Milford bus, then? The one she said she had passed when being driven in the Sharpes' car. Were the times wrong? But they had checked the times long ago and found they fitted nearly enough. The 'lighted sign' on the bus? Was the time too early for a sign to be lighted? But that would have been merely a slip of memory, not a discrediting factor in her statement.

He hoped passionately that Marion in her anxiety to obtain that 'one small piece of evidence' on their side was not exaggerating some trifling discrepancy into proof of dishonesty. The descent from hope would be worse than no hope at all.

This real worry almost obliterated the social worry of the lunch from his mind, and he ceased to care greatly whether Kevin enjoyed his meal at The Franchise or not. When Aunt Lin said to him covertly, as she set off for church: 'What do you think they'll give you for lunch, dear? I'm quite sure they live on those toasted flake things out of packets, poor things,' he said shortly: 'They know good wine when they taste it; that should please Kevin.'

'What has happened to young Bennet?' Kevin asked as they drove out to The Franchise.

'He wasn't asked to lunch,' Robert asked.

'I didn't mean that. What has happened to the strident suits and the superiority and *The Watchman* aggressiveness?'

'Oh, he has fallen out with *The Watchman* over this case.'

'Ah!'

'For the first time he is in a position to have actual personal knowledge of a case *The Watchman* is pontificating about, and it has been a bit of a shock to him, I think.'

'Is the reformation going to last?'

'Well, do you know, I shouldn't be a bit surprised if it did. Apart from the fact that he got to an age when they normally give up childish things, and was due for a change, I think he has been doing some revision and wondering if any of the other *Watchman* white-headed boys were any more worthy of championing than Betty Kane. Kotovich, for instance.'

'Hah! The patriot!' Kevin said expressively.

'Yes. Only last week he was holding forth on our duty to Kotovich – our duty to protect and cherish him, and eventually provide him with a British passport, I suppose. I doubt if today he would be quite so simple. He has grown up wonderfully in the last few days. I didn't know he even possessed a suit like the one he was wearing last night. It must be one he got to go to his school prize-giving in, for he certainly has worn nothing so sober since.'

'I hope for your sake it lasts. He has brains, the boy, and once he got rid of his circus tricks would be an asset to the firm.'

'Aunt Lin is distressed because he has split with Rosemary over The Franchise affair, and she is afraid he won't marry a bishop's daughter after all.'

'Hooray! More power to him! I begin to like the boy. You put a few wedges into that split, Rob – casual like – and see that he marries some nice stupid English girl who will give him five children and give the rest of the neighbourhood tennis parties between showers on Saturday afternoons. It's a much nicer kind of stupidity than standing up on platforms and holding forth on subjects you don't know the first thing about. Is this the place?'

'Yes, this is The Franchise.'

'A perfect "mystery house".'

'It wasn't a mystery house when it was built. The gates, as you can see, were scroll-work – rather nice work too – so that the whole place was visible from the road. It was the simple operation of backing the gate with the iron sheeting that converted the house from something quite ordinary to something rather secret.'

'A perfect house for Betty Kane's purpose, anyhow. What a piece of luck for her that she remembered it.'

Robert was to feel guilty afterwards that he had not had greater faith in Marion, both over the matter of Betty Kane's statement and over the lunch. He should have remembered how cool-minded she was, how analytic; and he should have remembered the Sharpe gift for taking people as they found them and its soothing effect on the persons concerned. The Sharpes had made no effort to live up to Aunt Lin's standard of hospitality, no effort to provide a formal dining-room lunch. They had set a

176

table for four in the window of the drawing-room where the sun fell on it. It was a cherrywood table, very pleasant in grain, but sadly needing polishing. The wine glasses, on the other hand, were polished to a diamond brilliance. (How like Marion, he thought, to concentrate on the thing that mattered and to ignore mere appearance.)

'The dining-room is an incredibly gloomy place,' Mrs Sharpe said. 'Come and see it, Mr Macdermott.'

That too was typical. No sitting round with their sherry making small talk. Come and see our horrible dining-room. And the visitor was part of the household before he knew it.

'Tell me,' Robert said to Marion as they were left alone, 'what is this about the –'

'No, I am not going to talk about it until after lunch. It is to be your liqueur. It is a piece of the most astonishing luck that I should have thought of it last night, when Mr Macdermott was coming to lunch today. It makes everything quite different. It won't stop the case, I suppose, but it does make everything different for us. It is the "small thing" that I was praying for to be evidence for *us*. Have you told Mr Macdermott?'

'About your message? No, I haven't said anything. I thought it better – not to.'

'Robert!' she said, looking at him with a quizzical amusement. 'You didn't trust me. You were afraid I was havering.'

'I was afraid you might be building more on a small foundation than – it would hold. I –'

'Don't be afraid,' she said reassuringly. 'It will hold. Would you like to come to the kitchen and carry the tray of soup for me?'

They had even managed the service without fuss or flurry. Robert carried the tray with four flat bowls of soup, and Marion came after him with a large dish under a Sheffield plate cover, and that seemed to be all. When they had drunk their soup, Marion put the large dish in front of her mother and a bottle of wine in front of Kevin. The dish was a *pot-au-feu* chicken with all its vegetables round it; and the wine was a Montrachet.

'A Montrachet!' Kevin said. 'You wonderful woman.'

'Robert told us you were a claret lover,' Marion said, 'but

what is left in old Mr Crowle's cellar is long past its best. So it was a choice between that and a very heavy red burgundy that is wonderful on winter evenings but not so good with one of the Staples' fowls on a summer day.'

Kevin said something about how seldom it was that women were interested in anything that did not bubble or, alternatively, explode.

'To be frank,' Mrs Sharpe said, 'If these parcels had been saleable we should probably have sold them, but we were exceedingly glad that they were too scrappy and varied for that. I was brought up to appreciate wine. My husband had a fairly good cellar, though his palate was not as good as mine. But my brother at Lessways had a better one, and a fine palate to match.'

'Lessways?' Kevin said, and looked at her as if searching for a resemblance. 'You're not Charlie Meredith's sister, are you?'

'I am. Did you know Charles? But you couldn't. You are too young.'

'The first pony I ever had of my own was bred by Charlie Meredith,' Kevin said. 'I had him for seven years and he never put a foot wrong.'

And after that, of course, both of them ceased to take any further interest in the others and not over-much in the food.

Robert caught Marion's amused and congratulatory glance at him, and said: 'You did yourself grave injustice when you said you couldn't cook.'

'If you were a woman you would observe that I have not cooked anything. The soup I emptied out of a can, heated it, and added some sherry and flavouring; the fowl I put into a pot just as it came from Staples, poured some boiling water over it, added everything I could think of, and left it on the stove with a prayer; the cream cheese also came from the farm.'

'And the wonderful rolls to go with the cream cheese?'

'Stanley's landlady made those.'

They laughed a little together, quietly.

Tomorrow she was going into the dock. Tomorrow she was going to be a public spectacle for the delight of Milford. But today her life was still her own and she could share amusement with him, could be content with the hour. Or so it seemed if her shining eyes were any evidence.

They took the cheese plates from under the noses of the other two, who did not even pause in their conversation to remark the action, carried the trays of dirty dishes away to the kitchen and made the coffee there. It was a great gloomy place with a floor of stone slabs and an old-fashioned sink that depressed him at sight.

'We put the range on only on Mondays, when the scrubbing is done,' Marion said, seeing his interest in the place. 'Otherwise we cook on the little oil-stove.'

He thought of the hot water that ran so instantly into the shining bath when he turned the tap this morning, and was ashamed. He could hardly visualize, after his long years of soft living, an existence where one's bathing was done in water that was heated over an oil burner.

'Your friend is a charmer, isn't he?' she said, pouring the hot coffee into its jug. 'A little Mephistophelian – one would be terribly afraid of him as opposing counsel – but a charmer.'

'It's the Irish,' Robert said gloomily. 'It comes as natural to them as breathing. Us poor Saxons plod along our brutish way and wonder how they do it.'

She had turned to give him the tray to carry, and so was facing him with their hands almost touching. 'The Saxons have the two qualities that I value most in the world – two qualities that explain why they have inherited the earth: kindness and dependability, or tolerance and responsibility, if you prefer the terms. Two qualities the Celt never had; which is why the Irish have inherited nothing but squabbles. Oh, damn, I forgot the cream. Wait a moment. It's keeping cold in the wash-house.' She came back with the cream and said, mock rustic: 'I have heard tell as how there's things called refrigerators in some folks' houses now, but we don't need none.'

And as he carried the coffee to the sunlight of the drawing-room he visualized the bone-chilling cold of those kitchen quarters in winter with no roaring range as there had been in the palmy days of the house when a cook had lorded it over half a dozen servants and you ordered coal by the wagon-load. He longed to take Marion away from the place. Where he would take her he did not quite know – his own home was filled with the aura of Aunt Lin. It would have to be a place where there was nothing to polish and nothing to carry and practically everything was done by pressing a button. He could not see Marion spending her old age in service to some pieces of mahogany.

As they drank their coffee he brought the conversation gently round to the possibility of their selling The Franchise at some time or other and buying a cottage somewhere.

'No one would buy the place,' Marion said. 'It is a white elephant: not big enough for a school, too remote for flats, and too big for a family these days. It might make a good madhouse,' she added thoughtfully, her eyes on the high pink wall beyond the window; and Robert saw Kevin's glance flash over her and run away again. 'It is quiet, at least – no trees to creak, or ivy to tap at the window-panes, or birds to go yap-yap-yap until you want to scream. It is a very peaceful place for tired nerves. Perhaps someone would consider it for that.'

So she liked the silence; the stillness that had seemed to him so dead. It was perhaps what she had longed for in her London life of noise and elbowing and demands; her life of fret and cramped quarters. The big, quiet, ugly house had been a haven. And now it was a haven no longer.

Some day – oh-please-God-let-it-happen – some day he would strip Betty Kane for ever of credit and love.

'And now,' Marion said, 'you are invited to inspect the "fatal attic".'

'Yes,' Kevin said, 'I should be greatly interested to see the things that the girl professed to identify. All her statements seemed to me the result of logical guesses – like the harder carpet on the second flight of stairs. Or the wooden commode – something that you would almost certainly find in a country house. Or the flat-topped trunk.'

'Yes, it was rather terrifying at the time, the way she kept hitting on things we had – and I hadn't had time to gather my wits – it was only afterwards I saw how little she really had identified in her statement. And she did make one complete

180

bloomer, only no one thought of it until last night. Have you got the statement, Robert?'

'Yes.' He took it out of his pocket.

They had climbed, she and Robert and Macdermott, the last bare flight of stairs and she led them into the attic. 'I came up here last night on my usual Saturday tour round the house with a mop. That is our solution to the housekeeping problem, in case you are interested. A good large mop well soaked in absorbent polish-stuff run over every floor once a week. It takes five minutes per room and keeps the dust at bay.'

Kevin was poking round the room and inspecting the view from the window. 'So this is the view she described,' he said.

'Yes,' Marion said, 'that is the view she described. And if I remember the words of her statement, as I remembered them last night, correctly, then she said something that she can't – Robert, would you read the bit where she describes the view from the window?'

Robert looked up the relevant passage and began to read. Kevin was bending slightly forward staring out of the little round window, and Marion was standing behind him, smiling faintly like a sibyl.

'"From the window of the attic,"' read Robert, '"I could see a high brick wall with a big iron gate in the middle of it. There was a road on the farther side of the wall, because I could see the telegraph posts. No, I couldn't see the traffic on it, because the wall was too high. Just the tops of lorry-loads sometimes. You couldn't see through the gate because it had sheets of iron on the inside. Inside the gate the carriage-way went straight for a little and then divided in two into a circle up to the door. No, it wasn't a garden, just – "'

'What!' yelled Kevin, straightening himself abruptly.

'What what?' Robert asked, startled.

'Read that last bit again, that bit about the carriage-way.'

'"Inside the gate the carriage-way went straight for a little and then divided in two into a circle up to the – "'

Kevin's shout of laughter stopped him. It was an abrupt monosyllable of amused triumph.

'You see?' Marion said into the sudden silence.

'Yes,' Kevin said softly, his pale bright eyes gloating on the view. 'That was something she didn't reckon with.'

Robert moved over as Marion gave way to let him have her place and so saw what they were talking about. The edge of the roof with its small parapet cut off the view of the courtyard before the carriage-way branched at all. No one imprisoned in that room would know about the two half-circles up to the doorway.

'You see,' Marion said, 'the Inspector read that description when we were all in the drawing-room. And all of us knew that the description was accurate – I mean, an accurate picture of what the courtyard is like; so we unconsciously treated it as something that was finished with. Even the Inspector. I remember his looking at the view from the window, but it was quite an automatic gesture. It didn't occur to any of us that it would not have been as described. Indeed, except for one tiny detail it was as described.'

'Except for one tiny detail,' Kevin said. 'She arrived in darkness and fled in darkness and she says she was locked in the room all the time, so she could have known nothing of that branching drive. What does she say, again, about her arrival, Rob?'

Robert looked it up and read:

'"The car stopped at last and the younger woman, the one with the black hair, got out and pushed open the big double gates on to a drive. Then she got back in and drove the car up to a house. No, it was too dark to see what kind of a house, except that it had steps up to the door. No, I don't remember how many steps; four or five, I think. Yes, definitely a small flight of them." And then she goes on about being taken to the kitchen for coffee.'

'So,' Kevin said. 'And her account of her flight? What time of night was that?'

'Some time after supper if I remember rightly,' Robert said, shuffling through the pages. 'After dark, anyhow. Here it is.' And he read:

'"When I got to the first landing, the one above the hall, I could hear them talking in the kitchen. There was no light in the hall. I went down the last flight, expecting every moment that one of them would come out and catch me, and then made a dash for the door. It wasn't locked and I ran straight out and down the steps to the gate and out on to the road. I ran along the road – yes, it was hard like a highroad – until I couldn't run any longer, and I lay in the grass till I was feeling able to go on."'

' "It was hard, like a highroad," ' Kevin quoted. 'The inference being that it was too dark to see the surface she was running on.'

There was a short silence.

'My mother thinks that this is enough to discredit her,' Marion said. She looked from Robert to Kevin and back again, without much hope. 'But you don't, do you?' It was hardly a question.

'No,' Kevin said. 'No. Not alone. She might wriggle out of it with a clever counsel's help. Might say that she had deduced the circle from the swing of the car when she arrived. What she would normally have deduced, of course, would be the ordinary carriage sweep. No one would spontaneously think of anything as awkward as that circular drive. It makes a pretty pattern, that's all – which is probably why she remembered it. I think this tit-bit should be kept as make-weight for the Assizes.'

'Yes, I thought you would say that,' Marion said. 'I'm not really disappointed. I was glad about it not because I thought that it would free us of the charge but because it frees us of the doubt that must have – must have –' She stammered unexpectedly, avoiding Robert's eyes.

'Must have muddied our crystal minds,' finished Kevin briskly, and cast a glance of pleased malice at Robert. 'How did you think of this last night when you came to sweep?'

'I don't know. I stood looking out of the window and at the view she described, and wishing that we might have just one small tiny, microscopic piece of evidence on *our* side. And then, without thinking, I heard Inspector Grant's voice reading that bit in the drawing-room. Most of the story he told us in his own words, you know. But the bits that brought him to The Franchise he read in the girl's words. I heard his voice – it's a nice voice – saying the bit about the circular carriage-way, and from where I was at that moment there was no circular carriage-way. Perhaps it was an answer to unspoken prayer.'

'So you still think that we had best "give" them tomorrow and bank everything on the Assizes?' Robert said.

'Yes. It makes no difference actually to Miss Sharpe and her mother. An appearance in one place is very like an appearance in another – except that the Assizes at Norton will probably be less unpleasant than a police court in one's home town. And the shorter their appearance tomorrow the better from their point of view. You have no evidence to put before the court tomorrow, so it should be a very short and formal affair. A parade of *their* evidence, an announcement that you reserve your defence, an application for bail, and *voilà*!'

This suited Robert well enough. He did not want to prolong tomorrow's ordeal for them; he had more confidence, in any case, in a judgement framed outside Milford. And most of all he did not want, now that it had come to a case, a half-decision, a dismissal. That would not be sufficient for his purpose where Betty Kane was concerned. He wanted the whole story of that month told in open court, in Betty Kane's presence. And by the time the Assizes opened at Norton, he would, please God, have the story ready to tell.

'Whom can we get to defend them?' he asked Kevin as they drove home to tea.

Kevin reached into a pocket, and Robert took it for granted that what he was looking for was a list of addresses. But what he produced was obviously an engagement book.

'What is the date of the Assizes at Norton, do you know?' he asked.

Robert told him and held his breath.

'It's just possible that I might be able to come down myself. Let me see, let me see.'

Robert let him see in complete silence. One word, he felt, might ruin the magic.

'Yes,' Kevin said. 'I don't see why I shouldn't – short of the unforeseen. I like your witches. It would give me great pleasure to defend them against that very nasty piece of work. How odd that she should be old Charlie Meredith's sister. One of the best, the old boy was. About the only approximately honest horse-coper known in history. I have never ceased to be grateful to him for that pony. A boy's first horse is very important. It colours his whole after-life – not only his attitude to horse-flesh; everything else as well. There is something in the trust and friendship that exists between a boy and a good horse that –'

Robert listened, relaxed and amused. He had realized, with a gentle irony untinged with any bitterness, that Kevin had given up any thought of the Sharpes' guilt long before the evidence of that view from the window was presented to him. It was not possible that old Charlie Meredith's sister could have abducted anyone.

17

'IT's a perpetual wonder to me,' Ben Carley said, eyeing the well-populated benches in the little court, 'how so many of the lieges have so little to do on a Monday morning. Though I must say it's some time since the gathering has had so much tone. Have you noticed the Sports Wear? Back row but one, in a yellow hat that doesn't go with her mauve powder *or* her hair. If she's left that little Godfrey girl in charge, she's going to be short of change tonight. I got that girl off when she was fifteen. She'd been swiping cash since she could walk and she's still swiping it. No female to be left alone with a till, believe me. And that Anne Boleyn woman. First time I've seen her in court. Though how she's avoided it so long I don't know. Her sister's for ever paying out cheques to cover her R.D. ones. No one's ever discovered what she does with the money. Someone blackmailing her, perhaps. I wonder who. I wouldn't put it past Arthur Wallis at the White Hart. Three different orders to pay each week, and another on the way, just won't come out of a potman's pay.'

Robert let Carley burble on without listening to him. He was only too conscious that the audience in court was not the usual Monday-morning collection of loafers putting off time until they opened. The news had gone round, by the mysterious Milford channels, and they had come to see the Sharpes charged. The normal drabness of the court was gay with women's clothes and its normal drowsy silence sibilant with their chatter.

One face he saw which should have been hostile but was oddly friendly: that of Mrs Wynn, whom he had last seen standing in her lovely little patch of garden in Meadowside Lane, Aylesbury. He could not think of Mrs Wynn as an enemy. He liked her, admired her, and was sorry for her in advance. He would have liked to go over and say how d'you do to her, but the game had been laid out on the squares now and they were chequers of different colour.

Grant had not appeared so far, but Hallam was there, talking to the sergeant who had come to The Franchise the night the hooligans wrecked the windows.

'How's your sleuth doing?' Carley asked during a pause in his running commentary.

'The sleuth's all right, but the problem is colossal,' Robert said. 'The proverbial needle just gives itself up by comparison.'

'One girl against the world,' mocked Ben. 'I'm looking forward to seeing this floosie in the flesh. I suppose after all the fan mail she's had and the offers of marriage and the resemblance to Saint Bernadette, she'll think a country police court too small an arena for her. Did she have any stage offers?'

'I wouldn't know.'

'I suppose Mama would repress them anyhow. That's her there with the brown suit, and she looks a very sensible woman to me. I can't think how she ever came to have a daughter like – Oh, but she was adopted, wasn't she? An Awful Warning. It's a constant reminder to me how little folk must know about the people they live with. There was a woman over at Ham Green had a daughter that was never out of her sight as far as she knew, but daughter walked out in a pet one day and didn't come back and frantic mother goes howling to the police, and police discover that the girl who has apparently never been away from mother for a night is a married woman with a child, and has merely collected child and gone to live with husband. See police records if not believing Ben Carley. Ah well, if you grow dissatisfied with your sleuth let me know and I'll give you the address of a very good one. Here we go.'

He rose in deference to the Bench, while continuing a monologue on the Bench's complexion, possible temper, and probable occupation yesterday.

Three routine cases were disposed of – old offenders apparently so used to the procedure that they anticipated the drill, and Robert half expected someone to say 'Wait for it, can't you!'

Then he saw Grant come in quietly and sit in an observer's position at the back of the Press bench, and he knew that the time had come.

They came in together when their names were called and took their places in the horrid little pew as if they were merely taking their places in church. It *was* rather like that, he thought: the quiet and observant eyes and the suggestion of waiting for a performance to begin. But he suddenly realized what he would be feeling if it were Aunt Lin in Mrs Sharpe's place, and was fully aware for the first time of what Marion must be suffering on her mother's behalf. Even if the Assizes saw them cleared of the charge, what would compensate them for what they had endured? What punishment fit Betty Kane's crime?

For Robert, being old-fashioned, believed in retribution. He might not go all the way with Moses – an eye was not always compensation for an eye – but he certainly agreed with Gilbert: the punishment should fit the crime. He certainly did not believe that a few quiet talks with the chaplain and a promise to reform made a criminal into a respect-worthy citizen. 'Your true criminal,' he remembered Kevin saying one night, after a long discussion on penal reform, 'has two unvarying characteristics, and it is these two characteristics which make him a criminal: monstrous vanity and colossal selfishness. And they are both as integral, as ineradicable as the texture of the skin. You might as well talk of "reforming" the colour of one's eyes.'

'But,' someone had objected, 'there have been monsters of vanity and selfishness who were not criminal.'

'Only because they have victimized their wives instead of their bank,' Kevin had pointed out. 'Tomes have been written trying to define the criminal, but it is a very simple definition after all. The criminal is a person who makes the satisfaction of his own immediate personal wants the mainspring of his actions. You can't cure him of his egoism, but you can make the indulgence of it not worth his while. Or almost not worth his while.'

Kevin's idea of prison reform, Robert remembered, was deportation to a penal colony: an island community where everyone worked hard. This was not a reform for the benefit of the prisoners. It would be a nicer life for the warders, Kevin said; and would leave more room in this crowded island for good citizen's houses and gardens; and since most criminals hated hard work more than they hated anything in this world, it would be a better deterrent than the present plan, which in Kevin's estimation was no more punitive than a third-rate public school.

Looking at the two figures in the dock Robert thought that in the 'bad old days' only the guilty were put in the pillory. Nowadays it was the untried who bore the pillory and the guilty went immediately into a safe obscurity. Something had gone wrong somewhere.

Old Mrs Sharpe was wearing the flat black satin hat in which she had appeared at his office on the morning of the *Ack-Emma* irruption into their affairs, and looked academic, respectable, but odd. Marion too was wearing a hat – less, he supposed, out of deference to the court than as some protection against the public gaze. It was a country felt with a short brim; and its orthodoxy lessened to some extent her normal air of being a law unto herself. With her black hair hidden and her brilliant eyes shadowed she looked no swarthier than a normal out-of-doors woman might. And though Robert missed the black hair and the brilliance, he thought that it was all to the good that she should look as 'ordinary' as possible. It might lessen the pecking-to-death instinct in her hostile fellows.

And then he saw Betty Kane.

It was the stir on the Press bench that told him she was in court. Normally the Press bench was occupied by two bored apprentices in the art of reporting: one for the *Milford Advertiser* (once weekly, on Fridays) and one combining the *Norton Courier* (twice weekly, Tuesdays and Fridays) with the *Larborough Times* and anyone else who would take the stuff. But today the Press bench was filled and the faces were neither young nor bored. They were the faces of men invited to a meal and quite ready for it. And Betty Kane was two-thirds of what they had come for.

Robert had not seen her since she stood in the drawing-room at The Franchise in her dark blue school coat, and he was surprised all over again by her youth and her candid innocence. In the weeks since he had first seen her she had grown into a monster in his mind: he thought of her only as the perverted creature who had lied two human beings into the dock. Now, seeing the actual physical Betty Kane again, he was nonplussed.

He *knew* that this girl and his monster were one, but he found it difficult to realize. And if he, who felt that he now knew Betty Kane so well, reacted like that to her presence, what effect would her child-like grace have on good men and true when the time came?

She was wearing 'week-end' clothes, not her school things. A cloudy blue outfit that made one think of forget-me-nots and wood-smoke and bluebells and summer distances, and was further calculated to bedevil the judgement of sober men. Her young and simple and very-well-brought-up hat stood back from her face and showed the charming brow and the wide-set eyes. Robert absolved Mrs Wynn, without even having to consider the matter, from any conscious dressing of the girl for the occasion, but was bitterly aware that if she had lain awake at nights devising the outfit it could not have served its purpose better.

When her name was called and she walked to the witness-stand, he stole a glance at the faces of those who could see her clearly. With the sole exception of Ben Carley – who was looking at her with the interest one accords a museum exhibit – there was only one expression on the faces of the men: a sort of affectionate compassion. The women, he observed, had not surrendered so easily. The more motherly ones obviously yearned to her youth and her vulnerability, but the younger ones were merely avid, without emotion other than curiosity.

'I – don't – believe – it!' Ben said, *sotto voce*, while she was taking the oath. 'You mean that child was on the loose for a month? I don't believe she's ever kissed anything but the book!'

'I'll bring witnesses to prove it,' muttered Robert, angry that even the worldly and cynical Carley was succumbing.

'You could bring ten irreproachable witnesses and still not get a jury to believe it; and it's the jury who count, my friend.'

Yes, what jury would believe any bad of her!

Watching her as she was led through her story, he reminded himself of Albert's account of her: the 'nicely brought-up girl' whom no one would have thought of as a woman at all, and the cool expertness with which she attached the man she had chosen.

She had a very pleasant voice: young and light and clear, without accent or affectation. And she told her tale like a model witness; volunteering no extras, explicit in what she did say. The Pressmen could hardly keep their eyes on their shorthand. The Bench was obviously doting. (God send there was something tougher at the Assizes!) The members of the police force were gently perspiring in sympathy. The body of the court breathless and motionless.

No actress had ever had a better reception.

She was quite calm, as far as anyone could see; and apparently unaware of the effect she was having. She made no effort to make a point or use a piece of information dramatically. And Robert found himself wondering whether the understatement was deliberate and whether she realized quite clearly how effective it was.

'And did you in fact mend the linen?'

'I was too stiff from the beating, that night. But I mended some later.'

Just as if she were saying: 'I was too busy playing bridge.' It gave an extraordinary air of truth to what she said.

Nor was there any sign of triumph in the account of her vindication. She had said this and that about the place of her imprisonment, and this and that had proved to be so. But she showed no overt pleasure in the fact. When she was asked if she recognized the women in the dock and if they were in fact the women who had detained and beaten her, she looked at them gravely for a moment of silence and then said that she did and they were.

'Do you want to examine, Mr Blair?'

'No, sir. I have no questions.'

This caused a slight stir of surprise and disappointment in the body of the court, who had looked forward to drama; but it was accepted by the initiates without remark; it was taken for granted that the case would go forward to another court.

Hallam had already given his statement, and the girl was now followed by the corroborative witnesses.

The man who had seen her picked up by the car proved to be a post-office sorter called Piper. He worked on a postal van which the L.M.S. ran between Larborough and London, and

191

he was dropped off at Mainshill station on the return journey because it was near his home. He was walking up the long, straight London road through Mainshill when he noticed that a young girl was waiting at the stop for the London coaches. He was still a long distance from her, but he noticed her because the London coach had overtaken him half a minute previously, before he had come within sight of the bus-stop; and when he saw her waiting there he realized that she must just have missed it. While he was walking towards her, but still some distance away, a car overtook him at a good pace. He did not even glance at it because his interest was concentrated on the girl and on whether when he came up with her he should stop and tell her that the London bus had passed. Then he saw the car slow down alongside the girl. She bent forward to talk to whoever was in it, and then got in herself and was driven away.

By this time he was near enough to describe the car, but not to read the number. He had not thought of reading the number anyhow. He was merely glad that the girl had got a lift so quickly.

He would not take an oath that the girl in question was the girl he had seen give evidence, but he was certain in his own mind. She had worn a palish coat – grey, he thought – and black slippers.

Slippers?

Well, those shoes with no straps across the instep.

Court shoes.

Well, court shoes, but he called them slippers. (And had every intention, his tone made it clear, of going on calling them slippers.)

'Do you want to examine, Mr Blair?'

'No, thank you, sir.'

Then came Rose Glyn.

Robert's first impression was of the vulgar perfection of her teeth. They reminded him of a false set made by a not very clever dentist. There surely never had been, never could be any natural teeth as flashily perfect as those Rose Glyn had produced as substitutes for her milk teeth.

The Bench did not like her teeth either, it seemed, and Rose soon stopped smiling. But her tale was lethal enough. She had been in the habit of going to The Franchise every Monday to clean the house. On a Monday in April she had been there as usual, and was preparing to leave in the evening when she heard screaming coming from upstairs somewhere. She thought something had happened to Mrs or Miss Sharpe and ran to the foot of the stairs to see. The screaming seemed to be far away, as if it came from the attic. She was going to go upstairs, but Mrs Sharpe came out of the drawing-room and asked her what she was doing. She said someone was screaming upstairs. Mrs Sharpe said nonsense, that she was imagining things, and wasn't it time that she was going home. The screaming had stopped then, and while Mrs Sharpe was talking Miss Sharpe came downstairs. Miss Sharpe went with Mrs Sharpe, and Mrs Sharpe said something about 'ought to be more careful'. She was frightened, she did not quite know why, and went away to the kitchen and took her money from where it was always left for her on the kitchen mantelpiece, and ran from the house. The date was 15 April. She remembered the date because she had decided that next time she went back, on the following Monday, she would give the Sharpes her week's notice; and she had in fact done that, and had not worked for the Sharpes since Monday, 29 April.

Robert was faintly cheered by the bad impression she was patently making on everyone. Her open delight in the dramatic, her Christmas Supplement glossiness, her obvious malice and her horrible clothes were unhappily contrasted with the restraint and good sense and good taste of her predecessor in the witness-box. From the expression on the faces of her audience she was summed up as a slut and no one would trust her with sixpence. But that did nothing to discount the evidence she had just given on oath.

Robert, letting her go on, wondered if there was any way of pinning that watch on her, so to speak. Being a country girl, unversed in the ways of pawnshops, it was unlikely that she had stolen that watch to sell it; she had taken it to keep for herself. That being so, was there perhaps some way of convicting her of theft and so discrediting her evidence to that extent?

She was succeeded by her friend Gladys Rees. Gladys was

as small and pale and skinny as her friend was opulent. She was scared and ill at ease, and took the oath hesitatingly. Her accent was so broad that even the Court found difficulty in following her, and the prosecution had several times to translate her wilder flights of English into something nearer common speech. But the gist of her evidence was clear. On the evening of Monday the 15th April she had gone walking with her friend, Rose Glyn. No, not anywhere special, just walking after supper. Up to High Wood and back. And Rose Glyn had told her that she was scared of The Franchise because she had heard someone screaming in an upstairs room, although there was supposed not to be anyone there. She, Gladys, knew that it was Monday the 15th that Rose had told her that, because Rose had said that when she went next week she was going to give notice. And she had given notice and had not worked for the Sharpes since Monday the 29th.

'I wonder what dear Rose has got on her,' Carley said, as she left the witness-box.

'What makes you think she has anything?'

'People don't come and perjure themselves for friendship – not even country morons like Gladys Rees. The poor silly little rat was frightened stiff. She would never have come voluntarily. No, that oleograph has a lever of some sort. Worth looking into if you're stuck, perhaps.'

'Do you happen to know the number of your watch?' he asked Marion as he was driving them back to The Franchise. 'The one Rose Glyn stole.'

'I didn't even know that watches had numbers,' Marion said.

'Good ones do.'

'Oh, mine was a good one, but I don't know anything about its number. It was very distinctive, though. It had a pale blue enamel face with gold figures.'

'Roman figures?'

'Yes. Why do you ask? Even if I got it back I could never bear to wear it after that girl.'

'It wasn't so much getting it back I thought of as convicting her of having taken it.'

'That would be nice.'

'Ben Carley calls her "the oleograph", by the way.'

194

'How lovely! That is just what she is like. Is that the little man you wanted to push us off on to, that first day?'

'That's the one.'

'I am so glad that I refused to be pushed.'

'I hope you will still be as glad when this case is over,' Robert said, suddenly sober.

'We have not yet thanked you for standing surety for our bail,' Mrs Sharpe said from the back of the car.

'If we began to thank him for all we owe him,' Marion said, 'there would be no end to it.'

Except, he thought, that he had enlisted Kevin Macdermott on their side – and that was an accident of friendship – what had he been able to do for them? They would go for trial at Norton little more than a fortnight hence and they had no defence whatever.

18

THE newspapers had a field-day on Tuesday.

Now that The Franchise affair was a court case, it could no longer provide a crusade for either the *Ack-Emma* or *The Watchman* – though the *Ack-Emma* did not fail to remind its gratified readers that on such and such a day *they* had said so and so, a plain statement which was on the surface innocent and unexceptionable but was simply loaded with the forbidden comment; and Robert had no doubt that on Friday *The Watchman* would be taking similar credit to itself, with similar discretion. But the rest of the Press, who had not so far taken any interest in a case that the police had no intention of touching, woke with a glad shout to report a case that was news. Even the soberer dailies held accounts of the court appearance of the Sharpes, with headings like EXTRAORDINARY CASE and UNUSUAL CHARGE. The less inhibited had full descriptions of the principal actors in the case, including Mrs Sharpe's hat and Betty Kane's blue outfit, pictures of The Franchise, the High Street in Milford, a school friend of Betty Kane, and anything else that was even approximately relevant.

And Robert's heart sank. Both the *Ack-Emma* and *The Watchman*, in their different ways, had used The Franchise affair as a stunt. Something to be used for its momentary worth and dropped tomorrow. But now it was a national interest, reported by every kind of paper from Cornwall to Caithness; and showed signs of becoming a *cause célèbre*.

For the first time he had a feeling of desperation. Events were hounding him, and he had no refuge. The thing was beginning to pile up into a tremendous climax at Norton and he had nothing to contribute to that climax; nothing at all. He felt as a man might feel if he saw a stacked heap of loaded crates begin to lean over towards him and had neither retreat nor a prop to stay the avalanche.

Ramsden grew more and more monosyllabic on the telephone and less and less encouraging. Ramsden was sore. 'Baffled' was a word used in boys' detective stories; it had not until now had even the remotest connexion with Alex Ramsden. So Ramsden was sore, monosyllabic, and dour.

The one bright spot in the days that followed the court at Milford was provided by Stanley, who tapped on his door on Thursday morning, poked his head in, and seeing that Robert was alone came in, pushing the door to with one hand and fishing in the pocket of his dungarees with the other.

'Morning,' he said. 'I think you ought to take charge of these. Those women at The Franchise have no sense at all. They keep pound notes in tea-pots and books and what not. If you're looking for a telephone number you're as likely as not to find a ten-shilling note marking the butcher's address.' He fished out a roll of money and solemnly counted twelve ten-pound notes on to the desk under Robert's nose.

'A hundred and twenty,' he said. 'Nice, ain't it?'

'But what *is* it?' Robert asked bewildered.

'Kominsky.'

'Kominsky?'

'Don't tell me you didn't have anything on! After the old lady giving us the tip herself. Mean to say you *forgot* about it?'

'Stan, I haven't even remembered lately that there was such a thing as the Guineas. So you backed it?'

'At sixties. And that's the tenth I told her she was on to, for the tip.'

'But – a tenth? You must have been plunging, Stan.'

'Twenty pounds. Twice as much as my normal ceiling. Bill did a bit of good too. Going to give his missus a fur coat.'

'So Kominsky won.'

'Won by a length and a half on a tight rein; and was that a turn up for the book!'

'Well,' Robert said, stacking the notes and banding them, 'if the worst comes to the worst and they end up bankrupt, the old lady can always do a fair trade as a tipster.'

Stanley eyed his face for a moment in silence, apparently not happy about something in his tone. 'Things are pretty bad, 'm?' he said.

'Fierce,' said Robert, using one of Stanley's own descriptions.

'Bill's missus went to the court,' Stan said, after a pause.

'She said she wouldn't believe that girl even if she told her there were twelve pennies in a shilling.'

'Oh?' Robert said, surprised. 'Why?'

'Much too good to be true, she said she was. She said no girl of fifteen was ever as good as that.'

'She's sixteen now.'

'All right, sixteen. She said she was fifteen once and so were all her girl friends, and that wide-eyed wonder didn't fool her for a moment.'

'I'm very much afraid it will fool a jury.'

'Not if you had an all-woman jury. I suppose there's no way of wangling that?'

'Not short of Herod measures. Don't you want to give this money to Mrs Sharpe yourself, by the way?'

'Not me. You'll be going out there some time today and you can give it to her if you like. But see you get it back and put it in the bank or they'll be picking it out of flower vases years hence and wondering when they put that there.'

Robert smiled as he put the money away in his pocket to the sound of Stanley's departing feet. Endlessly unexpected, people were. He would have taken it for granted that Stan would have revelled in counting those notes out in front of the old lady. But instead he had turned shy. That tale of money in teapots was just a tale.

Robert took the money out to The Franchise in the afternoon, and for the first time saw tears in Marion's eyes. He told the tale as Stanley had told it – tea-pots and all – and finished: 'So he made me his deputy;' and it was then that Marion's eyes had filled.

'Why did he mind about giving it to us?' she said, fingering the notes. 'He's not usually so – so –'

'I think it may be that he considers that you need it now, and that that makes it a delicate affair instead of a matter-of-fact one. When you gave him the tip you were just the well-off Sharpes who lived at The Franchise, and he would have turned over the proceeds to you with éclat. But now you are two women out on bail of £200 each in your personal recognizances and of a similar sum by one surety on behalf of you each; to say nothing of having the expenses of a counsel to come; and are therefore, I think, in Stan's mind not people that one can hand over money to easily.'

'Well,' said Mrs Sharpe, 'not all my tips have had a margin of a length-and-a-half on the right side. But I don't deny that I am very glad to see the percentage. It was very kind of the boy.'

'Should we keep as much as ten per cent?' Marion asked doubtfully.

'That was the arrangement,' Mrs Sharpe said equably. 'If it hadn't been for me he would be short by the amount of a bet on Bali Boogie at this moment. What *is* a Bali Boogie, by the way?'

'I am glad you came,' Marion said, ignoring her mother's quest for education, 'because something unexpected has happened. My watch has come back.'

'You mean you've found it?'

'No. Oh no. She sent it back through the post. Look!'

She produced a small, very dirty, white cardboard box, which contained her watch with the blue enamel face and the wrapping that had been round the watch. The wrapping was a square of pink tissue paper with a circular stamp reading SUN VALLEY, TRANSVAAL and had evidently started life embracing an orange. On a torn piece of paper was printed: I DON'T WANT NONE OF IT. The capital I was dotted like a small letter, after the fashion of illiterates.

'Why do you think she turned squeamish about it?' Marion wondered.

'I don't for a moment think she did,' Robert said. 'I couldn't imagine that girl ever relinquishing anything that her hand had closed over.'

'But she did. She sent it back.'

'No. Someone sent it back. Someone who was frightened. Someone with a rudimentary conscience, too. If Rose Glyn had wanted to be rid of it she would have thrown it into a pond without a second thought. But X wants to be rid of it and to make restitution at the same time. X has both a conscience and a frightened soul. Now who would have a bad conscience about you just now? Gladys Rees?'

'Yes, of course you are right about Rose. I should have thought of that. She never would have sent it back. She would have put her heel on it sooner. You think perhaps she gave it to Gladys Rees?'

'That might explain a lot. It might explain how Rose got her to court to back up that "screaming" story. I mean, if she had been the receiver of stolen goods. When you come to think of it, Rose could have very little chance of wearing a watch that the Staples people must quite often have seen on your wrist. It is much more likely that she was "large" with it in favour of her friend. "A little thing I picked up." Where does the Rees girl belong to?'

'I don't know where she belongs to – somewhere the other side of the county, I think. But she has come to work for that isolated farm beyond Staples.'

'Long ago?'

'I don't know. I don't think so.'

'So she could wear a new watch without question. Yes, I think it was Gladys who sent back your watch. If ever there was an unwilling witness it was Gladys on Monday. And if Gladys is shakable to the point of sending back your property, a faint hope begins to dawn.'

'But she has committed perjury,' Mrs Sharpe said. 'Even a moron like Gladys Rees must have some glimmering of awareness that that is not well seen in a British court.'

'She could plead that she was blackmailed into it – if someone suggested that course to her.'

Mrs Sharpe eyed him. 'Isn't there anything in English law about tampering with a witness?' she asked.

'Plenty. But I don't propose to do any tampering.'

'What do you propose to do?'

'I must think it over. It is a delicate situation.'

'Mr Blair, the intricacies of the law have always been beyond me, and are always likely to be, but you won't get yourself put away for contempt of court or something like that, will you? I can't imagine what the present situation would be like without your support.'

Robert said that he had no intention of getting himself put away for anything. That he was a blameless solicitor of unblemished reputation and high moral principles, and that she need have no fear for herself or for him.

'If we could knock the prop of Gladys Rees from under Rose's story it would undermine their whole case,' he said. 'It's their most valuable piece of evidence: that Rose had mentioned the screaming before there was any suggestion of a charge against you. I suppose you couldn't see Grant's face when Rose was giving evidence? A fastidious mind must be a great handicap in the C.I.D. It must be sad to have your whole case depend on someone you would hate to touch with a barge-pole. Now I must be getting back. May I take the little cardboard box and the scrap of paper with the printing?'

'It was clever of you to have seen that Rose would not have sent it back,' Marion said, putting the scrap of paper into the box and giving it to him. 'You should have been a detective.'

'Either that or a fortune-teller. Everything deduced from the egg-stain on the waistcoat. *Au revoir.*'

Robert drove back to Milford with his mind full of this new possibility. It was no solution to their predicament, but it might be a lifeline.

In the office he found Mr Ramsden waiting for him; long, grey, lean, and dour.

'I came to see you, Mr Blair, because it wasn't a thing that could be said over the telephone very well.'

'Well?'

'Mr Blair, we're wasting your money. Do you happen to know what the white population of the world is?'

'No, I don't.'

'Neither do I. But what you're asking me to do is to pick this girl out of the white population of the world. Five thousand men working for a year mightn't do it. One man might do it tomorrow. It's a matter of pure chance.'

'But it always has been that.'

'No. In the first days the chances were fair. We covered the obvious places. The port, the airports, the travel places, the best-known "honeymoon" places. And I didn't waste your time or money in any travelling. I have contacts in all the big towns and in a lot of the smaller ones, and I just send them a request saying: "Find out if such and such a person stayed at one of your hotels," and the answer is back in a few hours. Answers from all over Britain. Well, that done, we are left with

201

a small proposition called the rest of the world. And I don't like wasting your money, Mr Blair. Because that is what it will amount to.'

'Do I understand that you are giving up?'

'I don't put it like that, exactly.'

'You think I should give you notice because you have failed.'

Mr Ramsden stiffened noticeably at the word 'failed'.

'It's throwing good money away on a long chance. It isn't a business proposition, Mr Blair. It isn't even a good gamble.'

'Well, I have something for your consideration that is definite enough to please you, I think.' He fished the little cardboard box out of his pocket. 'One of the witnesses on Monday was a girl called Gladys Rees. Her role was to supply evidence that her friend Rose Glyn had talked to her about screams at The Franchise long before the police were interested in the place. Well, she supplied the evidence all right, but not *con amore*, as you might say. She was nervous, unwilling, and was obviously hating it – in contrast to her friend Rose, who was having the time of her life. One of my local colleagues suggested that Rose had got her there by pressure, but that didn't seem very likely at the time. This morning, however, the watch that Rose stole from Miss Sharpe came back by post in this box, with the printed message enclosed. Now Rose would never have bothered to return the watch; she has no conscience at all. Nor would she have written the note, having no desire to repudiate anything. The conclusion is inescapable, that it was Gladys who received the watch – Rose could not have worn it without detection anyhow – and that was how Rose got her to back up her lies.'

He paused to let Ramsden comment. Mr Ramsden nodded, but it was an interested nod.

'Now we can't approach Gladys with any kind of argument without being accused of intimidating witnesses. I mean, getting her to go back on her story before the Assizes. Kevin Macdermott could probably do it by force of personality and persistent questions, but I doubt it; and anyhow the Court might stop him before he had achieved anything. They are apt to look sideways on him when he begins to ride a witness.'

'They are.'

'What I want to do is to be able to put this printed scrap into court as evidence. To be able to say that it is Gladys Rees's writing. With the evidence that it was she who had the stolen watch, we make the suggestion that Rose used pressure on her to testify to what is not true. Macdermott assures her that if she was blackmailed into giving false evidence she will probably not be punished for it, and she breaks down and confesses.'

'So you want another specimen of Gladys Rees's printing.'

'Yes. And coming along just now I was thinking about it. I have the impression that her present job is her first one, so it can't be very long since she left school. Perhaps her school could furnish one. Or, anyhow, provide a starting-off place. It would be enormously to our advantage if we could come by a specimen without *provocateur* methods. Do you think you could do something about it?'

'I'll get you a specimen, yes,' Ramsden said; as who should say: Give me any reasonable commission and it will be executed. 'Did the Rees girl go to school here?'

'No, I understand she comes from the other side of the county.'

'All right, I'll find out. Where is she working now?'

'At an isolated place called Bratt's Farm, over the fields from Staples, the place behind The Franchise.'

'And about the search for the Kane girl –'

'Isn't there anything you could still do in Larborough itself? I can't teach you anything about your business, I know that, but she *was* in Larborough.'

'Yes, and where she was we traced her. In public places. But X may *live* in Larborough, for all we know. She may just have gone to ground there. After all, a month – or practically a month – is an odd time for that sort of disappearance, Mr Blair. That sort of thing usually ranges from a week-end to ten days, but no longer. She may just have gone home with him.'

'Do you think that is what happened?'

'No,' Ramsden said slowly. 'If you want my honest opinion, Mr Blair, it is that we have missed her at one of the exits.'

'Exits?'

'That she went out of the country, but looking so different

that that butter-wouldn't melt photograph didn't convey her at all.'

'Why different?'

'Well, I don't suppose she was provided with a phoney passport, so she would presumably travel as his wife.'

'Yes, of course. I took that for granted.'

'And she couldn't do that looking as she does. But with her hair swept up and some make-up on, she would look quite different. You have no idea the difference sweeping-up hairdressing makes to a woman. The first time I saw my wife with one I didn't recognize her. It made her so different, if you want to know, that I felt quite shy with her; and we'd been married twenty years.'

'So that's what you think happened. I expect you're right,' Robert said sadly.

'That's why I don't want to waste any more of your money, Mr Blair. Looking for the girl in the photograph is not much use, because the girl we're looking for didn't look a bit like that. When she *did* look like that, people recognized her at first glance. At the cinemas and what not. We traced her easily enough during her time on her own in Larborough. But from then on it's a complete blank. Her photograph doesn't convey her to anyone who saw her after she left Larborough.'

Robert sat doodling on Miss Tuff's nice fresh blotting-paper – a herring-bone pattern, very neat and decorative. 'You see what this means, don't you? We are sunk.'

'But you have this,' Ramsden protested, indicating the printed scrap of paper that had come with the watch.

'That merely destroys the police case. It doesn't disprove Betty Kane's story. If the Sharpes are ever to be rid of this thing the girl's story has to be shown to be nonsense. Our only chance of doing that is to find out where she was during those weeks.'

'Yes. I see.'

'I suppose you have checked on private owners?'

'Planes? Oh yes. The same thing goes there. We have no photograph of the man, so he might be any one of the hundreds of private owners who went abroad with female companions in the specified time.'

204

'Yes. Pretty well sunk. Not much wonder Ben Carley was amused.'

'You're tired, Mr Blair. You've been having a worrying time.'

'Yes. It isn't very often a country solicitor has something like this dumped on his shoulders,' Robert said wryly.

Ramsden regarded him with what amounted on the Ramsden visage to a smile. 'For a country solicitor,' he said, 'it seems to me you're not doing badly, Mr Blair. Not badly at all.'

'Thanks,' Robert said, really smiling. Coming from Alec Ramsden that was practically an O.M.

'I shouldn't let it get you down. You've got an insurance against the very worst happening – or will, when I get that printed evidence.'

Robert flung down the pen he had been doodling with. 'I'm not interested in insurance,' he said with sudden heat. 'I'm interested in justice. I have only one ambition in life at this moment. And that is to have Betty Kane's story disproved in open court – to have the full account of what she did during those weeks made public in her presence and duly backed up by irreproachable witnesses. What are our chances of that, do you think? And what – tell me – what have we left untried that could possibly help us?'

'I don't know,' Mr Ramsden said seriously. 'Prayer, perhaps.'

19

THIS, oddly enough, was also Aunt Lin's reaction.

Aunt Lin had become gradually reconciled to Robert's connexion with The Franchise affair as it moved from the provincial-unsavoury to the national-celebrated. It was, after all, no disgrace to be connected with a case that was reported in *The Times*. Aunt Lin did not, of course, read *The Times*, but her friends did. The vicar, and old Colonel Whittaker, and the girl at Boots, and old Mrs Warren from Weymouth (Swanage); and it was vaguely gratifying to think that Robert should be solicitor for the defence in a famous trial, even if the defence was against a charge of beating a helpless girl. And of course it had never even remotely shadowed her mind that Robert would not win the case. She had taken that quite placidly for granted. In the first place Robert himself was so clever; and in the second Blair, Hayward, and Bennet could not conceivably be connected with a failure. She had even regretted in her own mind, in passing, that his triumph would take place over at Norton and not at Milford, where everyone might be there to see.

So that the first hint of doubt came as a surprise to her. Not a shock, since she still could not visualize the prospect of failure. But definitely as a new thought.

'But, Robert,' she said, sweeping her foot round under the table in an effort to locate her footstool, 'you don't suppose for a moment that you are going to *lose* the case, do you?'

'On the contrary,' Robert said, 'I don't suppose for a moment that we shall win it.'

'Robert!'

'In trial by jury it is customary to have a case to put to the jury. So far we have no case. And I don't think that the jury is going to like that at all.'

'You sound quite pettish, dear. I think you are allowing the thing to get on your nerves. Why don't you take tomorrow afternoon off and arrange a golf four? You have hardly golfed at all lately and it can't be good for your liver. Not golfing, I mean.'

'I can't believe,' Robert said wonderingly, 'that I was ever interested in the fate of a "piece of gutta-percha" on a golf course. That must have been in some other life.'

'That is what I say, dear. You are losing your sense of proportion. Allowing this affair to worry you quite unnecessarily. After all, you have Kevin.'

'That I take leave to doubt.'

'What do you mean, dear?'

'I can't imagine Kevin taking time off and travelling down to Norton to defend a case that he is foreordained to lose. He has his quixotic moments, but they don't entirely obliterate his common sense.'

'But Kevin promised to come.'

'When he made that promise there was still time for a defence to materialize. Now we can almost count the days to the Assizes and still we have no evidence – and no prospect of any.'

Miss Bennet eyed him over her soup spoon. 'I don't think, you know, dear,' she said, 'that you have enough faith.'

Robert refrained from saying that he had almost none at all. Not, anyhow, where divine intervention in The Franchise affair was concerned.

'Have faith, my dear,' she said happily, 'and it will all come right. You'll see.' The charged silence that succeeded this evidently worried her a little, for she added: 'If I had known you were doubtful or unhappy about the case, dear, I should have said extra prayers about it long ago. I am afraid I took it for granted that you and Kevin would manage it between you.' 'It' being British justice. 'But now that I know you are worrying about it I shall almost certainly put up some special petitions.'

The matter-of-fact application-for-relief tone with which this was uttered restored Robert's good humour.

'Thank you, darling,' he said in his normal good-natured voice.

She laid the spoon down on her empty plate and sat back; and a small teasing smile appeared on her round, pink face. 'I know that tone,' she said. 'It means that you're humouring me. But there's no need to, you know. It's I who am right about this, and you are wrong. It says quite distinctly that faith will move mountains. The difficulty always is that it takes a quite

207

colossal faith to move a mountain, and it is practically impossible to assemble so large a faith; so mountains are practically never moved. But in lesser cases – like the present one – it is possible to have enough faith for the occasion. So instead of being deliberately hopeless, dear, do *try* to have some confidence in the event. Meanwhile I shall go along to St Matthew's this evening and spend a little time praying that you will be given a piece of evidence tomorrow morning. That will make you feel happier.'

When Alec Ramsden walked into his room next morning with the piece of evidence, Robert's first thought was that nothing could prevent Aunt Lin taking credit for it. Nor was there any hope of his not mentioning it, since the first thing she would ask him at luncheon, in bright, confident tones, would be: 'Well, dear, did you get the evidence I prayed for?'

Ramsden was both pleased with himself and amused; so much could be translated, at any rate, from the Ramsden idiom into common knowledge.

'I had better confess frankly, Mr Blair, that when you sent me to that school I had no great hopes. I went because it seemed to be as good a starting-place as any, and I might find out from the staff some good way of getting acquainted with Rees. Or, rather, letting one of my boys get acquainted. I had even worked out how we could get printed letters from her without any fuss, once one of my boys got off with her. But you're a wonder, Mr Blair. You had the right idea after all.'

'You mean you've got what we wanted!'

'I saw her form mistress and was quite frank about what we wanted and why. Well, as frank as need be. I said Gladys was suspected of perjury – a penal servitude affair – but that we thought she'd been blackmailed into giving evidence, and to prove it was blackmail we needed a sample of any printed letters she ever wrote. Well, when you sent me there I took it for granted that she would not have have printed a single letter since she left the kindergarten. But the form mistress – a Miss Baggaly – said to give her a minute to think. "Of course," she said, "she was very good at drawing, and if I have nothing perhaps the visiting art-mistress might have something. We like to keep good work when our pupils produce it." As a comfort for all the duds they have to put up with, I suppose, poor things. Well, I didn't have to see the art-mistress, because Miss Baggaly hunted through some things and produced this.'

He laid a sheet of paper down on the desk in front of Robert. It appeared to be a free-hand map of Canada, showing the principal divisions, towns, and rivers. It was inaccurate but very neat. Across the bottom was printed DOMINION OF CANADA. And in the right-hand corner was the signature: Gladys Rees.

'It seems that every summer, at breaking-up time, they have an exhibition of work, and they normally keep the exhibits until the next exhibition the following year. I suppose it would seem too callous just to toss them out the day after. Or perhaps they keep them to show to visiting big-wigs and inspectors. Anyhow, there were drawers full of the stuff. This,' he indicated the map, 'was a product of a competition – "Draw a map of any country from memory in twenty minutes" – and the three prize-winners had their answers exhibited. 'This was a "third equal".'

'I can hardly believe it,' Robert said, feasting his eyes on Gladys Rees's handiwork.

'Miss Baggaly was right about her being good with her hands. Funny when she stayed so illiterate. You can see where they corrected her dotted capital I's.'

You could indeed. Robert was gloating over the place.

'She has no mind, the girl, but a good eye,' he said, considering Gladys's idea of Canada. 'She remembered the shape of things, but not the names. And the spelling is entirely her own. I suppose the "third equal" was for the neat work.'

'Neat work for us, anyhow,' Ramsden said, laying down the scrap of paper that had come with the watch. 'Let us be thankful she didn't choose Alaska.'

'Yes,' Robert said. 'A miracle.' (Aunt Lin's miracle, his mind said.) 'Who is the best man at this sort of thing?'

Ramsden told him.

'I'll take it up to to town with me now, tonight, and have the report before morning, and I'll take it round to Mr Macdermott at breakfast-time, if that's all right with you.'

'Right?' said Robert. 'It's perfect.'

'I think it might be a good idea to finger-print them too – and the little cardboard box. There *are* judges who don't like handwriting experts, but the two together would convince even a judge.'

'Well,' Robert said, handing them over, 'at least my clients are not going to be sentenced to hard labour.'

'There's nothing like looking on the bright side,' Ramsden commented dryly; and Robert laughed.

'You think I'm ungrateful for such a dispensation. I'm not. It's a terrific load off my mind. But the real load is still there. Proving that Rose Glyn is a thief, liar, and blackmailer – with perjury thrown in as a sideline – leaves Betty Kane's story still untouched. And it is Betty Kane's story that we set out to disprove.'

'There's still time,' Ramsden said, but half-heartedly.

'About all there is time for is a miracle.'

'Well? Why not? They happen. Why shouldn't they happen to us? What time shall I telephone you tomorrow?'

But it was Kevin who telephoned on the morrow, full of congratulations and jubilation. 'You're a marvel, Rob. I'll make mincemeat of them.'

Yes, it would be a lovely little exercise in cat-and-mouse play for Kevin; and the Sharpes would walk out of the court 'free'. Free to go back to their haunted house and their haunted existence; two half-mad witches who had once threatened and beaten a girl.

'You don't sound very gay, Rob. Is it getting you down?'

Robert said what he was thinking: that the Sharpes saved from prison would still be in a prison of Betty Kane's making.

'Perhaps not, perhaps not,' Kevin said. 'I'll do my best with the Kane over that howler about the divided path. Indeed, if Miles Allison weren't prosecuting I could probably break her with it; but Miles will probably be quick enough to retrieve the situation. Cheer up, Rob. At the very least her credit will be seriously shaken.'

But shaking Betty Kane's credit was not enough. He knew just how little effect that would have on the general public. He had had a large experience lately of the woman-in-the-street and had been appalled by the general inability to analyse the simplest statement. Even if the newspapers were to report that small bit about the view from the window – and they would

210

probably be much too busy reporting the more sensational matter of Rose Glyn's perjury – even if they reported it, it would have no effect on the average reader. 'They tried to put her in the wrong, but they were very quickly put in their place.' That is all it would convey to them.

Kevin might successfully shake Betty Kane's credit with the Court, the reporters, the officials, and any critical minds who happened to be present; but on the present evidence he could do nothing to alter the strong feelings of partisanship that Betty Kane's case had aroused throughout the country. The Sharpes would stay condemned.

And Betty Kane would 'get away with it'.

That to Robert was a thought that was even worse than the prospect of the Sharpes' haunted life. Betty Kane would go on being the centre of an adoring family – secure, loved, hero-worshipped. The once easy-going Robert grew homicidal at the thought.

He had had to confess to Aunt Lin that a piece of evidence had turned up at the time specified in her prayers, but had pusillanimously refrained from telling her that the said evidence was good enough to destroy the police case. She would call that winning the case; and 'winning' to Robert meant something very different.

To Nevil too, it seemed. And for the first time since young Bennet came to occupy the back room that used to be his, Robert thought of him as an ally, a communal spirit. To Nevil, too, it was unthinkable that Betty Kane should 'get away with it'. And Robert was surprised all over again at the murderous rage that fills the pacifist-minded when their indignation is roused. Nevil had a special way of saying 'Betty Kane': as if the syllables were some poison he put in his mouth by mistake and he was spitting it out. 'Poisonous', too, was his favourite epithet for her – 'that poisonous creature'. Robert found him very comforting.

But there was little comfort in the situation. The Sharpes had accepted the news of their probable escape from a prison sentence with the same dignity that had characterized their acceptance of everything, from Betty Kane's first accusation to the serving of a summons and an appearance in the dock. But they too realized that the thing would be escape but not vindication. The police case would break down and they would get their verdict. But they would get it because in English law there was no middle course. In a Scots court the verdict would be Not Proven. And that, in fact, would be what the result of the Assizes verdict next week would amount to: merely that the police had not had good enough evidence to prove their case, not that the case was necessarily a bad one.

It was when the Assizes were only four days away that he confessed to Aunt Lin that the evidence did suffice to defeat the charge. The growing worry on that round, pink face was too much for him. He had meant merely to give her that sop and leave the matter there; but instead he found himself pouring it all out to her as he had poured out his troubles as a small boy, in the days when Aunt Lin was an omniscient and omnipotent angel and not just kind, silly Aunt Lin. She listened to this unexpected torrent of words – so different from the normal phrases of their meal-time intercourse – in surprised silence, her jewel-blue eyes attentive and concerned.

'Don't you see, Aunt Lin, it isn't victory; it's defeat,' he finished. 'It's a travesty of justice. It isn't a verdict we're fighting for; it's justice. And we have no hope of getting it. Not a ghost of a hope!'

'But why didn't you tell me all this, dear? Did you think I would not understand or agree, or something?'

'Well, you didn't feel as I did about –'

'Just because I didn't much like the look of those people at The Franchise – I must confess, dear, even now, that they aren't the kind of people I naturally take to – just because I didn't much like them doesn't mean that I am indifferent to seeing justice done, surely?'

'No, of course not; but you said quite frankly that you found Betty Kane's story believable, and so –'

'That,' said Aunt Lin calmly, 'was before the police court.'

'The court? But you weren't at the court.'

'No, dear, but Colonel Whittaker was, and he didn't like the girl at all.'

'Didn't he, indeed?'

'No. He was quite eloquent about it. He said he had once had

212

a – what-do-you-call-it – a lance-corporal in his regiment, or battalion or something, who was exactly like Betty Kane. He said he was an injured innocent who set the whole battalion by the ears and was more trouble than a dozen hard-cases. Such a nice expression: hard-cases, isn't it? He finished up in the greenhouse, Colonel Whittaker said.'

'The glasshouse.'

'Well, something like that. And as for the Glyn girl from Staples, he said that one glance at her and you automatically began to reckon the number of lies there would be per sentence. He didn't like the Glyn girl either. So you see, dear, you needn't have thought that I would be unsympathetic about your worry. I am just as interested in abstract justice as you are, I assure you. And I shall redouble my prayers for your success. I was going over to the Gleasons' garden party this afternoon, but I shall go along to St Matthew's instead and spend a quiet hour there. I think it is going to rain in any case. It always does rain at the Gleasons' garden party, poor things.'

'Well, Aunt Lin, I don't deny we need your prayers. Nothing short of a miracle can save us now.'

'Well, I shall pray for the miracle.'

'A last-minute reprieve with the rope round the hero's neck? That happens only in detective stories and the last few minutes of horse-operas.'

'Not at all. It happens every day somewhere in the world. If there was some way of finding out and adding up the times it happens you would no doubt be surprised. Providence does take a hand, you know, when other methods fail. You haven't enough faith, my dear, as I pointed out before.'

'I don't believe that an angel of the Lord is going to appear in my office with an account of what Betty Kane was doing for that month, if that is what you mean,' Robert said.

'The trouble with you, dear, is that you think of an angel of the Lord as a customer with wings, whereas he is probably a scruffy little man in a bowler hat. Anyhow, I shall pray very hard this afternoon, and tonight too, of course; and by to-morrow perhaps help will be sent.'

20

THE angel of the Lord was not a scruffy little man, as it turned out; and his hat was a regrettably Continental affair of felt with a tightly rolled brim turned up all round. He arrived at Blair, Hayward, and Bennet's about half-past eleven the following morning.

'Mr Robert,' old Mr Heseltine said, putting his head in at Robert's door, 'there's a Mr Lange in the office to see you. He –'

Robert, who was busy and not expecting angels of the Lord, and quite used to strangers turning up in the office and wanting to see him, said: 'What does he want? I'm busy.'

'He didn't say. He just said he would like to see you if you were not too busy.'

'Well, I'm scandalously busy. Find out tactfully what he wants, will you? If it is nothing important Nevil can deal with it.'

'Yes, I'll find out; but his English is very thick and he doesn't seem very willing to –'

'English? You mean, he has a lisp?'

'No, I mean his pronunciation of English isn't very good. He –'

'The man's a foreigner, you mean?'

'Yes. He comes from Copenhagen.'

'Copenhagen! Why didn't you tell me that before!'

'You didn't give me a chance, Mr Robert.'

'Show him in, Timmy, show him in. Oh, merciful heaven, do fairy-tales come true?'

Mr Lange was rather like one of the Norman pillars of Notre Dame. Just as round, just as high, just as solid and just as dependable-looking. Far away at the top of this great round, solid, erect pillar his face shone with friendly rectitude.

'Mr Blair?' he said. 'My name is Lange. I apologize for bothering you' – he failed to manage the *th* – 'but it was important. Important to you, I mean. At least, yes I think.'

'Sit down, Mr Lange.'

'Thank you, thank you. It is warm, is it not? This is perhaps the day you have your summer?' He smiled on Robert. 'That is an idiom of the English, that joke about one-day summer. I am greatly interested in the English idiom. It is because of my interest in English idiom that I come to see you.'

Robert's heart sank to his heels with the plummet swoop of an express lift. Fairy-tales, indeed. No; fairy-tales stay fairy-tales.

'Yes?' he said, encouragingly.

'I keep an hotel in Copenhagen, Mr Blair. The hotel of the Red Shoes it is called. Not, of course, because anyone wears red shoes there, but because of a tale of Andersen, which you perhaps may – '

'Yes, yes,' Robert said. 'It has become one of our tales too.'

'Ah, so! Yes. A great man, Andersen. So simple a man and now so international. It is a thing to marvel at. But I waste your time, Mr Blair, I waste your time. What was I saying?'

'About English idiom.'

'Ah, yes. To study English is my hubby.'

'Hobby,' Robert said involuntarily.

'Hobby. Thank you. For my bread and butter I keep an hotel – and because my father and his father kept one before me – but for a hub ... a hobby? yes, thank you ... for a hobby I study the idiomatic English. So every day the newspapers that they leave about are brought to me.'

'They?'

'The English visitors.'

'Ah, yes.'

'In the evening when they have retired the page collects the English papers and leaves them in my office. I am busy, often, and I do not have time to look at them, and so they go into the pile and when I have leisure I pick one up and study it. Do I make myself clear, Mr Blair?'

'Perfectly, perfectly, Mr Lange.' A faint hope was rising again. Newspapers?

'So it goes on. A few moments of leisure, a little reading in an English paper, a new idiom – perhaps two – all very without excitement. How do you say that?'

'Placid.'

215

'So. Placid. And then one day I take this paper from the pile, just as I might take any of the others, and I forget all about idiom.' He took from his capacious pocket a once-folded copy of the *Ack-Emma*, and spread it in front of Robert on the desk. It was the issue of Friday, May the 10th, with the photograph of Betty Kane occupying two-thirds of the page. 'I look at this photograph. Then I look inside and read the story. Then I say to myself that this is most extraordinary. Most extraordinary it is. The paper say this is the photograph of Betty Kann. Kann?'

'Kane.'

'Ah. So. Betty Kane. But it is also the photograph of Mrs Chadwick, who stay at my hotel with her husband.'

'What!'

Mr Lange looked pleased. 'You are interested? I so hoped you might be. I did so hope.'

'Go on. Tell me.'

'A fortnight they stayed with me. And it was most extraordinary, Mr Blair, because while that poor girl was being beaten and starved in an English attic, Mrs Chadwick was eating like a young wolf at my hotel – the cream that girl could eat, Mr Blair, even I, a Dane, was surprised – and enjoying herself very much.'

'Yes?'

'Well, I said to myself: It is after all a photograph. And although it is just the way she looked when she let down her hair to come to the ball –'

'Let it down!'

'Yes. She wore her hair brushed up, you see. But we had a ball with costume – costume?'

'Yes. Fancy Dress.'

'A. So. Fancy dress. And for her fancy dress she lets her hair hang down. Just like that there.' He tapped the photograph. 'So I say to myself: It is a photograph, after all. How often has one seen a photograph that does not in the least resemble the real person. And what has this girl in the paper to do, possibly, with little Mrs Chadwick, who is here with her husband during that time! So I am reasonable to myself. But I do not throw away the paper. No ; I keep it. And now and then I look at it. And each time I look at it I think: But that *is* Mrs Chadwick. So I am still puzzled, and going to sleep I think about it when I should be thinking about tomorrow's marketing. I seek explanation from myself. Twins, perhaps? But no; the Betty girl is an only child. Cousins. Coincidence. Doubles. I think of them all. At night I look at the photograph, and all come to pieces again. I think: But certainly beyond a doubt that is Mrs Chadwick. You see my dilemma?'

'Perfectly.'

'So when I am coming to England on business, I put the newspaper with the Arabic name – '

'Arabic? Oh yes, I see. I didn't mean to interrupt.'

'I put it into my bag, and after dinner one night I take it out and show it to my friend where I am staying. I am staying with a compatriot of mine in Bayswater, London. And my friend is instantly very excited and say: But it is now a police affair, and these women say that never have they seen the girl before. They have been arrested for what they are supposed to have done to this girl and they are about to be tried for it. And he calls to his wife: "Rita! Rita! Where is the paper of a week last Tuesday?" It is the kind of household, my friend's where there is always a paper of a week last Tuesday. And his wife comes with it and he shows me the account of the trial – no, the – the – '

'Court appearance.'

'Yes. The appearance in court of the two women. And I read how the trial is to be at some place in the country in a little more than a fortnight. Well, by now, that would be in a very few days. So my friend say: How sure are you, Einar, that that girl and your Mrs Chadwick are one? And I say: Very sure indeed I am. So he say: Here in the paper is the name of the solicitor for the women. There is no address, but this Milford is a very small place and he will be easy to find. We shall have coffee early tomorrow – that is breakfast – and you will go down to this Milford and tell what you think to this Mr Blair. So here I am, Mr Blair. And you are interested in what I say?'

Robert sat back, took out his handkerchief, and mopped his forehead. 'Do you believe in miracles, Mr Lange?'

'But of course. I am a Christian. Indeed, although I am not yet very old I have myself seen two.'

217

'Well, you have just taken part in a third.'

'So?' Mr Lange beamed. 'That makes me very content.'

'You have saved our bacon.'

'Bacon?'

'An English idiom. You have not only saved our bacon. You have practically saved our lives.'

'You think then, as I think, that they are are one person, that girl and my guest at the Red Shoes?'

'I haven't a doubt of it. Tell me, have you the dates of her stay with you?'

'Oh yes, indeed. Here they are. She and her husband arrived by air on Friday the 29th of March, and they left – again by air, I think, though of that I am not so certain – on the 15th of April, a Monday.'

'Thank you. And her "husband", what did he look like?'

'Young. Dark. Good-looking. A little – now, what is the word? Too-bright. Gaudy? No.'

'Flashy?'

'Ah. There is it – flashy. A little flashy, I think. I observe that he was not greatly approved of by the other Englishmen who came and went.'

'Was he just on holiday?'

'No, oh no. He was in Copenhagen on business.'

'What kind of business?'

'That I do not know, I regret.'

'Can't you even make a guess? What would he be most likely to be interested in Copenhagen?'

'That depends, Mr Blair, on whether he was interested in buying or selling.'

'What was his address in England?'

'London.'

'Beautifully explicit. Will you forgive me a moment while I telephone? Do you smoke?' He opened the cigarette box and pushed it towards Mr Lange.

'Milford 195. You will do me the honour of having lunch with me, Mr Lange, won't you? Aunt Lin? I have to go to London directly after lunch . . . Yes, for the night. Will you be an angel and pack a small bag for me? . . . Thank you, darling. And would it be all right if I brought someone back to take

pot-luck for lunch today? ... Oh, good ... Yes, I'll ask him.'
He covered the mouthpiece, and said: 'My aunt, who is actually my cousin, wants to know if you eat pastry?'

'Mr Blair!' Mr Lange said, with a wide smile and wide gesture for his girth. 'And you ask a Dane?'

'He loves it,' Robert said into the telephone. 'And I say, Aunt Lin. Were you doing anything important this afternoon? ... Because what I think you ought to do is go to St Matthew's and give thanks ... Your angel of the Lord has arrived.'

Even Mr Lange could hear Aunt Lin's delighted: '*Robert!* No, not really!'

'In the flesh ... No, not a bit scruffy ... Very tall and beautiful and altogether perfect for the part ... You'll give him a good lunch, won't you? ... Yes, that's who is coming to lunch. An angel of the Lord.'

He put down the telephone and looked up at the amused Mr Lange.

'And now, Mr Lange, let us go over to the Rose and Crown and have some bad beer.'

21

WHEN Robert went out to The Franchise, three days later, to drive the Sharpes over to Norton for the Assizes on the morrow, he found an almost bridal atmosphere about the place. Two absurd tubs of yellow wallflowers stood at the top of the steps, and the dark hall gleamed with flowers like a church decorated for a wedding.

'Nevil!' Marion said, with an explanatory wave of her hand to the massed glory. 'He said the house should be *en fête*.'

'I wish that I had thought of it,' Robert said.

'After the last few days, it surprises me that you can think at all. If it were not for you, it is not rejoicing we should be today!'

'If it weren't for a man called Bell, you mean.'

'Bell?'

'Alexander Bell. He invented the telephone. If it weren't for that invention we should still be groping in the dark. It will be months before I can look at a telephone without blenching.'

'Did you take turn about?'

'Oh no. We each had our own. Kevin and his clerk at his chambers, me at his little place in St Paul's Churchyard, Alec Ramsden and three of his men at his office and wherever they could find a telephone that they could use uninterruptedly.'

'That was six of you.'

'Seven of us with six telephones. And we needed them!'

'Poor Robert!'

'At first it was fun. We were filled with the exhilaration of the hunt, of knowing that we were on the right track. Success was practically in our laps. But by the time we had made sure that none of the Chadwicks in the London telephone book had any connexion with a Chadwick who had flown to Copenhagen on the 29th of March and that all the air line knew about him was that two seats had been booked from Larborough on the 27th, we had lost any feeling of fun we had started with. The Larborough information cheered us, of course. But after that it was pure slog. We found out what we sold to Denmark and what she bought from us, and divided them up between us.'

'The merchandise?'

'No, the buyers and sellers. The Danish tourist office was a godsend. They just poured information at us. Kevin, his clerk, and I took the exports, and Ramsden and his men took the imports. From then on it was a tedious business of being put through to managers and asking: "Have you a man called Bernard Chadwick working for you?" The number of firms who *haven't* got a Bernard Chadwick working for them is unbelievable. But I know a lot more about our exports to Denmark than I did before.'

'I have no doubt of it!'

'I was so sick of the telephone that when it rang at my end I nearly didn't pick it up. I had almost forgotten that telephones were two-way. A telephone was just a sort of quiz instrument that I could plug into offices all over the country. I stared at it for quite a while before I realized that it was, after all, a mutual affair and that someone was trying to call me for a change.'

'And it was Ramsden.'

'Yes, it was Alec Ramsden. He said: "We've got him. He buys porcelain and stuff for Brayne, Havard and Co."'

'I am glad it was Ramsden who unearthed him. It will comfort him for his failure to run down the girl.'

'Yes, he's feeling better about it now. After that it was a rush to interview the people we needed and to obtain subpoenas and what not. But the whole lovely result will be waiting for us in the court at Norton tomorrow. Kevin can hardly wait. His mouth waters at the prospect.'

'If it was ever in my power to be sorry for that girl,' Mrs Sharpe said, coming in with an over-night bag and dumping it on a mahogany wall-table in a way that would have turned Aunt Lin faint, 'it would be in a witness-box facing a hostile Kevin Macdermott.' Robert noticed that the bag, which had originally been a very elegant and expensive one – a relic of her prosperous early married life, perhaps – was now deplorably shabby. He decided that when he married Marion his present to the bride's mother would be a dressing-case – small, light, elegant, and expensive.

221

'It will never be in my power,' Marion said, 'to have even a passing sensation of sorrow for that girl. I would swat her off the earth's face as I would swat a moth in a cupboard – except that I am always sorry about the moth.'

'What had the girl intended to do?' Mrs Sharpe asked. 'Had she intended to go back to her people at all?'

'I don't think so,' Robert said. 'I think she was still filled with rage and resentment at ceasing to be the centre of interest at 39 Meadowside Lane. It is as Kevin said long ago: crime begins in egoism, inordinate vanity. A normal girl, even an emotional adolescent, might be heart-broken that her adopted brother no longer considered her the most important thing in his life; but she would work it out in sobs or sulks or being difficult, or deciding that she was going to renounce the world and go into a convent, or half a dozen other methods that the adolescent uses in the process of adjustment. But with an egoism like Betty Kane's there is no adjustment. She expects the world to adjust itself to her. The criminal always does, by the way. There was never a criminal who didn't consider himself ill-done by.'

'A charming creature,' Mrs Sharpe said.

'Yes. Even the Bishop of Larborough would find some difficulty in thinking up a case for her. His usual "environment" hobby-horse is no good this time. Betty Kane had everything that he recommends for the cure of the criminal: love, freedom to develop her talents, education, security. It's quite a poser for his lordship when you come to consider it, because he doesn't believe in heredity. He thinks that criminals are made and therefore can be unmade. "Bad blood" is just an old superstition in the Bishop's estimation.'

'Toby Byrne,' Mrs Sharpe said with a snort. 'You should have heard Charles' stable lads on him.'

'I've heard Nevil,' Robert said. 'I doubt if anyone could improve on Nevil's version of the subject.'

'Is the engagement definitely broken, then?' Marion asked.

'Definitely. Aunt Lin has hopes of the eldest Whittaker girl. She is a niece of Lady Mountleven and a grand-daughter of Karr's Krisps.'

Marion laughed with him. 'Is she nice, the Whittaker girl?' she asked.

'Yes. Fair, pretty, well-brought-up, musical, but doesn't sing.'

'I should like Nevil to get a nice wife. All he needs is some permanent interest of his own. A focus for his energies and his emotions.'

'At the moment the focus for both is The Franchise.'

'I know. He has been a dear to us. Well, I suppose it is time that we were going. If anyone had told me last week that I should be leaving The Franchise to go to a triumph at Norton I wouldn't have believed it. Poor Stanley can sleep in his own bed from now on, instead of guarding a couple of hags in a lonely house.'

'Isn't he sleeping here tonight?' Robert asked.

'No. Why should he?'

'I don't know. I don't like the idea of the house being left entirely empty.'

'The policeman will be round as usual on his beat. Anyhow, no one has even tried to do anything since the night they smashed our windows. It is only for tonight. Tomorrow we shall be home again.'

'I know. But I don't like it. Couldn't Stanley stay one more night? Until the case is over?'

'If they want to wreck our windows again,' Mrs Sharpe said, 'I don't suppose Stanley's being here will deter them.'

'No, I suppose not. I'll remind Hallam, anyhow, that the house is empty tonight,' Robert said, and left it there.

Marion locked the door behind them, and they walked to the gate, where Robert's car was waiting. At the gate Marion paused to look back at the house. 'It's an ugly old place,' she said, 'but it has one virtue. It looks the same all the year round. At mid-summer the grass gets a little burnt and tired-looking, but otherwise it doesn't change. Most houses have a "best" time – rhododendrons or herbaceous borders or virginia creeper or almond blossom, or something. But The Franchise is always the same. It has no frills. What are you laughing at, mother?'

'I was thinking how *bedizened* the poor thing looks with those tubs of wallflower.'

They stood there for a moment, laughing at the forbidding dirty-white house with its incongruous decoration of frivolity; and laughing, shut the gate on it.

But Robert did not forget; and before having dinner with Kevin at the Feathers in Norton he called the police station at Milford and reminded them that the Sharpes' house would be empty for that one night.

'All right, Mr Blair,' the sergeant said; 'I'll tell the man on the beat to open the gate and look round. Yes, we still have a key. That'll be all right.'

Robert did not quite see what that would achieve; but then he did not see what protection could be afforded in any case. Mrs Sharpe had said, if anyone was minded to break windows then the windows would inevitably be broken. He decided that he was being fussy and joined Kevin and his law friends with relief.

The law talks well, and it was late before Robert went to bed in one of the dark-panelled rooms that made the Feathers famous. The Feathers – one of the 'musts' of American visitors to Britain – was not only famous but up to date. Pipes had been led through the linenfold oak, wires through the beamed ceilings, and a telephone line through the oak planks of the floor. The Feathers had been providing comfort for the travelling public since 1480 and saw no reason why it should stop.

Robert fell asleep as soon as his head touched the pillow and the telephone at his ear had been ringing for some moments before he became aware of it.

'Well?' he said, still half-asleep. And became instantly wide awake.

It was Stanley. Could he come back to Milford? The Franchise was on fire.

'Badly?'

'It's got a good hold, but they think they can save it.'

'I'll be over as soon as I can make it.'

He made the twenty miles in a door-to-door time that the Robert Blair of a month ago would have considered reprehensible in the achievement of another and quite inconceivable as an achievement of his own. As he tore past his own home at the lower end of Milford High Street and out into the country beyond, he saw the glow against the horizon like the rising of a full moon. But the moon hung in the sky, a young silver moon in the pale summer night. And the glow of the burning Franchise wavered in sickening gusts that tightened Robert's heart with remembered horror.

At least there was no one in the building. He wondered if anyone had been there in time to rescue what was valuable from the house. Would there be anyone there who could distinguish what was valuable from what was worthless?

The gates were wide open and the courtyard – bright in the flames – was crowded with the men and machines of the Fire Service. The first thing he saw, incongruous on the grass, was the bead-work chair from the drawing-room; and a wave of hysteria rose in him. Someone had saved that, anyhow.

An almost unrecognizable Stanley grabbed his sleeve and said, 'There you are. I thought you ought to know, somehow.' Sweat trickled down his blackened face, leaving clear rivulets behind them, so that his young face looked seamed and old. 'There isn't enough water. We've got quite a lot of the stuff out. All the drawing-room stuff that they used every day. I thought that's what they'd want if it had to be a choice. And we flung out some of the upstairs stuff, but all the heavy stuff has gone up.'

Mattresses and bed-linen were piled on the grass out of the way of the firemen's boots. The furniture stood about on the grass as it had been set down, looking surprised and lost.

'Let's take the furniture farther away,' Stanley said. 'It's not safe where it is. Either some lighted bits will fall on it or one of those bastards will use it to stand on.' The bastards were the Fire Service, doing their sweating and efficient best.

So Robert found himself prosaically carting furniture through a fantastic scene, miserably identifying pieces that he had known in their proper sphere. The chair that Mrs Sharpe had considered Inspector Grant too heavy for; the cherry-wood table they had given Kevin luncheon at; the wall-table that Mrs Sharpe had dumped her bag down on only a few hours ago. The roar and crackle of the flames, the shoutings of the firemen, the odd mixture of moonlight, head-lights, and wavering flame, the mad juxtaposition and irrelevance of the bits of furniture, reminded him of how it felt to be coming round from an anaesthetic.

And then two things happened together. The first floor fell in with a crash. And as the new spout of flame lit the faces round him he saw two youths alongside whose countenances were alive with gloating. At the same moment he became aware that Stanley had seen them too. He saw Stanley's fist catch the farther one under the chin with a crack that could be heard even over the noise of the flames, and the gloating face disappeared into the darkness of the trampled grass.

Robert had not hit anyone since he gave up boxing when he left school, and he had no intention of hitting anyone now. His left arm seemed to do all that was necessary of its own accord. And the second leering face went down into obscurity.

'Neat,' remarked Stanley, sucking his broken knuckles. And then, 'Look!' he said.

The roof crumpled like a child's face when it is beginning to cry; like a melting negative. The little round window, so famous and so ill-reputed, leaned forward a little and sank slowly inwards. A tongue of flame leapt up and fell again. Then the whole roof collapsed into the seething mass below, falling two floors to join the red wreck of the rest of the interior. The men moved back from the furnace heat. The fire roared in unrestricted triumph into the summer night.

When at last it died away Robert noticed with a vague surprise that the dawn had come. A calm, grey dawn, full of promise. Quiet had come too; the roar and the shoutings had faded to the soft hiss of water on the smoking skeleton. Only the four walls stood, blurred and grimy, in the middle of the trampled grass. The four walls and the flight of steps with their warped iron railing. On either side of the doorway stood what remained of Nevil's gay little tubs, the soaked and blackened flowers hanging in unrecognizable shreds over their edges. Between them the square opening yawned into a black emptiness.

'Well,' said Stanley, standing beside him, 'that seems to be that.'

'How did it begin?' asked Bill, who had arrived too late to see anything but the wreck that was left.

'No one knows. It was well alight when P.C. Newsam arrived on his beat,' Robert said. 'What became of those two chaps, by the way?'

'The two we corrected?' Stanley said. 'They went home.'

'It's a pity that expression is no evidence.'

'Yes,' Stanley said. 'They won't get anyone for this, any more than they got anyone for the window-breaking. And I still owe someone for a crack on the head.'

'You nearly broke that creature's neck tonight. That ought to be some kind of compensation to you.'

'How are you going to tell them?' Stanley said. This obviously referred to the Sharpes.

'God knows,' Robert said. 'Am I to tell them first and let it spoil their triumph in court for them; or am I to let them have their triumph and face the awful comedown afterwards?'

'Let them have their triumph,' Stanley said. 'Don't mess it up.'

'Perhaps you are right, Stan. I wish I knew. I had better book rooms at the Rose and Crown for them.'

'They wouldn't like that,' Stan said.

'Perhaps not,' Robert said a shade impatiently. 'But they have no choice. Whatever they decide to do they will want to stay here a night or two to arrange about things, I expect. And the Rose and Crown is the best available.'

'Well,' Stanley said, 'I've been thinking. And I'm sure my landlady would be glad to have them. She's always been on their side, and she has a spare room, and they could have that sitting-room in front that she never uses; and it's very quiet down there, that last row of Council houses facing on the Meadows. I'm sure they'd rather have that than a hotel where they would be stared at.'

'They would indeed, Stan. I should never have thought of it. You think your landlady would be willing?'

'I don't think; I'm sure. They're her greatest interest in life at the moment. It would be like royalty coming to stay.'

'Well, find out definitely, would you, and telephone me a message to Norton? To the Feathers at Norton?'

22

IT seemed to Robert that at least half Milford had managed to pack itself into the court at Norton. Certainly a great many citizens of Norton were milling round the outer doors, vocal and frustrated; furious that when a case of national interest was being decided at 'their' Assizes they should be done out of their right to witness it by an influx of foreigners from Milford. Wily and deceitful foreigners, too, who had suborned the Norton youth to keep places in the queue for them – a piece of forethought which had not occurred to Norton adults.

It was very warm and the packed court stirred uneasily throughout the preliminaries and through most of Miles Allison's account of the crime. Allison was the antithesis of Kevin Macdermott, his fair, delicate face that of a type rather than a person. His light, dry voice was unemotional, his method matter-of-fact. And since the story he was telling was one which they had all read about and discussed until it was threadbare, they withheld their attention from him and amused themselves by identifying friends in court.

Robert sat turning over and over in his pocket the little oblong of pasteboard that Christina had pressed into his hand on his departure yesterday and rehearsing phrases for afterwards. The pasteboard was a bright Reckitt's blue and bore in gold letters the words: NOT A SPARROW SHALL FALL, and a picture in the right upper corner of a robin with an outsize red breast. How, wondered Robert, turning the little text over and over in his fingers, did you tell someone that they had no home any more?

The sudden movement of a hundred bodies and the subsequent silence brought him back to the court-room, and he realized that Betty Kane was taking the oath preparatory to giving evidence. 'Never kissed anything but the book,' Ben Carley had said of her appearance on a similar occasion. And that is what she looked like today. The blue outfit still made one think of youth and innocence, speedwell and camp-fire smoke and harebells in the grass. The tilted-back brim of her hat still showed the childish forehead with its charming hair line. And Robert, who knew now all about her life in the weeks she was missing, found himself being surprised all over again at sight of her. Plausibility was one of the first endowments of the criminal; but up to now such plausibility as he had had to deal with was of the old-soldier-ten-bob-note kind – easily recognized for what it was, the work of amateurs at the job. It occurred to him that for the first time he was seeing the real thing at work.

Once again she gave her evidence in model fashion, her clear young voice audible to everyone in court. Once again she had her audience breathless and motionless. The only difference this time was that the Bench was not doting. The Bench, indeed, if one was to judge by the expression on the face of Mr Justice Saye, was very far from doting. And Robert wondered how much the judge's critical gaze was due to natural distaste for the subject and how much to the conclusion that Kevin Macdermott would not be sitting there ready to defend the two women in the dock unless they had a thundering good defence.

The girl's own account of her sufferings did what her counsel's had not done: roused the audience to an emotional reaction. More than once they had given vent to a united sigh, a murmur of indignation; never overt enough to rank as a demonstration, and so bring down the Court's rebuke, but audible enough to show which way their sympathies lay. So that it was in a charged atmosphere that Kevin rose to cross-examine.

'Miss Kane,' began Kevin in his gentlest drawl, 'you say that it was dark when you arrived at The Franchise. Was it *really* so dark?'

This question, with its coaxing tone, made her think that he did not want it to be dark, and she reacted as he intended.

'Yes. Quite dark,' she said.

'Too dark to see the outside of the house?'

'Yes, much too dark.'

He appeared to give that up and try a new tack.

'Then the night you escaped. Perhaps that was not quite dark?'

'Oh yes. That was even darker, if possible.'

'So that you could not possibly have seen the outside of the house on some occasion?'

'Never.'

'Never. Well, having settled that point, let us consider what you say you could see from the window of your prison in the attic. You said in your statement to the police, when you were describing this unknown place where you were imprisoned, that the carriage-way from the gate to the door "went straight for a little and then divided in two into a circle up to the door."'

'Yes.'

'How did you know it did that?'

'How did I know it? I could see it.'

'From where?'

'From the window in the attic. It looked out on the court-yard in front of the house.'

'But from the window in the attic it is possible to see only the straight part of the carriage-way. The edge of the roof cuts off the rest. How did you know that the carriage-way divided in two and made a circle up to the door?'

'I saw it!'

'How?'

'From that window.'

'You want us to understand that you see on a different principle from ordinary beings? On the principle of the Irish-man's gun that shoots round corners. Or is it all done by mirrors?'

'It is the way I described!'

'Certainly it is the way you described; but what you des-cribed was the view of the courtyard as seen by, let us say, someone looking over the wall at it; not by someone looking at it from the window in the attic – which you assure us was your only view of it.'

'I take it,' said the Court, 'that you have a witness to the extent of the view from the window.'

'Two, my lord.'

'One with normal vision will be sufficient,' said the Court dryly.

'So you cannot explain how, speaking to the police that day

in Aylesbury, you described a peculiarity that you could not possibly have known about if your story was true. Have you ever been abroad, Miss Kane?'

'Abroad?' she said, surprised by the change of subject. 'No.'

'Never?'

'No, never.'

'You have not, for instance, been to Denmark lately? To Copenhagen, for instance.'

'No.' There was no change in her expression, but Robert thought that there was the faintest uncertainty in her voice.

'Do you know a man called Bernard Chadwick?'

She was suddenly wary. Robert was reminded of the subtle change in an animal that has been relaxed and becomes attentive. There is no alteration in pose, no actual physical change. On the contrary, there is only an added stillness, an awareness.

'No.' The tone was colourless, uninterested.

'He is not a friend of yours.'

'No.'

'You did not, for instance, stay with him at a hotel in Copenhagen?'

'No.'

'Have you stayed with anyone in Copenhagen?'

'No, I have never been abroad at all.'

'So that if I were to suggest that you spent those missing weeks in a hotel in Copenhagen and not in an attic at The Franchise, I should be mistaken.'

'Quite mistaken.'

'Thank you.'

Miles Allison, as Kevin had anticipated, rose to retrieve the situation.

'Miss Kane,' he said, 'you arrived at The Franchise by car.'

'Yes.'

'And that car, you say in your statement, was driven up to the door of the house. Now, if it was dark, as you say, there must have been side-lights on the car, if not head-lights; which would illuminate not only the carriage-way but most of the courtyard.'

'Yes,' she broke in, before he could put it to her, 'yes, of course I must have seen the circle then. I knew I had seen it,

231

I knew it.' She glanced at Kevin for a moment, and Robert was reminded of her face when she saw that she had guessed correctly about the suitcases in the cupboard that first day at The Franchise. If she knew what Kevin had waiting for her, Robert thought, she would have no spare thought for a passing triumph.

She was succeeded in the witness-box by Carley's 'oleograph', who had bought both a new frock and a new hat for her appearance at Norton – a tomato-red frock and a puce hat with a cobalt ribbon and a pink rose – and looked more luscious and more revolting than ever. Again Robert was interested to note how her relish of her part discounted, even with this more emotional audience, the effect of what she said. They didn't like her, and in spite of their *parti pris* attitude their English distrust of malice cooled their minds towards her. When Kevin, cross-examining, suggested that she had in fact been dismissed and had not 'given in her notice' at all, there was a So-that's-it! expression on every second face in court. Apart from an attempt to shake her credit, there was not much that Kevin could do with her, and he let her go. He was waiting for her poor stooge.

The stooge, when she arrived, looked even less happy than she had looked in the police court at Milford. The much more impressive array of robes and wigs clearly shook her. Police uniforms were bad enough, but in retrospect they seemed positively home-like compared with this solemn atmosphere, this ritual. If she was out of her depth in Milford, she was obviously drowning here. Robert saw Kevin's considering eye on her, analysing and understanding; deciding on his approach. She had been scared stiff by Miles Allison in spite of his patient quietness, evidently regarding anything in a wig and gown as hostile and a potential dispenser of penalties. So Kevin became her wooer and protector.

It was positively indecent, the caress that Kevin could get into his voice, Robert thought, listening to his first sentences to her. The soft, unhurried syllables reassured her. She listened for a moment and then began to relax. Robert saw the small, skinny hands that had been clutched so tightly together on the rail of the box slacken and spread slowly to a prone position.

232

He was asking about her school. The fright had faded from her eyes and she was answering quite calmly. Here, she quite obviously felt, was a friend.

'Now, Gladys, I am going to suggest to you that you did not want to come here today and give evidence against these two people at The Franchise.'

'No, I didn't. Indeed I didn't!'

'But you came,' he said; not accusing, just making the statement.

'Yes,' she said, shamefaced.

'Why? Because you thought it was your duty?'

'No, oh no.'

'Was it because someone forced you to come?'

Robert saw the judge's instant reaction to this, but so, out of the tail of his eye, did Kevin. 'Someone who held something over your head?' finished Kevin smoothly, and his lordship paused. 'Someone who said: "You say what I tell you to say or I'll tell about you"?'

She looked half-hopeful, half-bewildered. 'I don't know,' she said, falling back on the escape of the illiterate.

'Because if anyone made you tell lies by threatening what they would do to you if you didn't, they can be punished for it.'

This was clearly a new idea to her.

'This court, all these people you see here, have come here today to find out the truth about something. And his lordship up there would deal very sternly with anyone who had used threats to make you come here and say something that was not true. What is more, there is a very heavy punishment for persons who take an oath to speak truth and tell what is not true; but if it so happened that they had been frightened into telling lies by someone threatening them, then the person who would be punished most would be the person who made the threats. Do you understand that?'

'Yes,' she said in a whisper.

'Now I am going to suggest to you what really happened, and you will tell me whether I am right.' He waited for her agreement, but she said nothing, so he went on. 'Someone – a friend of yours, perhaps – took something from The Franchise. Let us say a watch. She did not want the watch herself, perhaps, and so she handed it on to you. It may be that you did not want to take it, but your friend is perhaps a domineering person and you did not like to refuse her gift. So you took it. Now I suggest that presently that friend proposed to you that you should back up a story she was going to tell in court and you, being averse to telling lies, said no. And that then she said to you: "If you don't back me up I shall say that you took that watch from The Franchise one day when you came to see me" – or some other threat of that sort.'

He paused a moment, but she merely looked bewildered.

'Now, I suggest that because of those threats you did actually go to a police court and did actually back up your friend's untrue story, but that when you got home you were sorry and ashamed. So sorry and ashamed that the thought of keeping that watch any longer was unbearable to you. And that you then wrapped up the watch and sent it back to The Franchise by post with a note saying: "I don't want none of it." ' He paused. 'I suggest to you, Gladys, that that is what really happened.'

But she had had time to take fright. 'No,' she said. 'No, I never had that watch.'

He ignored the admission and said smoothly: 'I am quite wrong about that?'

'Yes. It wasn't me sent back the watch.'

He picked up a paper and said, still mildly: 'When you were at that school we were talking about, you were very good at drawing. So good that you had things put up for show at the school exhibition.'

'I have here a map of Canada – a very neat map – which was one of your exhibits and which indeed won you a prize. You have signed it here in the right-hand corner, and I have no doubt that you were proud to sign such a neat piece of work. I expect you will remember it.'

It was taken across the court to her, while Kevin added:

'Ladies and gentlemen of the jury, it is a map of Canada which Gladys Rees made in her last year at school. When his lordship has inspected it he will no doubt pass it on to you.' And then, to Gladys: 'You made that map yourself?'

'Yes.'

'And wrote your name in the corner?'

'Yes.'

'And printed DOMINION OF CANADA across the bottom?'

'Yes.'

'You printed those letters across the bottom that read: DOMINION OF CANADA. Good. Now, I have here the scrap of paper on which someone wrote the words: I DON'T WANT NONE OF IT. This scrap of paper, with its printed letters, was enclosed with the watch that was sent back to The Franchise – the watch that had gone missing while Rose Glyn was working there. And I suggest that the printing of I DON'T WANT NONE is the same as the printing of DOMINION OF CANADA. That it was written by the same hand. And that that hand was yours.'

'No,' she said, taking the scrap of paper as it was handed to her and putting it hastily down on the ledge as though it might sting her. 'I never. I never sent back no watch.'

'You didn't print those letters that read: I DON'T WANT NONE OF IT?'

'No.'

'But you did print those letters that read DOMINION OF CANADA?'

'Yes.'

'Well, later in this case I shall bring evidence that these two printings are by the same hand. In the meantime the jury can inspect them at their leisure and arrive at their own conclusions. Thank you.'

'My learned friend has suggested to you,' said Miles Allison, 'that pressure was brought on you to come here. Is there any truth in that suggestion?'

'No.'

'You did not come here because you were frightened of what might happen to you if you didn't?'

She took some time to think over this, evidently disentangling it in her mind. 'No,' she ventured at last.

'What you said in the witness-box at the police court and what you have said today is the truth?'

'Yes.'

'Not something that someone suggested you might say?'

'No.'

But the impression that was left with the jury was just that: that she was an unwilling witness repeating a story that was someone else's invention.

That ended the evidence for the prosecution, and Kevin went straight on with the matter of Gladys Rees – on the house-wife principle of 'getting her feet clear' before he began the real work of the day.

A handwriting expert gave evidence that the two samples of printing which had been put into court were by the same hand. Not only had he no doubt about it, but he had rarely been given an easier task. Not only were letters duplicated in the two samples but combinations of letters were similarly duplicated, combinations such as DO and AN and ON. As it was evident that the jury had already made up their minds for themselves on this point – no one who saw the two samples could doubt that they were by the same hand – Allison's suggestion that experts could be wrong was automatic and half-hearted. Kevin demolished it by producing his fingerprint witness, who deposed that the same fingerprints were to be found on each. And Allison's suggestion that the fingerprints might not be those of Gladys Rees was a last-stand effort. He had no wish that the court might put it to the test.

Now that he had established the fact that Gladys Rees had, when she made her first declaration, been in possession of a watch stolen from The Franchise and had returned it immediately after that declaration with a conscience-stricken note, Kevin was free to deal with Betty Kane's story. Rose Glyn and her story had been sufficiently discredited for the police to be already laying their heads together. He could safely leave Rose to the police.

When Bernard William Chadwick was called there was a craning forward and a murmur of interrogation. This was a name that the newspaper readers did not recognize. What could he be doing in the case? What was he here to say?

He was there to say that he was a buyer of porcelain, fine china, and fancy goods of various kinds for a wholesale firm in London. That he was married and lived with his wife in a house in Ealing.

'You travel for your firm?' Kevin said.

'Yes.'

'In March this year did you pay a visit to Larborough?'

'Yes.'

'While you were in Larborough did you meet Betty Kane?'

'Yes.'

'How did you meet her?'

'She picked me up.'

There was an instant and concerted protest from the body of the court. Whatever discrediting Rose Glyn and her ally had suffered, Betty Kane was still sacrosanct. Betty Kane, who looked so much like Bernadette, was not to be spoken of lightly.

The judge rebuked them for the demonstration, involuntary though it had been. He also rebuked witness. He was not quite clear, he inferred, what 'picking up' involved and would be grateful if the witness would confine himself to standard English in his replies.

'Will you tell the court just how you did meet her,' Kevin said.

'I had dropped into the Midland lounge for tea one day and she – er – began to talk to me. She was having tea there.'

'Alone?'

'Quite alone.'

'You did not speak to her at first?'

'I didn't even notice her.'

'How did she call attention to her presence, then?'

'She smiled, and I smiled back and went on with my papers. I was busy. Then she spoke to me. Asked what the papers were and so on.'

'So the acquaintance progressed.'

'Yes. She said she was going to the flicks – to the pictures – and wouldn't I come too? Well, I was finished for the day and she was a cute kid, so I said yes, if she liked. The result was that she met me next day and went out to the country in my car with me.'

'On your business trips, you mean.'

'Yes; she came for the ride and we would have a meal somewhere in the country and tea before she went home to her aunt's place.'

'Did she talk about her people to you?'

'Yes, she said how unhappy she was at home, where no one took any notice of her. She had a long string of complaints about her home, but I didn't take much notice of them. She looked a pretty sleek little outfit to me.'

'A what?' said the judge.

'A well-cared-for young girl, my lord.'

'Yes?' Kevin said. 'And how long did this idyll in Larborough persist?'

'It turned out that we were leaving Larborough on the same day. She was going back to her people because her holiday was over – she had already extended it so that she could run about with me – and I was due to fly to Copenhagen on business. She then said she had no intention of going home and asked me to take her with me. I said nothing doing. I didn't think she was so much of an innocent child as she seemed in the lounge at the Midland – I knew her better by that time – but I still thought she was inexperienced. She was only sixteen, after all.'

'She told you she was sixteen?'

'She had her sixteenth birthday in Larborough,' Chadwick said with a wry twist of the mouth under the small dark moustache. 'It cost me a gold lip-stick.'

Robert looked across at Mrs Wynn and saw her cover her face with her hands. Leslie Wynn, sitting beside her, looked unbelieving and blank.

'You had no idea that actually she was still fifteen?'

'No. Not until the other day.'

'So when she made the suggestion that she should go with you, you considered her an inexperienced child of sixteen?'

'Yes.'

'Why did you change your mind about her?'

'She – convinced me that she wasn't.'

'Wasn't what?'

'Inexperienced.'

'So after that you had no qualms about taking her with you on the trip abroad?'

'I had qualms in plenty, but by then I had learned – what fun she could be, and I couldn't have left her behind if I had wanted to.'

'So you took her abroad with you?'

'Yes.'

'As your wife?'

'Yes, as my wife.'

'You had no qualms about any anxiety her people might suffer?'

'No. She said she still had a fortnight's holiday to come and that her people would take it for granted that she was still with her aunt in Larborough. She had told her aunt that she was going home, but had told her people that she was staying on. And as they never wrote to each other it was unlikely that her not being in Larborough would become known to her people.'

'Do you remember the date on which you left Larborough?'

'Yes; I picked her up at a coach stop in Mainshill on the afternoon of March the 28th. That was where she would normally have got her bus home.'

Kevin left a pause after this piece of information so that its full significance should have a chance. Robert, listening to the momentary quiet, thought that if the courtroom were empty the silence could not be more absolute.

'So you took her with you to Copenhagen. Where did you stay?'

'At the Red Shoes Hotel.'

'For how long?'

'A fortnight.'

There was a faint murmur of comment or surprise at that. 'And then?'

'We came back to England together on the 15th of April. She had told me that she was due home on the 16th. But on the way over she told me that she had actually been due back on the 11th and would now have been missing for four days.'

'She misled you deliberately?'

'Yes.'

'Did she say why she had misled you?'

'Yes. So that it would be impossible for her to go back. She said she was going to write to her people and say that she had

239

a job and was quite happy and that they were not to look for her or worry about her.'

'She had no compunction about the suffering that would cause parents who had been devoted to her?'

'No. She said her home bored her so much she could scream.'

Against his will Robert's eyes went to Mrs Wynn, and came away again at once. It was crucifixion.

'What was your reaction to the new situation?'

'I was angry to begin with. It put me in a spot.'

'Were you worried about the girl?'

'No, not particularly.'

'Why?'

'By that time I had learned that she was very well able to take care of herself.'

'What exactly do you mean by that?'

'I mean: whoever was going to suffer in any situation she created, it wouldn't be Betty Kane.'

The mention of her name suddenly reminded the audience that the girl they had just been hearing about was 'the' Betty Kane. 'Their' Betty Kane. The one like Bernadette. And there was a small uneasy movement, a taking of breath.

'So?'

'After a lot of rag-chewing —'

'Of what?' said his lordship.

'After a lot of discussion, my lord.'

'Go on,' said his lordship, 'but do confine yourself to English, standard or basic.'

'After a lot of talk I decided the best thing to do would be to take her down to my bungalow on the river near Bourne End. We used it for week-ends in the summer and for summer holidays, but only rarely for the rest of the year.'

'When you say "we", you mean your wife and you?'

'Yes. She agreed to that quite readily, and I drove her down.'

'Did you stay there with her that night?'

'Yes.'

'And on the following nights?'

'The following night I spent at home.'

'In Ealing.'

'Yes.'

'And afterwards?'

'For a week after that I spent most nights at the bungalow.'

'Was your wife not surprised that you did not sleep at home?'

'Not unbearably.'

'And how did the situation at Bourne End disintegrate?'

'I went down one night and found that she had gone.'

'What did you think had happened to her?'

'Well, she had been growing very bored for the last day or two – she found housekeeping fun for about three days, but not more, and there wasn't much to do down there – so when I found she had gone I took it that she was tired of me and had found someone or something more exciting.'

'You learned later where she had gone, and why?'

'Yes.'

'You heard the girl Betty Kane give evidence today?'

'I did.'

'Evidence that she had been forcibly detained in a house near Milford.'

'Yes.'

'That is the girl who went with you to Copenhagen, stayed there for a fortnight with you, and subsequently lived with you in a bungalow near Bourne End?'

'Yes, that is the girl.'

'You have no doubt about it?'

'No.'

'Thank you.'

There was a great sigh from the crowd as Kevin sat down and Bernard Chadwick waited for Miles Allison. Robert wondered if Betty Kane's face was capable of showing any emotion other than fear and triumph. Twice he had seen it pulse with triumph and once – when old Mrs Sharpe crossed the drawing-room towards her that first day – he had seen it show fear. But for all the emotion it showed just now she might have been listening to a reading of fat stock prices. Its effect of inward calm, he decided, must be the result of physical construction. The result of wide-set eyes and placid brow and inexpressive small mouth always set in the same childish pout. It was that physical construction that had hidden, all those years, the real Betty

241

Kane even from her intimates. A perfect camouflage, it had been. A façade behind which she could be what she liked. There it was now, the mask, as childlike and calm as when he had first seen it above her school coat in the drawing-room at The Franchise; although behind it its owner must be seething with unnameable emotions.

'Mr Chadwick,' Miles Allison said, 'this is a very *belated* story, isn't it?'

'Belated?'

'Yes. This case has been a matter for press-report and public comment for the past three weeks, or thereabouts. You must have known that two women were being wrongfully accused – if your story was true. If, as you say, Betty Kane was with you during those weeks, and not, as she says, in the house of these two women, why did you not go straight to the police and tell them so?'

'Because I didn't know anything about it.'

'About what?'

'About the prosecution of these women. Or about the story that Betty Kane had told.'

'How was that?'

'Because I have been abroad again for my firm. I knew nothing about this case until a couple of days ago.'

'I see. You have heard the girl give evidence and you have heard the doctor's evidence as to the condition in which she arrived home. Does anything in your story explain that?'

'No.'

'It was not you who beat the girl?'

'No.'

'You say you went down one night and found her gone.'

'Yes.'

'She had packed up and gone?'

'Yes; so it seemed at the time.'

'That is to say, all her belongings and the luggage that contained them had disappeared with her.'

'Yes.'

'And yet she arrived home without belongings of any sort, and wearing only a dress and shoes.'

'I didn't know that till much later.'

'You want us to understand that when you went down to the bungalow you found it tidy and deserted, with no sign of any hasty departure.'

'Yes. That's how I found it.'

When Mary Frances Chadwick was summoned to give evidence there was what amounted to a sensation in court, even before she appeared. It was obvious that this was 'the wife'; and this was fare that not even the most optimistic queuer outside the court had anticipated.

Frances Chadwick was a tallish, good-looking woman, a natural blonde with the clothes and figure of a girl who has 'modelled' clothes; but growing a little plump now and, if one was to judge from the good-natured face, not much caring.

She said that she was indeed married to the previous witness, and lived with him in Ealing. They had no children. She still worked in the clothes trade now and then – not because she needed to, but for pocket-money and because she liked it. Yes, she remembered her husband's going to Larborough and his subsequent trip to Copenhagen. He arrived back from Copenhagen a day later than he promised and spent that night with her. During the following week she began to suspect that her husband had developed an interest elsewhere. The suspicion was confirmed when a friend told her that her husband had a guest at their bungalow on the river.

'Did you speak to your husband about it?' Kevin asked.

'No. That wouldn't have been any solution. He attracts them like flies.'

'What did you do, then? Or plan to do?'

'What I always do with flies.'

'What is that?'

'I swat them.'

'So you proceeded to the bungalow with the intention of swatting whatever fly was there.'

'That's it.'

'And what did you find at the bungalow?'

'I went late in the evening hoping I would catch Barney there too –'

'Barney is your husband?'

243

'And how. I mean, yes,' she added hastily, catching the judge's eye.

'Well?'

'The door was unlocked, so I walked straight in and into the sitting-room. A woman's voice called from the bedroom: "Is that you, Barney? I've been so lonely for you." I went in and found her lying on the bed in the kind of négligée you used to see in vamp films about ten years ago. She looked a mess and I was a bit surprised at Barney. She was eating chocolates out of an enormous box that was lying on the bed alongside her. Terribly nineteen-thirty, the whole set-up.'

'Please confine your story to the essentials, Mrs Chadwick.'

'Yes. Sorry. Well, we had the usual exchange –'

'The usual?'

'Yes. The what-are-you-doing-here stuff. The wronged wife and the light-of-love, you know. But for some reason or other she got in my hair. I don't know why. I had never cared very much on other occasions. I mean, we just had a good row without any real hard feelings on either side. But there was something about this little tramp that turned my stomach. So –'

'Please, Mrs Chadwick!'

'All right. Sorry. But you did say tell it in my own words. Well, there came a point where I couldn't stand this floo – I mean, I got to a stage when she riled me past bearing. I pulled her off the bed and gave her a smack on the side of the head. She looked so surprised it was funny. It would seem no one had ever hit her in her life. She said: "You hit me!" Just like that; and I said: "A lot of people are going to hit you from now on, my poppet", and gave her another one. Well, from then on it was just a fight. I own quite frankly that the odds were all on my side. I was bigger for one thing and in a flaming temper. I tore that silly négligée off her, and it was ding-dong till she tripped over one of her mules that was lying on the floor, and went sprawling. I waited for her to get up, but she didn't, and I thought she had passed out. I went into the bathroom to get a cold wet cloth and mopped her face. And then I went into the kitchen to make some coffee. I had cooled off by then and thought she would be glad of something when she had cooled off too. I brewed the coffee and left it to stand. But when I got back to the bedroom I found that the faint had been all an act. The little – the girl had lit out. She had had time to dress, so I took it for granted that she had dressed in a hurry and gone.'

'And did you go too?'

'I waited for an hour, thinking Barney might come – my husband. All the girl's things were lying about, so I slung them all into her suitcase and put it in the cupboard under the stairs to the attic. And I opened all the windows. She must have put her scent on with a ladle. And then when Barney didn't come I went away. I must just have missed him, because he did go down that night. But a couple of days later I told him what I had done.'

'And what was his reaction?'

'He said it was a pity her mother hadn't done the same thing ten years ago.'

'He was not worried as to what had become of her?'

'No. I was, a bit, until he told me her home was only over at Aylesbury. She could quite easily cadge a lift that distance.'

'So he took it for granted that she had gone home?'

'Yes. I said, hadn't he better make sure – after all, she was a kid.'

'And what did he say in answer to that?'

'He said: "Frankie, my girl, that 'kid' knows more about self-preservation than a chameleon." '

'So you dismissed the affair from your mind?'

'Yes.'

'But it must have come to your mind again when you read accounts of The Franchise affair?'

'No, it didn't.'

'Why was that?'

'For one thing, I never knew the girl's name. Barney called her Liz. And I just didn't connect a fifteen-year-old schoolgirl who was kidnapped and beaten somewhere in the Midlands with Barney's bit. I mean, with the girl who was eating choco-lates on my bed.'

'If you had realized that the girls were identical, you would have told the police what you knew about her?'

'Certainly.'

'You would not have hesitated owing to the fact that it was you who had administered the beating?'

'No. I would administer another tomorrow if I got the chance.'

'I will save my learned friend a question and ask you: Do you intend to divorce your husband?'

'No. Certainly not.'

'This evidence of yours and his is not a neat little piece of public collusion?'

'No. I wouldn't need collusion. But I have no intention of divorcing Barney. He's fun and he's a good provider. What more do you want in a husband?'

'I wouldn't know,' Robert heard Kevin murmur. Then in his normal voice he asked her to state that the girl she had been talking about was the girl who had given evidence; the girl who was now sitting in court. And so thanked her and sat down.

But Miles Allison made no attempt to cross-examine. And Kevin moved to call his next witness. But the foreman of the jury was before him.

The jury, the foreman said, would like his lordship to know that they had all the evidence they required.

'What was this witness that you were about to call, Mr Macdermott?' the judge asked.

'He is the owner of the hotel in Copenhagen, my lord. To speak of their having stayed there over the relevant period.'

The judge turned inquiringly to the foreman.

The foreman consulted the jury.

'No, my lord; we don't think it is necessary, subject to your lordship's correction, to hear the witness.'

'If you are satisfied that you have heard enough to arrive at a true verdict – and I cannot myself see that any further evidence would greatly clarify the subject – then so be it. Would you like to hear counsel for the defence?'

'No, my lord, thank you. We have reached our verdict already.'

'In that case any summing-up by me would be markedly redundant. Do you want to retire?'

'No, my lord. We are unanimous.'

23

'WE had better wait until the crowd thins out,' Robert said. 'Then they'll let us out the back way.'

He was wondering why Marion looked so grave, so un-rejoicing. Almost as if she were suffering from shock. Had the strain been as bad as all that?'

As if aware of his puzzlement, she said: 'That woman. That poor woman. I can't think of anything else.'

'Who?' Robert said stupidly.

'The girl's mother. Can you imagine anything more frightful? To have lost the roof over one's head is bad – Oh yes, Robert my dear, you don't have to tell us.' She held out a late edition of the *Larborough Times* with a stop-press paragraph reading: THE FRANCHISE, HOUSE MADE FAMOUS BY MILFORD ABDUCTION CASE, BURNT TO THE GROUND LAST NIGHT. 'Yesterday that would have seemed to me an enormous tragedy. But compared with that woman's calvary it seems an incident. What *can* be more shattering than to find that the person you have lived with and loved all those years not only doesn't exist but has never existed? That the person you have loved so much not only doesn't love you but doesn't care two hoots about you and never did? What is there *left* for someone like that? She can never again take a step on to green grass without wondering if it is bog.'

'Yes,' Kevin said, 'I couldn't bear to look at her. It was indecent, what she was suffering.'

'She has a charming son,' Mrs Sharpe said. 'I hope he will be a comfort to her.'

'But don't you *see*,' Marion said, 'she *hasn't* got her son. She has nothing now. She thought she had Betty. She loved her and was as sure of her as she loved and was sure of her son. Now the very foundations of her life have given way. How is she to judge any longer, if appearances can be so deceptive? No, she has nothing. Just a desolation. I am bleeding inside for her.'

Kevin slipped an arm into hers and said: 'You have had

sufficient trouble of your own lately without saddling yourself with another's. Come; they'll let us go now, I think. Did it please you to see the police converging, in that polite, casual way of theirs, on the perjurers?'

'No; I could think of nothing but that woman's crucifixion.' So she too had thought of it as that.

Kevin ignored her. 'And the indecent scramble for a telephone that the Press indulged in the moment his lordship's red tail was through the door? You will be vindicated at great length in every newspaper in Britain, I promise you. It will be the most public vindication since Dreyfus. Wait here for me while I get out of these. I shan't be a moment.'

'I suppose we had best go to a hotel for a night or two?' Mrs Sharpe said. 'Have we any belongings at all?'

'Yes, quite a few, I'm glad to say,' Robert told her; and described what had been saved. 'But there is an alternative to the hotel.' And he told them of Stanley's suggestion.

So it was to the little house on the outer rim of the 'new' town that Marion and her mother came back; and it was in the front room at Miss Sim's that they sat down to celebrate – a sober little group: Marion, her mother, Robert and Stanley. Kevin had had to go back to town. There was a large bunch of garden flowers on the table which had come with one of Aunt Lin's best notes. Aunt Lin's warm and gracious little notes had as little actual meaning as her 'Have you had a busy day, dear?' but they had the same cushioning effect on life. Stanley had come in with a copy of the *Larborough Times*, which carried on its front page the first report of the trial. The report was printed under a heading which read ANANIAS ALSO RAN.

'Will you golf with me tomorrow afternoon?' Robert asked Marion. 'You have been cooped up too long. We can start early, before the two-rounders have finished their lunch, and have the course to ourselves.'

'Yes, I should like that,' she said. 'I suppose tomorrow life will begin again and be just the usual mixture of good and bad. But tonight it is just a place where dreadful things can happen to one.'

When he called for her on the morrow, however, all seemed well with life. 'You can't imagine what bliss it is,' she said.

248

'Living in this house, I mean. You just turn a tap and hot water comes out.'

'It is also very educational,' Mrs Sharpe said.

'Educational?'

'You can hear every word that is said next door.'

'Oh, come, mother! Not every word!'

'Every third word,' amended Mrs Sharpe.

So they drove out to the golf-course in high spirits, and Robert decided that he would ask her to marry him when they were having tea in the club-house afterwards. Or would there be too many people interrupting there, with their kind words on the result of the trial? Perhaps on the way home again?

He had decided that the best plan was to leave Aunt Lin in possession of the old house – the place was so much hers that it was unthinkable that she should not live there until she died – and to find a small place for Marion and himself somewhere else in Milford. It would not be easy, these days, but if the worst came to the worst they could make a tiny flat on the top floor of Blair, Hayward, and Bennet's. It would mean removing the records of two hundred years or so; but the records were rapidly arriving at museum quality and should be moved in any case.

Yes, he would ask her on the way home again.

This resolution lasted until he found that the thought of what was to come was spoiling his game. So on the ninth green he suddenly stopped waggling his putter at the ball and said: 'I want you to marry me, Marion.'

'Do you, Robert?' She picked her own putter out of her bag and dropped the bag at the edge of the green.

'You will, won't you?'

'No, Robert dear, I won't.'

'But, Marion! Why? Why not, I mean.'

'Oh – as the children say, "because".'

'Because why?'

'Half a dozen reasons, any one of them good by itself. For one, if a man is not married by the time he is forty, then marriage is not one of the things he wants out of life – just something that has overtaken him, like flu and rheumatism and

249

income-tax demands. I don't want to be just something that has overtaken you.'

'But that is –'

'Then I don't think that I should be in the least an asset to Blair, Hayward, and Bennet. Even –'

'I'm not asking you to marry Blair, Hayward, and Bennet.'

'Even the proof that I didn't beat Betty Kane won't free me of being "the woman in the Kane case": an uncomfortable sort of wife for the senior partner. It wouldn't do you any good, Robert, believe me.'

'Marion, for heaven's sake! Stop –'

'Then you have Aunt Lin and I have my mother. We couldn't just park them like pieces of chewing-gum. I not only love my mother, I like her. I admire her and enjoy living with her. You, on the other hand, are used to being spoiled by Aunt Lin – oh yes, you are! – and would miss far more than you know all the creature comforts and the cosseting that I wouldn't know how to give you – and wouldn't give you if I knew how,' she added, flashing a smile at him.

'Marion, it is *because* you don't cosset me that I want to marry you. Because you have an adult mind and a –'

'An adult mind is very nice to go to dinner with once a week, but after a lifetime with Aunt Lin you would find it a very poor exchange for good pastry in an uncritical atmosphere.'

'There is one thing you haven't even mentioned,' Robert said.

'What is that?'

'Don't you care for me at all?'

'Yes; I care for you a great deal. More than I have ever cared for anyone, I think. That is, partly, why I won't marry you. The other reason has to do with myself.'

'With you?'

'You see, I am *not* a marrying woman. I don't want to put up with someone else's crochets, someone else's demands, someone else's colds in the head. Mother and I suit each other perfectly because we make no demands on each other. If one of us has a cold in the head she retires to her room without fuss and doses her disgusting self until she is fit for human society again. But no husband would do that. He would expect sympathy – even though he brought on the cold himself by pulling off clothes when he grew warm instead of waiting sensibly to get cool – sympathy and attention and feeding. No, Robert. There are a hundred thousand women just panting to look after some man's cold. Why pick on me?'

'Because you are that one woman in a hundred thousand and I love you.'

She looked slightly penitent. 'I sound flippant, don't I? But what I say is good sound sense.'

'But, Marion, it is a lonely life –'

'A "full" life in my experience is usually full only of other people's demands.'

'– and you will not have your mother for ever.'

'Knowing mother as I do, I have no doubt that she will out-live me with perfect ease. You had better hole out: I see old Colonel Whittaker's four on the horizon.'

Automatically he pushed his ball into the hole. 'But what will you do?' he asked.

'If I don't marry you?'

He ground his teeth. She was right: perhaps her mocking habit of mind would not be a comfort to live with.

'What had you and your mother thought of doing now that you have lost The Franchise?'

She delayed over her answer, as if it were difficult to say, fussing with her bag, and keeping her back to him.

'We are going to Canada,' she said.

'Going away!'

She still had her back to him. 'Yes.'

He was aghast. 'But, Marion, you can't. And why to Canada?'

'I have a cousin who is a professor at McGill. A son of mother's only sister. He wrote some time ago to ask mother if we would go out to keep house for him, but by that time we had inherited The Franchise and were very happy in England. So we said no. But the offer is still open. And we – we both will be glad to go now.'

'I see.'

'Don't look so downcast. You don't know what an escape you are having, my dear.'

They finished the round in a business-like silence.

But driving back to Sin Lane after having dropped Marion at Miss Sim's, Robert smiled wryly to think that to all the new experiences that knowing the Sharpes had brought to him was now added that of being a rejected suitor. The final and perhaps the most surprising one.

Three days later, having sold to a local dealer what had been saved of their furniture and to Stanley the car he so much despised, they left Milford by train. By the odd toy train that ran from Milford to the junction at Norton. And Robert came to the junction with them to see them on to the fast train.

'I always had a passion for travelling light,' Marion said, referring to their scanty luggage, 'but I never imagined it would be indulged to the extent of travelling with an over-night case to Canada.'

But Robert could not think of small-talk. He was filled with a misery and desolation that he had not known since his small soul was filled with woe at going back to school. The blossom foamed along the line side, the fields were burnished with buttercups, but the world for Robert was grey ash and drizzle.

He watched the London train bear them away and went home wondering how he could support Milford without the hope of seeing Marion's thin, brown face at least once a day.

But on the whole he supported it very well. He took to golfing of an afternoon again; and although a ball would always in the future be for him a 'piece of gutta-percha', his form had not seriously deteriorated. He rejoiced Mr Heseltine's heart by taking an interest in work. He suggested to Nevil that between them they might sort and catalogue the records in the attic and perhaps make a book of them. By the time Marion's good-bye letter from London came, three weeks later, the soft folds of life in Milford were already closing round him.

MY VERY DEAR ROBERT (wrote Marion),

This is a hasty *au revoir* note, just to let you know that we are both thinking of you. We leave on the morning plane to Montreal the day after tomorrow. Now that the moment is almost here we have discovered that what we both remember are the good and lovely things, and that the rest fades to comparative insignificance. This may be only nostalgia in advance. I don't know. I only know that it will always be happiness to remember you. And Stanley, and Bill – and England.

Our united love to you, and our gratitude,

MARION SHARPE

He laid the letter down on his brass and mahogany desk. Laid it down in the afternoon patch of sunlight.

Tomorrow at this time Marion would no longer be in England. It was a desolating thought, but there was nothing to do but be sensible about it. What, indeed, was there to do about it?

And then three things happened at once.

Mr Heseltine came in to say that Mrs Lomax wanted to alter her will again, and would he go out to the farm immediately?

Aunt Lin rang up and asked him to call for the fish on his way home.

And Miss Tuff brought in his tea.

He looked for a long moment at the two digestive biscuits on the plate. Then, with a gentle finality, he pushed the tray out of his way and reached for the telephone.

24

THE summer rain beat on the airfield with a dreary persistence. Every now and then the wind would lift it and sweep the terminus buildings with it in one long brush-stroke. The covered way to the Montreal plane was open on either side and the passengers bent their heads against the weather as they filed slowly into it. Robert, moving up at the tail of the queue, could see Mrs Sharpe's flat black satin hat and the short strands of white hair being blown about.

By the time he boarded the plane they were seated and Mrs Sharpe was already burrowing in her bag. As he walked up the aisle between the seats Marion looked up and saw him. Her face lighted with welcome and surprise.

'Robert!' she said. 'Have you come to see us off?'

'No,' Robert said. 'I'm travelling by this plane.'

'Travelling!' she said, staring. 'You *are*?'

'It's a public conveyance, you know.'

'I know. But – you're going to Canada?'

'I am.'

'What for?'

'To see my sister in Saskatchewan,' Robert said demurely. 'A much better pretext than a cousin at McGill.'

She began to laugh, softly and consumedly.

'Oh, Robert my dear,' she said, 'you can't imagine how revolting you are when you look smug!'

FOR THE BEST IN PAPERBACKS, LOOK FOR THE

In every corner of the world, on every subject under the sun, Penguin represents quality and variety – the very best in publishing today.

For complete information about books available from Penguin – including Pelicans, Puffins, Peregrines and Penguin Classics – and how to order them, write to us at the appropriate address below. Please note that for copyright reasons the selection of books varies from country to country.

In the United Kingdom: For a complete list of books available from Penguin in the U.K., please write to *Dept E.P., Penguin Books Ltd, Harmondsworth, Middlesex, UB7 0DA*

In the United States: For a complete list of books available from Penguin in the U.S., please write to *Dept BA, Penguin, 299 Murray Hill Parkway, East Rutherford, New Jersey 07073*

In Canada: For a complete list of books available from Penguin in Canada, please write to *Penguin Books Canada Ltd, 2801 John Street, Markham, Ontario L3R 1B4*

In Australia: For a complete list of books available from Penguin in Australia, please write to the *Marketing Department, Penguin Books Australia Ltd, P.O. Box 257, Ringwood, Victoria 3134*

In New Zealand: For a complete list of books available from Penguin in New Zealand, please write to the *Marketing Department, Penguin Books (NZ) Ltd, Private Bag, Takapuna, Auckland 9*

In India: For a complete list of books available from Penguin, please write to *Penguin Overseas Ltd, 706 Eros Apartments, 56 Nehru Place, New Delhi, 110019*

In Holland: For a complete list of books available from Penguin in Holland, please write to *Penguin Books Nederland B.V., Postbus 195, NL–1380AD Weesp, Netherlands*

In Germany: For a complete list of books available from Penguin, please write to *Penguin Books Ltd, Friedrichstrasse 10–12, D–6000 Frankfurt Main 1, Federal Republic of Germany*

In Spain: For a complete list of books available from Penguin in Spain, please write to *Longman Penguin España, Calle San Nicolas 15, E–28013 Madrid, Spain*

Also by Josephine Tey

THE DAUGHTER OF TIME

Many readers of this book will remember that great historical play *Richard of Bordeaux* by Gordon Daviot. Josephine Tey and Gordon Daviot were the same person; and in this unusual detective novel, as in *The Franchise Affair*, Miss Tey delves into history to reconstruct a crime. This time it is a crime committed in the tumultuous fifteenth century.

'A detective story with a very considerable difference. Ingenious, stimulating and very enjoyable' – J. W. Lambert in the *Sunday Times*

'Most people will find *The Daughter of Time* as interesting and enjoyable a book as they will meet in a month of Sundays' – Marghanita Laski in the *Observer*

BRAT FARRAR

If Patrick had really committed suicide, then who was the mysterious young man calling himself Brat Farrar, who had returned to claim the family inheritance?

'Josephine Tey has always been absolutely reliable in producing original and mysterious plots with interesting characters and unguessable endings' – Marghanita Laski in the *Spectator*

'A brilliant mystery' – *Books and Bookmen*